Plato to Alexander Pope

BACKGROUNDS OF MODERN CRITICISM

Plato to Alexander Pope

Backgrounds of Modern Criticism

Edited by

WALTER and VIVIAN SUTTON

THE ODYSSEY PRESS · INC · New York

The insets on the cover show Plato and Alexander Pope. The background illustration of Dante is from a painting by Jean Léon Géróme, 1824–1904.

A Note on the Texts

In preparing this collection of essays in criticism, we have aimed at accuracy and readability. The texts of the selections by English writers are based on the first editions, although some corrections have been incorporated. Jowett's translation of Plato and Butcher's Aristotle have been closely followed. In the other translations, changes in vocabulary and phrasing have been introduced, to a greater or lesser degree, in the interest of accuracy and idiomatic expression. The spelling and punctuation of all selections have been modernized to conform to current American usage.

The texts of Sidney's *Defense of Poesy* and Dryden's *Essay of Dramatic Poesy* have been somewhat reduced by the elimination of nonessential supporting detail—without damage, we think, to the full presentation of the writer's argument.

Syracuse University   WALTER SUTTON

State University College of Forestry   VIVIAN SUTTON
at Syracuse University

Contents

CONTENTS

Plato to Alexander Pope

BACKGROUNDS OF MODERN CRITICISM

Introduction

Although modern criticism is most directly indebted to the romantic revolution of the nineteenth century, its backgrounds extend from the classic age of Greece to the Augustan age of John Dryden and Alexander Pope. Of the two giants of Greek thought, Aristotle was the greater influence on the development of criticism until the close of the neoclassical period of the seventeenth and eighteenth centuries. The romantic writers and critics, however, felt a special affinity for Platonism, which lent support to their transcendentalist theories. Both Plato and Aristotle remain figures to be reckoned with, and a knowledge of their distinctive positions is necessary for an understanding of modern criticism and its backgrounds.

Through the mouth of Socrates in the dialogue of *Ion,* Plato described the poet as one inspired by his Muse and raised to eloquence through a divine madness. But Plato, the lover of reason, distrusted irrationality in any form. He considered the poet a purveyor of false knowledge, in contrast to his superior, the rationally enlightened philosopher. Because of his unreliability and his appeal to men's passions rather than their reason, the poet was banned from Plato's ideal Republic.

Despite his inhospitable treatment of poets, Plato's thought has much in common with romantic and later literary theory. Although Plato belittled poetry as an imitation of imitations because it merely *re*presents the fleeting forms of nature which are themselves imperfect copies of the pre-existing eternal forms or "ideas," he also explained poetry as the product of inspiration, or the poet's seizure by a supernatural force for which he is merely the mouthpiece. Without sharing Plato's misgivings about inspiration, the romantics, the later symbolist poets, and the surrealists after them also thought of poetry as the spontaneous expression of a reality underlying the forms of nature that provide the imperfect medium of the poet's symbolic expression.

[1]

Ironically, Plato himself was, as Sir Philip Sidney observed, of all philosophers "the most poetical." He often expressed his ideas symbolically through images, allegories, and myths. Perhaps the best known of these is the symbolic image of the cave in Book VII of *The Republic:* here the illusion of man's sensory experience is represented by shadows cast on the wall of the cave (the prison house of the senses) by an artificial light, whereas the true reality of the upper world of forms and ideas can be seen only in the sunlight of reason.

The theory of forms was supported by Plato's doctrine of *anamnesis,* the belief that knowledge is the recollection of ideas beheld in a previous state of existence. It should be clear that Plato's eternal forms and ideas are in effect *archetypes*—a term introduced by his neoplatonic followers. In the *Fifth Enniad* Plotinus spoke of the intelligible world of ideas as the archetype of the world of the senses, and in the *Sixth Enniad* of the material forms of the sense world as themselves archetypes to the extent that they were "illuminated by ideas." The terminology and the thought point to a bridge, important though not direct, between the philosophy of Plato and the assumptions of later myth critics like Maud Bodkin, even though these critics have been most directly influenced by the work of comparative anthropologists like Sir James Frazer and by the psychology of Carl Jung. Despite its ostensibly scientific formulation, Jung's idea of the collective unconscious as a pool of memory containing patterns of "forgotten" but still potent racial experiences that can be reanimated by the archetypal patterns of art and ritual is very close to Plato's theory of forms and the related doctrine of anamnesis. In this perspective, Jung and the myth and archetype critics who made use of his ideas can be seen to have their place in the tradition of Platonic idealism despite their altered terminology and frame of reference.

Unlike Plato, Aristotle praised poetry as a source of knowledge. In his eyes poetry was "a more philosophical and a higher thing than history" because it deals in universal normative truth, whereas the truths of history are limited and factual.

In approaching literature as a natural phenomenon to be analyzed and classified, Aristotle was the first of the great theorist critics of Western literature. In keeping with his breadth of interest and vision, he attempted to explain literature in three principal ways: formally, as a structure of elements or "parts" to be viewed as an organic whole; historically, as a product of evolutionary development in the arts; and functionally, as a cultural expression adapted to the needs of its audience and society. It is in the discussion of function that Aristotle developed his famous and much debated theory of the tragic *katharsis* or purgation of the emotions of pity and fear.

The systematic but incomplete treatment of literature in the *Poetics* is without doubt the most influential single piece of criticism ever written. Although it is limited largely to a consideration of tragedy and (to a lesser degree) epic, it has proved to be an inexhaustible source of ideas and terms for critics engaged in the continuing discussion of the nature and function of literature. In the hands of seventeenth and eighteenth century critics, however, the principles that Aristotle had set forth as the result of his observations were converted into dogma in an attempt to regulate the literary expression of the age. The most clear-cut example of this transformation of Aristotle was the development of the neoclassical doctrine of the unities of time, place, and action.

Thus Aristotle became associated with a tradition of genre or type criticism that attempted to classify and judge literature on the basis of pre-existing standards, usually identified as "Aristotelian" or "neo-Aristotelian." But for some later critics Aristotle has remained a model of the open-minded inquirer who, like the scientist, studies his subject inductively and develops his conclusions without personal bias.

The later stages of the classical period are represented in this volume by Horace's *Art of Poetry* and Longinus' *On the Sublime.* Horace, the poet-critic of Rome's Augustan age, wrote as the consolidator and steward of conventional principles rather than as a breaker of new ground. Conservative, aristocratic, and urbane in temper, his epistolary essay of the first century B.C. was a model of reasonableness, decorum, and gracefully turned wit. Poetry and polite learning were linked by Horace in his famous definition of the function of poetry: *Aut prodesse volunt, aut delectare poetae; / Aut simul et jucunda et idonea dicere vitae* ("Poets wish either to profit or delight, or to combine enjoyment and usefulness in what they write").

Writing in the first century of the Christian era, "Longinus," the unknown author of *Peri Hypsous,* or *On the Sublime,* examined the qualities of literature that contribute to its "height" or excellence. He was especially interested in the effect of intensity and the devices by which it may be achieved. Although Longinus took into account the ideas of earlier critics, including Aristotle, he did not simply accept traditional principles but questioned and tested them in the light of his own experience and reactions: "I am not satisfied with the definition of amplification generally given by authorities on rhetoric." He pointed out faults as well as virtues, even in Homer, who (like Shakespeare in a later age) stood as the touchstone and focus of attention for generations of classical critics.

Longinus' responsiveness to the emotional values of literature and, even more, to its power of expressing the sense of transport or ecstasy appealed to eighteenth century readers who found in this voice from the classical past a sanction for their growing interest in "sensibility" and in the suprarational powers of literature. Present day readers tend to be less interested in the idea of transport than in Longinus' skill in analyzing, through examples, the ways in which literary language is charged with intellectual and emotional associations.

The centuries between Longinus and Dante brought a shift from a humanistic to a religious emphasis in all the arts. In the letter to the General Can Grande della Scala of Verona in which he explained the plan of his *Commedia,* Dante borrowed from St. Thomas Aquinas a scheme of interpreting literary meanings on four levels ranging from the literal to the anagogical. For Dante, his highest mission as a poet was to exemplify the moral and philosophic truths of his deeply Christian vision. Concentrating on the formal dimension of meaning, Dante was didactic and rationalistic in discussing his own work, taking no account of the complex poetic values arising from the interaction of such other elements as sound, imagery, and emotion. Nor did he, in his letter, give any hint of his achievement as the founder of a literature in his native Italian tongue. Although Dante's symmetrical scheme for composing and explaining the *Commedia* was appropriate to his own age of systematic theology, his idea of a hierarchical closed cosmos, reflected in his four-level system of meanings, is alien to the modern mind. More easily accepted is his recognition of the polysemous or plurisignificant nature of poetic language—a view that invites a variety of approaches to the literary work, which is seen as a verbal complex of many meanings.

The revival and dissemination of classical learning during the Renaissance brought a resurgence of humanism and a freeing of the arts from religious domination. After several centuries during which Aquinas and the medieval schoolmen devoted themselves to Christianizing Aristotle as a moral philosopher, critics and poets rediscovered the *Poetics,* and Aristotle's literary theory helped to shape the new growth of secular drama. In England the two most important figures in Renaissance criticism were Sir Philip Sidney, who died before the full flowering of Elizabethan literature, and Ben Jonson, who lived through the great years as a practicing playwright and younger contemporary of Shakespeare.

Sidney wrote his *Defense of Poesy* (published posthumously in 1595) as a reply to Puritan attacks upon poetry. Championing poetry as an ancient fount of knowledge, the source of morality and wisdom, and thus superior to philosophy and history, Sidney anticipated a later view that poetry or imaginative literature provides a "completer" knowledge because it combines the "general notion" or universal of the philosopher with the "particular example" of the historian. A model of the Renaissance nobleman, Sidney regarded the knowledge provided by poetry not only as food for contemplation but also as a guide to conduct. He accepted Aristotle's idea of poetry as imitation and developed it further as he argued that, because of its freedom from confinement to literal fact, poetry can provide man with ideals and patterns for the "virtuous action" which is his highest goal.

The younger Ben Jonson, a commoner, did not let his respect for classical learning and his admiration for Aristotle, whom he praised as "the first accurate critic and truest judge," interfere with his independent judgments of earlier writers and contemporaries. In *Timber, or Discoveries* 1640–41), a posthumously published collection of random observations, he recommended that the Ancients be followed as "guides not commanders." As a student of Aristotle, Jonson stressed the need for wholeness and unity of plot; his own plays were to be praised by Dryden for their regularity, proportion, and observance of the unities.

Like Sidney, Jonson believed in the didactic function of literature.

In his role as critic-teacher, he urged the beginning writer to imitate models (though not slavishly), to exercise his own style through repetitive practice, and to study diligently. But he insisted on the independence of the poet from the prescriptive rules of the grammarian and philosopher. Like Sidney again, he pointed to the connection between literature and an active life in society, and he appealed to the authority of Aristotle for his claim that the study of poetry "offers to mankind a certain rule and pattern of living well and happily, disposing us to all civil offices of society."

The neoclassicism for which Ben Jonson was an early spokesman came to its fullest development in England during the Restoration and eighteenth century, the age of Dryden and Pope. In Europe and in England neoclassicism developed partly as a reaction against the enthusiasm and, as it seemed, undisciplined extravagance of Renaissance art, hence an intensified stress on the need for authority and rules and for the subordination of the individual to social norms. Shakespeare must be schooled—as he was, by Dryden and others, who "improved" his rude genius. With the growing vogue of decorum, urbanity, and polish, the masculine vigor of Jonson gave way to the easy smoothness of Dryden and Pope, who, even though they engaged in the deadly personal satire so satisfying to their age, lacked the intellectual and moral rigor of their predecessors. For all their cultivation and breadth of knowledge, they were not so much original thinkers as synthesizers and adapters of established principles and, especially in the case of Dryden, skillful mediators of differing opinions.

The years following the restoration of Charles II in 1660 brought John Dryden fame as a critic, a dramatist, and a poet with a special gift for satire. Because of his critical essays and prefaces, Dryden was called by Samuel Johnson "the father of English criticism." In the dialogue of *An Essay of Dramatic Poesy* (1668), written in the easy, flexible, conversational style for which Dryden has been admired, Neander, Dryden's spokesman, arbitrates the debate and delivers the final comments on the opinions set forth by the other speakers.

In the *Essay*, the working definition of a play provided by Lisideius, "a just and lively image of human nature, representing its passions and humors, and the changes of fortune to which it is subject, for the delight and instruction of mankind," shows the mingled influence of Aristotle's idea of imitation and Horace's description of the function of poetry as profit and delight. Out of these two authorities, says Crites, "have been extracted the famous rules which the French call *Des Trois Unitez,* or The Three Unities, which ought to be observed in every regular play, namely, of Time, Place, and Action." Taking exception to Crites' unqualified endorsement of the rules, Neander approves the principle but argues against the servile observation of the unities that has resulted in "that dearth of plot and narrowness of imagination" that he finds in the French drama.

Dryden singled out Ben Jonson from his contemporaries because of his regularity and through Neander examined Jonson's *Epicoene: or, The Silent Woman* in the first extended analysis of a single work in English criticism. Dryden contributed to a lively controversy of his time in his discussion and defense of the use of rhyme on the stage, a subject of interest to later poets and critics who have attempted to revive verse drama on the modern stage.

Like Horace's *Art of Poetry,* Alexander Pope's *Essay on Criticism* (1711) was composed as a comprehensive restatement of accepted views rather than an original contribution to poetic or critical theory. Pope's "authorities," more than fifty in all, included not only the Greek and Roman classic writers but also many of his immediate neoclassic forebears, such as Boileau, whose *Art Poétique* (1674) served as a model for the *Essay,* and John Dryden, to whom Pope gave precedence among English poets and critics.

In beginning his poem Pope reconciled the rival authorities of nature and tradition by identifying natural law with the principles formulated by the Ancients and subordinating nature to tradition: "Those rules of old discovered, not devised, / Are nature still, but nature methodized." He then took up the proper standards and procedures for criticism and the qualities of the ideal critic and opposed these to the abuses of partial and biased criticism. But as Dr. Johnson noted in his life of Pope, there is no direct thrust of argument in the *Essay.* Although certain subjects recur, sections could be transposed without altering the general effect of the poem. Its most distinctive feature is the epigrammatic quality of its component parts.

Pope's command of the metrical conventions of his time shows to advantage in his treatment of the subject of prosody through contrapuntal examples of good and bad verses and in his demonstration of the necessary relationship of sound and sense.

A recurrent theme is "wit" as essential to poetry, and the *Essay* is remarkable for the many variations of meaning Pope managed to ring upon the term, so important for his age. But despite all discussion and attempts at definition by many writers, "wit," as an aesthetic virtue and a significant critical term, declined with the eighteenth century and in the nineteenth suffered almost complete eclipse by the romantic "imagination."

The conventions on which the neoclassical writer and critic depended were soon to be blasted by the romantic revolution. Premonitory rumblings could be heard as early as the mid-eighteenth century as Samuel Johnson bluntly attacked the arbitrary rules and terminology of neoclassical genre criticism. Despite Johnson's ingrained conservatism and loyalty to the neoclassical principle of general or universal truth, he was a rebel against the Augustan age (and closer to ours) in his habitual method of reading closely and subjecting rules and generalizations to the test of his experience.

The romantic rejection of the authority of the past has left a deep mark on the twentieth century. For most writers and critics the idea of prescriptive rules is unthinkable. But this healthy attitude of creative and critical independence does not mean that the earlier critics have had their say. The meaning and value of the works of great minds cannot be limited to what the past has found in them.

The continuing reexamination of Aristotle's *Poetics*, for example, is rewarding and salutary in many ways. One is the exploratory spirit it reveals. Tentative insights and careful notations are surer stimulants and finer examples for the beginning critic than dogmatic pronouncements. There is also an essential humanism in Aristotle's idea of art: his awareness that the imitation of character and event satisfies the human desire to "know" through recognition and to express common aspirations in the face of all obstacles. Finally, there is his acute observation that a command of metaphor "is the mark of genius, for to make good metaphors implies an eye for resemblances."

An "eye for resemblances" is a necessary qualification for the critic as well as the poet. Without this gift he would be able to distinguish neither the formal patterns of organization in a work, nor the place of a work within a larger body of literature, nor the relationships between literature and experience. The resemblances, to be sure, are never fixed and unchanging. There is a continuous shift and renewal of perspective from generation to generation and from age to age. It is largely for this reason that the works of the great critics, like the classics of imaginative literature they discuss, are inexhaustible to analysis and meditation.

Plato

(427?–347 B.C.)

The idealist philosophy of Plato has had a profound though largely indirect influence upon literary study and criticism. In *The Republic* Plato describes poetry and art as an imitation, not of true reality, but of the forms of nature, which are themselves merely imitations or imperfect reflections of the eternal unchanging forms or "ideas" that constitute essential reality. Because this higher reality can be apprehended only through man's reason, not his senses, philosophy is the guide to truth, while poetry and the representative arts, mere imitations of imitations, remain two removes away. In the dialogue of *Ion* Plato sets forth through his spokesman Socrates the idea of poetry as inspiration and of the poet as one who, possessed by his Muse and transported out of his senses, sings not by art but by a "power divine." This exalted view of the poet as prophet and seer, so attractive to later romantics, has sometimes been cited as a tribute to the poet's genius. It is undercut, however, as Socrates proceeds to demonstrate through adroit questioning of the rhapsode Ion that neither the poet, who is inspired by his Muse, nor his critic-interpreter the rhapsode, who is inspired by the poet, is the master of an "art" in the sense of a specialized technical or "scientific" knowledge. Pleasantly but remorselessly Socrates maneuvers Ion into a position where he must acknowledge that his own criticism of Homer is the product of inspiration rather than "art," or scientific method. The end of the dialogue leaves both the poet and his critic at an unmistakably implied disadvantage to the philosopher.

So too in Book X of *The Republic* Plato speaks of the poet as one who appeals to men's passions rather than to their reason. It is not surprising then that the imitative poet, because he is a threat to civic virtue, is excluded from the ideal state, where the philosopher-leaders will admit no poetry other than "hymns to the gods and praises of famous men." In spite of these objections, Plato's own manner of expression has struck many readers as poetic, depending as it does on fictional dialogue and the extensive use of analogies, metaphors, and myths. The idea that inspiration is the motive not only of the poet but also of the philosophic lover of beauty and truth pervades Plato's writings. His doctrine of noumenal forms or "ideas" reflected in the forms of the lower world of nature has affinities with the assumptions of later myth and archetype critics. Despite his banishment of poets from his ideal state, Plato's own tenure in the republic of letters has survived two thousand years.

The best known and most used edition of Plato's works in English is Benjamin Jowett, *The Dialogues of Plato* (3rd edition, 1892).

ION

Socrates: Welcome, Ion. Are you from your native city of Ephesus?

Ion: No, Socrates, but from Epidaurus, where I attended the festival of Asclepius.

And do the Epidaurians have contests of rhapsodes at the festival?

O yes, and of all sorts of musical performers.

And were you one of the competitors—and did you succeed?

I obtained the first prize of all, Socrates.

Well done, and I hope that you will do the same for us at the Panathenaea.

And I will, please heaven.

I often envy the profession of a rhapsode, Ion, for you have always to wear fine clothes, and to look as beautiful as you can is a part

The text is based on that of Benjamin Jowett, ed., *The Dialogues of Plato* (3rd edition, 1892).

of your art. Then, again, you are obliged to be continually in the company of many good poets, and especially of Homer, who is the best and most divine of them, and to understand him, and not merely learn his words by rote, is a thing greatly to be envied. And no man can be a rhapsode who does not understand the meaning of the poet. For the rhapsode ought to interpret the mind of the poet to his hearers, but how can he interpret him well unless he knows what he means? All this is greatly to be envied.

Very true, Socrates; interpretation has certainly been the most laborious part of my art, and I believe myself able to speak about Homer better than any man and that neither Metrodorus of Lampsacus nor Stesimbrotus of Thasos nor Glaucon nor any one else who ever was had as good ideas about Homer as I have or as many.

I am glad to hear you say so, Ion; I see that you will not refuse to acquaint me with them.

Certainly, Socrates, and you really ought to hear how exquisitely I render Homer. I think that the Homeridae should give me a golden crown.

I shall take an opportunity of hearing your embellishments of him at some other time. But just now I should like to ask you a question: Does your art extend to Hesiod and Archilochus, or to Homer only?

To Homer only; he is in himself quite enough.

Are there any things about which Homer and Hesiod agree?

Yes; in my opinion there are a good many.

And can you interpret better what Homer says or what Hesiod says about these matters in which they agree?

I can interpret them equally well, Socrates, where they agree.

But what about matters in which they do not agree?—for example, about divination, of which both Homer and Hesiod have something to say?

Very true.

Would you or a good prophet be a better interpreter of what these two poets say about divination, not only when they agree, but when they disagree?

A prophet.

And if you were a prophet, would you be able to interpret them when they disagree as well as when they agree?

Clearly.

But how did you come to have this skill about Homer only and not about Hesiod or the other poets? Does not Homer speak of the same themes which all other poets handle? Is not war his great argument? and does he not speak of human society and of intercourse of men, good and bad, skilled and unskilled, and of the gods conversing with one another and with mankind and about what happens in heaven and in the world below and the generations of gods and heroes? Are not these the themes of which Homer sings?

Very true, Socrates.

And do not the other poets sing of the same?

Yes, Socrates, but not in the same way as Homer.

What, in a worse way?

Yes, in a far worse.

And Homer in a better way?

He is incomparably better.

And yet surely, my dear friend Ion, in a discussion about arithmetic, where many people are speaking and one speaks better than the rest, there is somebody who can judge which of them is the good speaker?

Yes.

And he who judges of the good will be the same as he who judges of the bad speakers?

The same.

And he will be the arithmetician?

Yes.

Well, and in discussions about the wholesomeness of food, when many persons are speaking and one speaks better than the rest, will he who recognizes the better speaker be a different person from him who recognizes the worse or the same?

Clearly the same.

And who is he, and what is his name?

The physician.

And speaking generally, in all discussions in which the subject is the same and many men are speaking, will not he who knows the good know the bad speaker also? For if he does not know the bad, neither will he know the good when the same topic is being discussed.

True.

Is not the same person skillful in both?

Yes.

And you say that Homer and the other poets, such as Hesiod and Archilochus, speak of the same things, although not in the same way, but the one speaks well and the other not so well?

Yes, and I am right in saying so.

And if you knew the good speaker, you would also know the inferior speakers to be inferior?

That is true.

Then, my dear friend, can I be mistaken in saying that Ion is equally skilled in Homer and in other poets, since he himself acknowledges that the same person will be a good judge of all those who speak of the same things and that almost all poets do speak of the same things?

Why then, Socrates, do I lose attention and go to sleep and have absolutely no ideas of the least value when any one speaks of any other poet, but when Homer is mentioned, I wake up at once and am all attention and have plenty to say?

The reason, my friend, is obvious. No one can fail to see that you speak of Homer without any art or knowledge. If you were able to speak of him by rules of art, you would have been able to speak of all other poets, for poetry is a whole.

Yes.

And when any one acquires any other art as a whole, the same may be said of them. Would you like me to explain my meaning, Ion?

Yes, indeed, Socrates; I very much wish that you would, for I love to hear you wise men talk.

O that we were wise, Ion, and that you could truly call us so, but you rhapsodes and actors and the poets whose verses you sing are wise, whereas I am a common man, who only speak the truth. For consider what a very commonplace and trivial thing is this which I have said, a thing which any man might say: that when a man has acquired a knowledge of a whole art, the inquiry into good and bad is one and the same. Let us consider this matter. Is not the art of painting a whole?

Yes.

And there are and have been many painters good and bad?

Yes.

And did you ever know any one who was skillful in pointing out the excellences and defects of Polygnotus the son of Aglaophon, but incapable of criticizing other painters and, when the work of any other painter was produced, went to sleep and was at a loss and had no ideas, but when he had to give his opinion about Polygnotus, or whoever the painter might be, and about him only, woke up and was attentive and had plenty to say?

No, indeed, I have never known such a person.

Or did you ever know of any one in sculpture who was skillful in expounding the merits of Daedalus the son of Metion or of Epeius the son of Panopeus or of Theodorus the Samian or of any individual sculptor but, when the works of sculptors in general were produced, was at a loss and went to sleep and had nothing to say?

No, indeed; no more than the other.

And if I am not mistaken, you never met with any one among flute-players or harp-players or singers to the harp or rhapsodes who was able to discourse of Olympus or Thamyras or Orpheus or Phemius the rhapsode of Ithaca, but was at a loss when he came to speak of Ion of Ephesus and had no notion of his merits or defects?

I cannot deny what you say, Socrates. Nevertheless I am conscious in my own self, and the world agrees with me in thinking that I do speak better and have more to say about Homer than any other man. But I do not speak equally well about others—tell me the reason of this.

I perceive, Ion, and I will proceed to explain to you what I imagine to be the reason of this. The gift which you possess of speaking excellently about Homer is not an art, but, as I was just saying, an inspiration; there is a divinity moving you like that contained in the stone which Euripides calls a magnet, but which is commonly known as the stone of Heraclea. This stone not only attracts iron rings, but also imparts to them a similar power of attracting other rings, and sometimes you may see a number of pieces of iron and rings suspended from one another so as to form quite a long chain, and all of them derive their power of suspension from the original stone. In like manner the Muse first of all inspires men herself, and from these inspired persons a chain of other persons is suspended who take the inspiration. For all good poets, epic as well as lyric, compose their beautiful poems not by art, but because they are inspired and possessed. And as the Corybantian revellers when they dance are not in their right mind, so the lyric poets are not in their right mind when they are composing their beautiful strains, but when falling under the power of music and meter, they are inspired and possessed like Bacchic maidens who draw milk and honey from the rivers when they are under the influence of Dionysus but not when they are in their right mind. And the soul of the lyric poet does the same, as they themselves say, for they tell us that they bring songs from honeyed fountains, culling them out of the gardens and dells of the Muses, they, like the bees, winging their way from flower to flower. And this is true. For the poet is a light and winged and holy thing, and there is no invention in him until he has been inspired and is out of his senses, and the mind is no longer in him. When he has not attained to this state, he is powerless and is unable to utter his oracles. Many are the noble words in which poets speak concerning the actions of men, but like yourself when speaking about Homer, they do not speak of them by any rules of art. They are simply inspired to utter that to which the Muse impels them and that only, and when inspired, one of them will make dithyrambs, another hymns of praise, another choral strains, another epic or iambic verses, and he who is good at one is not good at any other kind of verse, for not by art does the poet sing, but by power divine. Had he learned by rules of art, he would have known how to speak not of one theme only, but of all, and therefore God takes away the minds of poets and uses them as his ministers, as he also uses diviners and holy prophets, in order that we who hear them may know them to be speaking not of themselves who utter these priceless words in a state of unconsciousness, but that God himself is the speaker and that through them he is conversing with us. And Tynnichus the Chalcidian affords a striking instance of what I am saying: he wrote nothing that any one would care to remember but the famous paean which is in every one's mouth, one of the finest poems ever written, simply an invention of the Muses, as he himself says. For in this way the God would seem to indicate to us and not allow us to doubt that these beautiful poems are not human or the work of man, but divine and the work of

God, and that the poets are only the interpreters of the Gods by whom they are severally possessed. Was not this the lesson which the God intended to teach when by the mouth of the worst of poets he sang the best of songs? Am I not right, Ion?

Yes, indeed, Socrates, I feel that you are, for your words touch my soul, and I am persuaded that good poets by a divine inspiration interpret the things of the Gods to us.

And you rhapsodists are the interpreters of the poets?

There again you are right.

Then you are the interpreters of interpreters?

Precisely.

I wish you would frankly tell me, Ion, what I am going to ask of you: When you produce the greatest effect upon the audience in the recitation of some striking passage, such as the apparition of Odysseus leaping forth on the floor, recognized by the suitors and casting his arrows at his feet, or the description of Achilles rushing at Hector or the sorrows of Andromache, Hecuba, or Priam, are you in your right mind? Are you not carried out of yourself, and does not your soul in an ecstasy seem to be among the persons or places of which you are speaking, whether they are in Ithaca or in Troy or whatever may be the scene of the poem?

That proof strikes home to me, Socrates. For I must frankly confess that at the tale of pity my eyes are filled with tears, and when I speak of horrors, my hair stands on end and my heart throbs.

Well, Ion, and what are we to say of a man who at a sacrifice or festival, when he is dressed in holiday attire and has golden crowns upon his head of which nobody has robbed him, appears weeping or panic-stricken in the presence of more than twenty thousand friendly faces, when there is no one despoiling or wronging him, is he in his right mind or is he not?

No, indeed, Socrates, I must say that, strictly speaking, he is not in his right mind.

And are you aware that you produce similar effects on most spectators?

Only too well, for I look down upon them from the stage and behold the various emotions of pity, wonder, sternness, stamped upon their countenances when I am speaking, and I am obliged to give my very best attention to them, for if I make them cry, I myself shall laugh, and if I make them laugh, I myself shall cry when the time for payment arrives.

Do you know that the spectator is the last of the rings which, as I am saying, receive the power of the original magnet from one another? The rhapsode like yourself and the actor are intermediate links, and the poet himself is the first of them. Through all these the God sways the souls of men in any direction which he pleases and makes one man hang down from another. Thus there is a vast chain of dancers and masters and undermasters of choruses who are suspended as if from the stone at the side of the rings which hang down from the Muse. And every poet has some Muse from whom he is suspended and by whom he is said to be possessed, which is nearly the same thing, for he is taken hold of. And from these first rings, which are the poets, depend others, some deriving their inspiration from Orpheus, others from Musaeus, but the greater number are possessed and held by Homer. Of whom, Ion, you are one, and are possessed by Homer, and when any one repeats the words of another poet, you go to sleep and know not what to say, but when any one recites a strain of Homer, you wake up in a moment and your soul leaps within you and you have plenty to say, for not by art or knowledge about Homer do you say what you say, but by divine inspiration and by possession, just as the Corybantian revellers too have a quick perception of that strain only which is appropriated to the God by whom they are possessed and have plenty of dances and words for that, but take no heed of any other. And you, Ion, when the name of Homer is mentioned, have plenty to say and have nothing to say of others. You ask, "Why is this?" The answer is that you praise Homer not by art but by divine inspiration.

That is good, Socrates, and yet I doubt whether you will ever have eloquence enough to persuade me that I praise Homer only when I am mad and possessed, and if you could hear me speak of him, I am sure you would never think this to be the case.

I should like very much to hear you, but not until you have answered a question which I have to ask. On what part of Homer do you speak well?—not surely about every part.

There is no part, Socrates, about which I do not speak well; of that I can assure you.

Surely not about things in Homer of which you have no knowledge?

And what is there in Homer of which I have no knowledge?

Why, does not Homer speak in many passages about arts? For example, about driving; if I can only remember the lines I will repeat them.

I remember and will repeat them.

Tell me then what Nestor says to Antilochus, his son, where he bids him be careful of the turn at the horse-race in honor of Patroclus.

"Bend gently," he says, "in the polished chariot to the left of them and urge the horse on the right hand with whip and voice and slacken the rein. And when you are at the goal, let the left horse draw near yet so that the nave of the well-wrought wheel may not even seem to touch the extremity and avoid catching the stone." [*Iliad*, XXIII, 335.]

Enough. Now, Ion, will the charioteer or the physician be the better judge of the propriety of these lines?

The charioteer, clearly.

And will the reason be that this is his art, or will there be any other reason?

No, that will be the reason.

And every art is appointed by God to have knowledge of a certain work, for that which we know by the art of the pilot we do not know by the art of medicine?

Certainly not.

Nor do we know by the art of the carpenter that which we know by the art of medicine?

Certainly not.

And this is true of all the arts, that which we know with one art we do not know with the other? But let me ask a prior question: You admit that there are differences of arts?

Yes.

You would argue, as I should, that when one art is of one kind of knowledge and another of another, they are different?

Yes.

Yes, surely, for if the subject of knowledge were the same, there would be no meaning in saying that the arts were different, if they both gave the same knowledge. For example, I know that here are five fingers, and you know the same. And if I were to ask whether

I and you became acquainted with this fact by the help of the same art of arithmetic, you would acknowledge that we did?

Yes.

Tell me, then, what I was intending to ask you, whether this holds universally? Must the same art have the same subject of knowledge, and different arts other subjects of knowledge?

That is my opinion, Socrates.

Then he who has no knowledge of a particular art will have no right judgment of the sayings and doings of that art?

Very true.

Then which will be a better judge of the lines which you were reciting from Homer, you or the charioteer?

The charioteer.

Why, yes, because you are a rhapsode and not a charioteer.

Yes.

And the art of the rhapsode is different from that of the charioteer?

Yes.

And if a different knowledge, then a knowledge of different matters?

True.

You know the passage in which Hecamede, the concubine of Nestor, is described as giving to the wounded Machaon a posset, as he says, "Made with Pramnian wine, and she grated cheese of goat's milk with a grater of bronze and at his side placed an onion which gives a relish to drink." [*Iliad*, XI, 639–640.] Now would you say that the art of the rhapsode or the art of medicine was better able to judge of the propriety of these lines?

The art of medicine.

And when Homer says, "And she descended into the deep like a leaden plummet which, set in the horn of ox that ranges in the fields, rushes along carrying death among the ravenous fishes" [*Iliad*, XXIV, 80.], will the art of the fisherman or of the rhapsode be better able to judge whether these lines are rightly expressed or not?

Clearly, Socrates, the art of the fisherman.

Come now, suppose that you were to say to me: "Since you, Socrates, are able to assign different passages in Homer to their corresponding arts, I wish that you would tell me what are the passages of which the excellence ought to be judged by the prophet and prophetic art," and you will see how readily and truly I shall answer you. For there are many such passages, particularly in the *Odyssey*, as, for example, the passage in which Theoclymenus the prophet of the house of Melampus says to the suitors, "Wretched men! what is happening to you? Your heads and your faces and your limbs underneath are shrouded in night, and the voice of lamentation bursts forth and your cheeks are wet with tears. And the vestibule is full and the court is full of ghosts descending into the darkness of Erebus and the sun has perished out of heaven and an evil mist is spread abroad." [XX, 351.] And there are many such passages in the *Iliad* also, as for example in the description of the battle near the rampart, where he says, "As they were eager to pass the ditch, there came to them an omen: a soaring eagle, holding back the people on the left, bore a huge bloody dragon in his talons, still living and panting; nor had he yet resigned the strife, for he bent back and smote the bird which carried him on the breast by the neck, and he in pain let him fall from him to the ground into the midst of the multitude. And the eagle, with a cry, was borne afar on the wings of the wind." [XII, 200.] These are the sorts of things which I should say that the prophet ought to consider and determine.

And you are quite right, Socrates, in saying so.

Yes, Ion, and you are right also. And as I have selected from the *Iliad* and *Odyssey* for you passages which describe the office of the prophet and the physician and the fisherman, do you, who know Homer so much better than I do, Ion, select for me passages which relate to the rhapsode and the rhapsode's art and which the rhapsode ought to examine and judge of better than other men.

All passages, I should say, Socrates.

Not all, Ion, surely. Have you already forgotten what you were saying? A rhapsode ought to have a better memory.

Why, what am I forgetting?

Do you not remember that you declared the art of the rhapsode to be different from the art of the charioteer?

Yes, I remember.

And you admitted that being different they would have different subjects of knowledge?

Yes.

Then upon your own showing the rhapsode and the art of the rhapsode will not know everything?

I should exclude certain things, Socrates.

You mean to say that you would exclude pretty much the subjects of the other arts. As he does not know all of them, which of them will he know?

He will know what a man and what a woman ought to say and what a freeman and what a slave ought to say and what a ruler and what a subject.

Do you mean that a rhapsode will know better than the pilot what the ruler of a sea-tossed vessel ought to say?

No, the pilot will know best.

Or will the rhapsode know better than the physician what the ruler of a sick man ought to say?

He will not.

But he will know what a slave ought to say?

Yes.

Suppose the slave to be a cowherd; the rhapsode will know better than the cowherd what he ought to say in order to soothe the infuriated cows?

No, he will not.

But he will know what a spinning-woman ought to say about the working of wool?

No.

At any rate he will know what a general ought to say when exhorting his soldiers?

Yes, that is the sort of thing which the rhapsode will be sure to know.

Well, but is the art of the rhapsode the art of the general?

I am sure that I should know what a general ought to say.

Why, yes, Ion, because you may possibly have a knowledge of the art of the general as well as of the rhapsode, and you may also have a knowledge of horsemanship as well as of the lyre, and then you would know when horses were well or ill managed. But suppose I were to ask you: By the help of which art, Ion, do you know whether horses are well managed, by your skill as a horseman or as a performer on the lyre, what would you answer?

I should reply, by my skill as a horseman.

And if you judged of performers on the lyre, you would admit that you judged of them as a performer on the lyre and not as a horseman?

Yes.

And in judging of the general's art, do you judge of it as a general or a rhapsode?

To me there appears to be no difference between them.

What do you mean? Do you mean to say that the art of the rhapsode and of the general is the same?

Yes, one and the same.

Then he who is a good rhapsode is also a good general?

Certainly, Socrates.

And he who is a good general is also a good rhapsode?

No, I do not say that.

But you do say that he who is a good rhapsode is also a good general.

Certainly.

And you are the best of Hellenic rhapsodes?

Far the best, Socrates.

And are you the best general, Ion?

To be sure, Socrates, and Homer was my master.

But then, Ion, what in the name of goodness can be the reason why you, who are the best of generals as well as the best of rhapsodes in all Hellas, go about as a rhapsode when you might be a general? Do you think that the Hellenes want a rhapsode with his golden crown and do not want a general?

Why, Socrates, the reason is that my countrymen, the Ephesians, are the servants and soldiers of Athens and do not need a general, and you and Sparta are not likely to have me, for you think that you have enough generals of your own.

My good Ion, did you never hear of Apollodorus of Cyzicus?

Who may he be?

One who, though a foreigner, has often been chosen their general by the Athenians, and there is Phanosthenes of Andros and Heraclides of Clazomenae, whom they have also appointed to the command of their armies and to other offices, although aliens, after they had shown their merit. And will they not choose Ion the Ephesian to be their general and honor him, if he prove himself worthy? Were not the Ephesians originally Athenians, and Ephesus is no mean city? But, indeed, Ion, if you are correct in saying that by art and knowledge you are able to praise Homer, you do not deal fairly with me, and after all your professions of knowing many glorious things about Homer and promises that you would exhibit them, you are only a deceiver and so far from exhibiting the art of which you are a master, will not, even after my repeated entreaties, explain to me the nature of it. You have literally as many forms as Proteus, and now you go all manner of ways, twisting and turning, and, like Proteus, become all manner of people at once and at last slip away from me in the disguise of a general in order that you may escape exhibiting your Homeric lore. And if you have art, then, as I was saying, in falsifying your promise that you would exhibit Homer, you are not dealing fairly with me. But if, as I believe, you have no art, but speak all these beautiful words about Homer unconsciously under his inspiring influence, then I acquit you of dishonesty and shall only say that you are inspired. Which do you prefer to be thought, dishonest or inspired?

There is a great difference, Socrates, between the two alternatives, and inspiration is by far the nobler.

Then, Ion, I shall assume the nobler alternative and attribute to you in your praises of Homer inspiration and not art.

THE REPUBLIC

From Book X

Socrates: Of the many excellences which I perceive in the order of our State, there is none which upon reflection pleases me better than the rule about poetry.

Glaucon: To what do you refer?

To the rejection of imitative poetry, which certainly ought not to be received; as I see far more clearly now that the parts of the soul have been distinguished.

/ What do you mean?

Speaking in confidence, for I should not like to have my words repeated to the tragedians and the rest of the imitative tribe—but I do not mind saying to you that all poetical imitations are ruinous to the understanding of the hearers and that the knowledge of their true nature is the only antidote to them.

Explain the purport of your remark. . . .

Well, then, here are three beds: one existing in nature, which is made by God, as I think that we may say, for no one else can be the maker?

No.

There is another which is the work of the carpenter?

Yes.

And the work of the painter is a third?

Yes.

Beds, then, are of three kinds, and there are three artists who superintend them: God, the maker of the bed, and the painter?

Yes, there are three of them.

God, whether from choice or from necessity, made one bed in nature and one only; two or more such ideal beds neither ever have been nor ever will be made by God.

Why is that?

Because even if He had made but two, a third would still appear behind them which both of them would have for their idea, and that would be the ideal bed and not the two others.

Very true.

God knew this, and He desired to be the real maker of a real bed, not a particular maker of a particular bed, and therefore He created a bed which is essentially and by nature one only.

So we believe.

Shall we then speak of Him as the natural author or maker of the bed?

Yes, inasmuch as by the natural process of creation he is the author of this and of all other things.

And what shall we say of the carpenter? Is not he also the maker of the bed?

Yes.

But would you call the painter a creator and maker?

Certainly not.

Yet if he is not the maker, what is he in relation to the bed?

I think that we may fairly designate him as the imitator of that which the others make.

Good; then you call him who is third in the descent from nature an imitator?

Certainly.

And the tragic poet is an imitator, and therefore, like all other imitators, he is thrice removed from the king and from the truth?

That appears to be so. . . .

Now do you suppose that if a person were able to make the original as well as the image he would seriously devote himself to the image-making branch? Would he allow imitation to be the ruling principle of his life, as if he had nothing higher in him?

I should say not.

The real artist, who knew what he was imitating, would be interested in realities and not in imitations and would desire to leave as memorials of himself works many and fair; and, instead of being the author of encomiums, he would prefer to be the theme of them.

Yes, that would be to him a source of much greater honor and profit.

. . . The poet with his words and phrases may be said to lay on the colors of the several arts, himself understanding their nature only enough to imitate them; and other people, who are as ignorant as he is and judge only from his words, imagine that if he speaks of cobbling or of military tactics or of anything else, in meter and harmony and rhythm, he speaks very well—such is the sweet influence which melody and rhythm by nature have. And I think that you must have observed again and again what a poor appearance the tales of poets make when stripped of the colors which music puts upon them and recited in simple prose.

Yes. . . .

Thus far then we are pretty well agreed that the imitator has no knowledge worth mentioning of what he imitates. Imitation is only a kind of play or sport, and the tragic poets, whether they write in iambic or heroic verse, are imitators in the highest degree?

Very true.

And now tell me, I conjure you, has not imitation been shown by us to be concerned with that which is thrice removed from the truth?

Certainly.

And what is the faculty in man to which imitation is addressed?

What do you mean?

I will explain: The body which is large when seen near appears small when seen at a distance?

True.

And the same object appears straight when looked at out of the water and crooked when in the water; and the concave becomes convex, owing to the illusion about colors to which the sight is liable. Thus every sort of confusion is revealed within us, and this is that weakness of the human mind on which the art of conjuring and of deceiving by light and shadow and other ingenious devices imposes, having an effect upon us like magic.

True.

And the arts of measuring and numbering and weighing come to the rescue of the human understanding (there is the beauty of them), and the apparent greater or less, or more or heavier, no longer have the mastery over us but give way before calculation and measure and weight?

Most true.

And this, surely, must be the work of the calculating and rational principle in the soul?

To be sure.

And when this principle measures and certifies that some things are equal or that some are greater or less than others, there occurs an apparent contradiction?

True.

But were we not saying that such a contradiction is impossible: the same faculty cannot have contrary opinions at the same time about the same thing?

Very true.

Then that part of the soul which has an opinion contrary to measure is not the same with that which has an opinion in accordance
with measure?

True.

And the better part of the soul is likely to be that which trusts to
measure and calculation?

Certainly.

And that which is opposed to them is one of the inferior principles of the soul?

No doubt.

This was the conclusion at which I was seeking to arrive when I
said that painting or drawing and imitation in general, when doing
their own proper work, are far removed from truth, and the companions and friends and associates of a principle within us which is
equally removed from reason, and that they have no true or healthy
aim.

Exactly.

The imitative art is an inferior who marries an inferior and has
inferior offspring.

Very true.

And is this confined to the sight only, or does it extend to the
hearing also, relating in fact to what we term poetry?

Probably the same would be true of poetry. . . .

Then the imitative poet who aims at being popular is not by nature
made nor is his art intended to please or to affect the rational principle in the soul; but he will prefer the passionate and fitful temper,
which is easily imitated?

Clearly.

And now we may fairly take him and place him by the side of the
painter, for he is like him in two ways: first, inasmuch as his creations
have an inferior degree of truth—in this, I say, he is like him; and he is
also like him in being concerned with an inferior part of the soul;
and therefore we shall be right in refusing to admit him into a well
ordered state because he awakens and nourishes and strengthens
the feelings and impairs the reason. As in a city when the evil are
permitted to have authority and the good are put out of the way, so
in the soul of man, as we maintain, the imitative poet implants an

evil constitution, for he indulges the irrational nature which has no discernment of greater and less but thinks the same thing at one time great and at another small. He is a manufacturer of images and is very far removed from the truth.

Exactly.

But we have not yet brought forward the heaviest count in our accusation: the power which poetry has of harming even the good (and there are very few who are not harmed) is surely an awful thing?

Yes, certainly, if the effect is what you say.

Hear and judge: The best of us, as I conceive, when we listen to a passage of Homer or one of the tragedians in which he represents some pitiful hero who is drawling out his sorrows in a long oration or weeping and smiting his breast—the best of us, you know, delight in giving way to sympathy and are in raptures with the excellence of the poet who stirs our feelings most.

Yes, of course I know.

But when any sorrow of our own happens to us, then you may observe that we pride ourselves on the opposite quality—we would fain be quiet and patient; this is the manly part, and the other which delighted us in the recitation is now deemed to be the part of a woman.

Very true.

Now can we be right in praising and admiring another who is doing that which any one of us would abominate and be ashamed of in his own person?

No, that is certainly not reasonable.

Nay, quite reasonable from one point of view.

What point of view?

If you consider that when in misfortune we feel a natural hunger and desire to relieve our sorrow by weeping and lamentation and that this feeling, which is kept under control in our own calamities, is satisfied and delighted by the poets, the better nature in each of us, not having been sufficiently trained by reason or habit, allows the sympathetic element to break loose because the sorrow is another's, and the spectator fancies that there can be no disgrace to himself in praising and pitying anyone who comes telling him what a good man

he is and making a fuss about his troubles; he thinks that the pleasure
is a gain, and why should he be supercilious and lose this and the
poem too? Few persons ever reflect, as I should imagine, that from the
evil of other men something of evil is communicated to themselves.
And so the feeling of sorrow which has gathered strength at the sight
of the misfortunes of others is with difficulty repressed in our own.

How very true!

And does not the same hold also of the ridiculous? There are jests
which you would be ashamed to make yourself, and yet on the comic
stage or indeed in private, when you hear them, you are greatly
amused by them and are not at all disgusted at their unseemliness.
The case of pity is repeated: there is a principle in human nature
which is disposed to raise a laugh, and this which you once restrained by reason because you were afraid of being thought a buffoon
is now let out again, and having stimulated the risible faculty at the
theater you are betrayed unconsciously to yourself into playing the
comic poet at home.

Quite true.

And the same may be said of lust and anger and all the other
affections, of desire and pain and pleasure, which are held to be
inseparable from every action—in all of them poetry feeds and waters
the passions instead of drying them up: she lets them rule although
they ought to be controlled if mankind are ever to increase in happiness and virtue.

I cannot deny it.

Therefore, Glaucon, whenever you meet with any of the eulogists
of Homer declaring that he has been the educator of Hellas and that
he is profitable for education and for the ordering of human things
and that you should take him up again and again and get to know
him and regulate your whole life according to him, we may love and
honor those who say these things (they are excellent people, as far
as their lights extend) and we are ready to acknowledge that Homer
is the greatest of poets and first of tragedy writers, but we must remain firm in our conviction that hymns to the gods and praises of
famous men are the only poetry which ought to be admitted into our
State. For if you go beyond this and allow the honeyed muse to
enter, either in epic or lyric verse, not law and the reason of man-

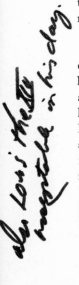

kind, which by common consent have ever been deemed best, but pleasure and pain will be the rulers in our State.

That is most true.

And now, since we have reverted to the subject of poetry, let this our defense serve to show the reasonableness of our former judgment in sending away out of our State an art having the tendencies which we have described, for reason constrained us. But that she may not impute to us any harshness or want of politeness, let us tell her that there is an ancient quarrel between philosophy and poetry, of which there are many proofs, such as the saying of "the yelping hound howling at her lord" or of one "mighty in the vain talk of fools" and "the mob of sages circumventing Zeus" and the "subtle thinkers who are beggars after all"; and there are innumerable other signs of ancient enmity between them. Notwithstanding this, let us assure our sweet friend and the sister arts of imitation that if she will only prove her title to exist in a well ordered state we shall be delighted to receive her. We are very conscious of her charms, but we may not on that account betray the truth. I dare say, Glaucon, that you are as much charmed by her as I am, especially when she appears in Homer?

Yes indeed, I am greatly charmed.

Shall I propose then that she be allowed to return from exile, but upon this condition only: that she make a defense of herself in lyrical or some other meter?

Certainly.

And we may further grant to those of her defenders who are lovers of poetry and not yet poets the permission to speak in prose on her behalf: let them show not only that she is pleasant but also useful to states and to human life, and we will listen in a kindly spirit, for if this can be proved we shall surely be the gainers—I mean if there is a use in poetry as well as a delight?

Certainly, we shall be the gainers.

If her defense fails, then, my dear friend, like other persons who are enamored of something but put a restraint upon themselves when they think their desires are opposed to their interests, so too must we after the manner of lovers give her up, though not without a struggle. We too are inspired by that love of poetry which the education of noble states has implanted in us, and therefore we would have her appear at her best and truest, but so long as she is unable to make good her defense, this argument of ours shall be a charm to us, which we will repeat to ourselves while we listen to her strains, that we may not fall away into the childish love of her which captivates the many. At all events we are well aware that poetry, being such as we have described, is not to be regarded seriously as attaining to the truth, and he who listens to her, fearing for the safety of the city which is within him, should be on his guard against her seductions and make our words his law.

Aristotle

(384–322 B.C.)

Pupil of Plato and tutor to Alexander, Aristotle stands beside his teacher as one of the two greatest seminal minds of the Greek classic age. He is also, by virtue of the *Poetics*, the founder of literary criticism and the first in a long line of theorist critics of Western literature. He accepts the idea of poetry and art as imitation without questioning as Plato had done the reality of the natural events and objects represented by the artist. Rather than the philosopher viewing literature as an alien discipline, he is truly the literary critic focusing on the formal elements of works as objects of study. Where Plato is transcendentalistic and idealistic, Aristotle is empirical and "scientific" in his analysis and classification of the literature of his age. He is also more friendly than Plato to poets and poetry. Whereas Plato distrusts the false knowledge of poetry and draws an invidious contrast between the poet and the philosopher, Aristotle praises the knowledge provided by the poet and compares him favorably with the historian, saying that poetry, because it deals in universal ideas and truths, is more philosophic than history, which deals in particulars. Since its revival during the Renaissance, the *Poetics* has stimulated a continuing discussion of its main topics: art as imitation; the literary genres, especially tragedy and to a lesser extent the epic; the problem of the unities, less urgent for Aristotle than for later neoclassical critics; and the nature of poetic diction and metaphor.

In discussing tragedy, the principal subject of his incomplete treatise, Aristotle considers its historical development, its constituent parts, its function of purging the emotions of pity and fear, the aims of characterization, and the character of the hero or protagonist. Aristotle, who begins the *Poetics* by stating his intention of following the "order of nature" in treating poetry in relation to its observable classes, is far more inductive and exploratory—and thus "modern" in spirit—than more dogmatic neoclassical followers who used his work as the foundation of a prescriptive genre criticism. The greatest debt of later critics to Aristotle is for his classic formulation of basic principles that must be made new as they are reexamined, revised, and reformulated in terms of the needs of each succeeding age.

Of numerous editions of the *Poetics* in English, the most familiar and useful to students of literature is S. H. Butcher, *Aristotle's Theory of Poetry and Fine Art with a Critical Text and Translation of "The Poetics"* (4th edition, 1907). The introductory essay by John Gassner in the Dover Publications edition of Butcher's work (1951) is an excellent example of a modern critic's revaluation of the *Poetics*.

POETICS

I

I propose to treat of poetry in itself and of its various kinds, noting the essential quality of each, to inquire into the structure of the plot as requisite to a good poem, into the number and nature of the parts of which a poem is composed, and similarly into whatever else falls within the same inquiry. Following, then, the order of nature, let us begin with the principles which come first.

The text is based on the translation by S. H. Butcher, *Aristotle's Theory of Poetry and Fine Art with a Critical Text and Translation of "The Poetics"* (4th edition, 1907).

Epic poetry and tragedy, comedy also and dithyrambic poetry, and the music of the flute and of the lyre in most of their forms are all in their general conception modes of imitation. They differ, however, from one another in three respects—the medium, the objects, the manner or mode of imitation, being in each case distinct.

For as there are persons who, by conscious art or mere habit, imitate and represent various objects through the medium of color and form, or again by the voice, so in the arts above mentioned, taken as a whole, the imitation is produced by rhythm, language, or harmony, either singly or combined.

Thus in the music of the flute and of the lyre, harmony and rhythm alone are employed, also in other arts, such as that of the shepherd's pipe, which are essentially similar to these. In dancing, rhythm alone is used without harmony, for even dancing imitates character, emotion, and action by rhythmical movement.

There is another art which imitates by means of language alone, and that either in prose or verse—which verse, again, may either combine different meters or consist of but one kind—but this has hitherto been without a name. For there is no common term we could apply to the mimes of Sophron and Xenarchus and the Socratic dialogues on the one hand, and, on the other, to poetic imitations in iambic, elegiac, or any similar meter. People do indeed add the word "maker" or "poet" to the name of the meter and speak of elegiac poets or epic (that is, hexameter) poets as if it were not the imitation that makes the poet, but the verse that entitles them all indiscriminately to the name. Even when a treatise on medicine or natural science is brought out in verse, the name of poet is by custom given to the author, and yet Homer and Empedocles have nothing in common but the meter, so that it would be right to call the one poet, the other physicist rather than poet. On the same principle, even if a writer in his poetic imitation were to combine all meters, as Chaeremon did in his Centaur, which is a medley composed of meters of all kinds, we should bring him too under the general term *poet*. So much then for these distinctions.

There are, again, some arts which employ all the means above mentioned—namely, rhythm, tune, and meter. Such are dithyrambic and nomic poetry, and also tragedy and comedy, but between them the difference is that in the first two cases these means are all employed in combination, in the latter, now one means is employed, now another.

Such, then, are the differences of the arts with respect to the medium of imitation.

II

Since the objects of imitation are men in action, and these men must be either of a higher or a lower type (for moral character mainly answers to these divisions, goodness and badness being the distinguishing marks of moral differences), it follows that we must represent men either as better than in real life or as worse or as they are. It is the same in painting. Polygnotus depicted men as nobler than they are, Pauson as less noble; Dionysius drew them true to life.

Now it is evident that each of the modes of imitation above mentioned will exhibit these differences and become a distinct kind in imitating objects that are thus distinct. Such diversities may be found even in dancing, flute-playing, and lyre-playing. So again in language, whether prose or verse unaccompanied by music. Homer, for example, makes men better than they are; Cleophon, as they are; Hegemon the Thasian, the inventor of parodies, and Nicochares, the author of the *Deiliad,* worse than they are. The same thing holds good of dithyrambs and nomes; here too one may portray different types, as Timotheus and Philoxenus differed in representing their Cyclopes. The same distinction marks off tragedy from comedy, for comedy aims at representing men as worse, tragedy as better than in actual life.

III

There is still a third difference—the manner in which each of these objects may be imitated. For the medium being the same, and the objects the same, the poet may imitate by narration—in which case he can either take another personality as Homer does or speak in his own person, unchanged—or he may present all his characters as living and moving before us.

These, then, as we said at the beginning, are the three differences which distinguish artistic imitation—the medium, the objects, and the manner. So that from one point of view Sophocles is an imitator of the same kind as Homer, for both imitate higher types of character; from another point of view, of the same kind as Aristophanes, for both imitate persons acting and doing. Hence, some say, the name of "drama" is given to such poems, as representing action. For the same reason the Dorians claim the invention of both tragedy and comedy. The claim to comedy is put forward by the Megarians, not only by those of Greece proper, who allege that it originated under their democracy, but also by the Megarians of Sicily, for the poet Epicharmus, who is much earlier than Chionides and Magnes, belonged to that country. Tragedy too is claimed by certain Dorians of the Peloponnese. In each case they appeal to the evidence of language. Villages, they say, are by them called *kōmai*, by the Athenians *dēmoi*, and they assume that comedians were so named not from *kōmazein*, "to revel," but because they wandered from village to village (*kata kōmas*), being excluded contemptuously from the city. They add also that the Dorian word for "doing" is *dran*, and the Athenian, *prattein*.

This may suffice as to the number and nature of the various modes of imitation.

IV

Poetry in general seems to have sprung from two causes, each of them lying deep in our nature. First, the instinct of imitation is implanted in man from childhood, one difference between him and other animals being that he is the most imitative of living creatures, and through imitation he learns his earliest lessons, and no less universal is the pleasure felt in things imitated. We have evidence of this in the facts of experience. Objects which in themselves we view with pain we delight to contemplate when reproduced with minute fidelity, such as the forms of the most ignoble animals and of dead bodies. The cause of this again is that to learn gives the liveliest pleasure, not only to philosophers but to men in general, whose capacity, however, of learning is more limited. Thus the reason why men enjoy seeing a likeness is that in contemplating it they find themselves learning or inferring, and saying perhaps, "Ah, that is he." For if you happen not to have seen the original, the pleasure will be due not to the imitation as such, but to the execution, the coloring, or some such other cause.

Imitation, then, is one instinct of our nature. Next there is the instinct for harmony and rhythm, meters being manifestly sections of rhythm. Persons, therefore, starting with this natural gift developed by degrees their special aptitudes, till their rude improvisations gave birth to poetry.

Poetry now diverged in two directions, according to the individual character of the writers. The graver spirits imitated noble actions and the actions of good men. The more trivial sort imitated the actions of meaner persons, at first composing satires, as the former did hymns to the gods and the praises of famous men. A poem of the satirical kind cannot indeed be put down to any author earlier than Homer, though many such writers probably there were. But from Homer onward, instances can be cited: his own *Margites*, for example, and other similar compositions. The appropriate meter was also here introduced; hence the measure is still called the iambic or lampooning measure, being that in which people lampooned one another. Thus the older poets were distinguished as writers of heroic or of lampooning verse.

As in the serious style Homer is pre-eminent among poets, for he alone combined dramatic form with excellence of imitation, so he too first laid down the main lines of comedy by dramatizing the ludicrous instead of writing personal satire. His *Margites* bears the same relation to comedy that the *Iliad* and *Odyssey* do to tragedy. But when tragedy and comedy came to light, the two classes of poets still followed their natural bent: the lampooners became writers of comedy, and the epic poets were succeeded by tragedians, since the drama was a larger and higher form of art.

Whether tragedy has as yet perfected its proper types or not and whether it is to be judged in itself or in relation also to the audience, this raises another question. Be that as it may, tragedy—as also comedy—was at first mere improvisation. The one originated with the leaders of the dithyramb, the other with those of the phallic songs, which are still in use in many of our cities. Tragedy advanced by slow degrees; each new element that showed itself was in turn developed. Having passed through many changes, it found its natural form, and there it stopped.

Aeschylus first introduced a second actor; he diminished the importance of the chorus and assigned the leading part to the dialogue. Sophocles raised the number of actors to three and added scene-painting. Moreover, it was not till late that the short plot was discarded for one of greater compass, and the grotesque diction of the earlier satyric form for the stately manner of tragedy. The iambic measure then replaced the trochaic tetrameter which was originally employed when the poetry was of the satyric[1] order and had greater affinities with dancing. Once dialogue had come in, nature herself discovered the appropriate measure. For the iambic is, of all measures, the most colloquial: we see it in the fact that conversational speech runs into iambic form more frequently than into any other kind of verse—rarely into hexameters, and only when we drop the colloquial intonation. The additions to the number of episodes or acts, and the other improvements of which tradition tells, must be taken as already described, for to discuss them in detail would doubtless be a large undertaking.

V

Comedy is, as we have said, an imitation of characters of a lower type—not, however, in the full sense of the word *bad*, the ludicrous being merely a subdivision of the ugly. It consists in some defect or ugliness which is not painful or destructive. To take an obvious example, the comic mask is ugly and distorted but does not imply pain.

The successive changes through which tragedy passed and the authors of these changes are well known, whereas comedy has had no history because it was not at first treated seriously. It was late before

---

[1] The reference is to the earlier satyr play, with its chorus of satyrs, and not to satire.

Tragedy
Aristotle

the Archon granted a comic chorus to a poet; the performers were till then voluntary. Comedy had already taken definite shape when comic poets, distinctively so called, are heard of. Who introduced masks or prologues or increased the number of actors—these and other similar details remain unknown. As for the plot, it came originally from Sicily, but of Athenian writers Crates was the first who, abandoning the iambic or lampooning form, generalized his themes and plots.

Epic poetry agrees with tragedy insofar as it is an imitation in verse of characters of a higher type. They differ in that epic poetry admits but one kind of meter and is narrative in form. They differ, again, in their length, for tragedy endeavors, as far as possible, to confine itself to a single revolution of the sun, or but slightly to exceed this limit, whereas the epic action has no limits of time. This, then, is a second point of difference, though at first the same freedom was admitted in tragedy as in epic poetry.

Of their constituent parts, some are common to both, some peculiar to tragedy. Whoever, therefore, knows what is good or bad tragedy, knows also about epic poetry, for all the elements of an epic poem are found in tragedy, but the elements of a tragedy are not all found in the epic poem.

VI

Of the poetry which imitates in hexameter verse and of comedy, we will speak hereafter. Let us now discuss tragedy, resuming its formal definition, as resulting from what has been already said.

Tragedy, then, is an imitation of an action that is serious, complete, and of a certain magnitude; in language embellished with each kind of artistic ornament, the several kinds being found in separate parts of the play; in the form of action, not of narrative; through pity and fear effecting the proper purgation [*katharsis*] of these emotions. By "language embellished," I mean language into which rhythm, harmony, and song enter. By "the several kinds in separate parts," I mean that some parts are rendered through the medium of verse alone, others again with the aid of song.

Now, as tragic imitation implies persons acting, it necessarily fol-

TRAGECY
PLOT
ALTION

lows, in the first place, that spectacular equipment will be a part of tragedy. Next, song and diction, for these are the medium of imitation. By "diction" I mean the mere metrical arrangement of the words; as for "song," it is a term whose sense every one understands.

Again, tragedy is the imitation of an action, and an action implies personal agents who necessarily possess certain distinctive qualities both of character and thought, for it is by these that we qualify actions themselves, and these—thought and character—are the two natural causes from which actions spring, and on actions again all success or failure depends. Hence, the plot is the imitation of the action, for by plot I here mean the arrangement of the incidents. By character I mean that in virtue of which we ascribe certain qualities to the agents. Thought is required wherever a statement is proved, or, it may be, a general truth enunciated. Every tragedy, therefore, must have six parts, which parts determine its quality—namely, plot, character, diction, thought, spectacle, song. Two of the parts constitute the medium of imitation, one the manner, and three the objects of imitation. And these complete the list. These elements have been employed, we may say, by the poets to a man; in fact, every play contains spectacular elements as well as character, plot, diction, song, and thought.

But most important of all is the structure of the incidents. For tragedy is an imitation, not of men, but of an action and of life, and life consists in action, and its end is a mode of action, not a quality. Now character determines men's qualities, but it is by their actions that they are happy or the reverse. Dramatic action, therefore, is not with a view to the representation of character: character comes in as subsidiary to the actions. Hence the incidents and the plot are the end of a tragedy, and the end is the chief thing of all. Again, without action there cannot be a tragedy; there may be without character. The tragedies of most of our modern poets fail in the rendering of character, and of poets in general this is often true. It is the same in painting, and here lies the difference between Zeuxis and Polygnotus. Polygnotus delineates character well; the style of Zeuxis is devoid of ethical quality. Again, if you string together a set of speeches expressive of character and well finished in point of diction and thought, you will not produce the essential tragic effect nearly so well as with

a play which, however deficient in these respects, yet has a plot and
artistically constructed incidents. Besides which, the most powerful
elements of emotional interest in tragedy—*peripeteia* or reversal of intention, and recognition scenes—are parts of the plot. A further proof
is that novices in the art attain to finish of diction and precision of
portraiture before they can construct the plot. It is the same with
almost all the early poets.

The plot, then, is the first principle and, as it were, the soul of a
tragedy; character holds the second place. A similar fact is seen in
painting. The most beautiful colors, laid on confusedly, will not give
as much pleasure as the chalk outline of a portrait. Thus tragedy is
the imitation of an action and of the agents, mainly with a view to the
action.

Third in order is thought, that is, the faculty of saying what is
possible and pertinent in given circumstances. In the case of oratory,
this is the function of the political art and of the art of rhetoric: and
so indeed the older poets make their characters speak the language of
civic life; the poets of our time, the language of the rhetoricians.

Character is that which reveals moral purpose, showing what kind of
things a man chooses or avoids. Speeches, therefore, which do not
make this manifest, or in which the speaker does not choose or avoid
anything whatever, are not expressive of character. Thought, on the
other hand, is found where something is proved to be or not to be
or a general maxim is enunciated.

Fourth among the elements enumerated comes diction, by which
I mean, as has been already said, the expression of the meaning in
words; and its essence is the same both in verse and prose.

Of the remaining elements song holds the chief place among the
embellishments.

The spectacle has indeed an emotional attraction of its own, but
of all the parts it is the least artistic and connected least with the art
of poetry. For the power of tragedy, we may be sure, is felt even
apart from representation and actors. Besides, the production of spectacular effects depends more on the art of the stage machinist than
on that of the poet.

VII

These principles being established, let us now discuss the proper structure of the plot, since this is the first and most important part of tragedy.

Now, according to our definition, tragedy is an imitation of an action that is complete, and whole, and of a certain magnitude, for there may be a whole that is wanting in magnitude. A whole is that which has a beginning, a middle, and an end. A beginning is that which does not itself follow anything by causal necessity, but after which something naturally is or comes to be. An end, on the contrary, is that which itself naturally follows some other thing, either by necessity, or as a rule, but has nothing following it. A middle is that which follows something as some other thing follows it. A well constructed plot, therefore, must neither begin nor end at haphazard, but conform to these principles.

Again, a beautiful object, whether it be a picture of a living organism or any whole composed of parts, must not only have an orderly arrangement of parts but must also be of a certain magnitude, for beauty depends on magnitude and order. Hence an exceedingly small picture cannot be beautiful, for the view of it is confused, the object being seen in an almost imperceptible moment of time. Nor, again, can one of vast size be beautiful, for as the eye cannot take it all in at once, the unity and sense of the whole is lost for the spectator, as for instance if there were a picture a thousand miles long. As, therefore, in the case of animate bodies and pictures a certain magnitude is necessary, and a magnitude which may be easily embraced in one view, so in the plot a certain length is necessary, and a length which can be easily embraced by the memory. The limit of length in relation to dramatic competition and sensuous presentment is no part of artistic theory. For had it been the rule for a hundred tragedies to compete together, the performance would have been regulated by the water clock—as indeed we are told was formerly done. But the limit as fixed by the nature of the drama itself is this: the greater the length, the more beautiful will the piece be by reason of its size, provided that the whole be perspicuous. And, to define the matter roughly, we may say that the proper magnitude is comprised within such limits that the sequence of events, according to the law of probability or necessity, will admit of a change from bad fortune to good or from good fortune to bad.

VIII

Unity of plot does not, as some persons think, consist in the unity of the hero. For infinitely various are the incidents in one man's life, which cannot be reduced to unity, and so, too, there are many actions of one man out of which we cannot make one action. Hence the error, as it appears, of all poets who have composed a *Heracleid*, a *Theseid*, or other poems of the kind. They imagine that as Heracles was one man, the story of Heracles must also be a unity. But Homer, as in all else he is of surpassing merit, here too—whether from art or natural genius—seems to have happily discerned the truth. In composing the *Odyssey* he did not include all the adventures of Odysseus—such as his wound on Parnassus or his feigned madness at the mustering of the host—incidents between which there was no necessary or probable connection, but he made the *Odyssey*, and likewise the *Iliad*, to center round an action that in our sense of the word is one. As, therefore, in the other imitative arts, the imitation is one when the object imitated is one, so the plot, being an imitation of an action, must imitate one action and that a whole, the structural union of the parts being such that, if any one of them is displaced or removed, the whole will be disjointed and disturbed. For a thing whose presence or absence makes no visible difference is not an organic part of the whole.

IX

It is, moreover, evident from what has been said that it is not the function of the poet to relate what has happened, but what may happen—what is possible according to the law of probability or necessity. The poet and the historian differ not by writing in verse or in prose. The work of Herodotus might be put into verse, and it would still be a species of history, with meter no less than without it. The true difference is that one relates what has happened, the other what may happen. Poetry, therefore, is a more philosophical and a higher thing than history, for poetry tends to express the universal, history the particular. By the universal I mean how a person of a certain type will on occasion speak or act, according to the law of probability or necessity, and it is this universality at which poetry aims in the names she attaches to the personages. The particular is, for example, what Alcibiades did or suffered. In comedy this is already apparent, for here the poet first constructs the plot on the lines of probability and then inserts characteristic names, unlike the lampooners who write about particular individuals. But tragedians still keep to real names, the reason being that what is possible is credible. What has not happened we do not at once feel sure to be possible, but what has happened is manifestly possible; otherwise it would not have happened. Still there are some tragedies in which there are only one or two well known names, the rest being fictitious. In others, none are well known—as in Agathon's *Antheus*, where incidents and names alike are fictitious—and yet they give none the less pleasure. We must not, therefore, at all costs keep to the received legends which are the usual subjects of tragedy. Indeed, it would be absurd to attempt it, for even subjects that are known are known only to a few, and yet give pleasure to all. It clearly follows that the poet or "maker" should be the maker of plots rather than of verses, since he is a poet because he imitates, and what he imitates are actions. And even if he chances to take a historical subject, he is none the less a poet, for there is no reason why some events that have actually happened should not conform to the law of the probable and possible, and in virtue of that quality in them he is their poet or maker.

Of all plots and actions the episodic are the worst. I call a plot "episodic" in which the episodes or acts succeed one another without probable or necessary sequence. Bad poets compose such pieces by their own fault, good poets, to please the players, for, as they write show pieces for competition, they stretch the plot beyond its capacity and are often forced to break the natural continuity.

But again, tragedy is an imitation not only of a complete action, but of events terrible and pitiful. Such an effect is best produced when the events come on us by surprise, and the effect is heightened when, at the same time, they follow as cause and effect. The tragic wonder will then be greater than if they happened of themselves or by accident, for even coincidences are most striking when they have an air of design. We may instance the statue of Mitys at Argos, which fell upon his murderer while he was a spectator at a festival and killed him. Such events seem not to be due to mere chance. Plots, there-fore, constructed on these principles are necessarily the best.

X

Plots are either simple or complex, for the actions in real life, of which the plots are an imitation, obviously show a similar distinction. An action which is one and continuous in the sense above defined I call simple when the change of fortune takes place without reversal of intention and without recognition.

A complex action is one in which the change is accompanied by such reversal or by recognition, or by both. These last should arise from the internal structure of the plot, so that what follows should be the necessary or probable result of the preceding action. It makes all the difference whether any given event is a case of *propter hoc* or *post hoc*.

XI

Reversal of intention is a change by which the action veers round to its opposite, subject always to our rule of probability or necessity. Thus in the *Oedipus* the messenger comes to cheer Oedipus and free him from his alarms about his mother, but by revealing who he is he produces the opposite effect. Again, in the *Lynceus*, Lynceus is being led away to his death, and Danaus goes with him, meaning to slay him, but the outcome of the action is that Danaus is killed and Lynceus saved.

Recognition, as the name indicates, is a change from ignorance to knowledge, producing love or hate between the persons destined by the poet for good or bad fortune. The best form of recognition is coincident with a reversal of intention, as in the *Oedipus*. There are indeed other forms. Even inanimate things of the most trivial kind may sometimes be objects of recognition. Again, we may recognize or discover whether a person has done a thing or not. But the recognition which is most intimately connected with the plot and action is, as we have said, the recognition of persons. This recognition, combined with reversal, will produce either pity or fear, and actions producing these effects are those which, by our definition, tragedy represents. Moreover, it is upon such situations that the issues of good or bad fortune will depend. Recognition, then, being between persons, it may happen that one person only is recognized by the other—when the latter is already known—or it may be necessary that the recognition should be on both sides. Thus Iphigenia is revealed to Orestes by the sending of the letter, but another act of recognition is required to make Orestes known to Iphigenia.

Two parts then of the plot—reversal of intention and recognition—turn upon surprises. A third part is the tragic incident. The tragic incident is a destructive or painful action, such as death on the stage, bodily agony, wounds, and the like.

XII

The parts of tragedy which must be treated as elements of the whole have been already mentioned. We now come to the quantitative parts—the separate parts into which tragedy is divided—namely, *prologue, episode, exodos, choric song*, this last being divided into *parodos* and *stasimon*. These are common to all plays; peculiar to some are the songs of actors from the stage and the *kommoi*.

The *prologos* is that entire part of a tragedy which precedes the *parodos* of the chorus. The *episode* is that entire part of a tragedy which is between complete choric songs. The *exodos* is that entire part of a tragedy which has no choric song after it. Of the choric part the *parodos* is the first undivided utterance of the chorus; the *stasimon* is a choric ode without anapests or trochaic tetrameters; the *kommos* is a joint lamentation of chorus and actors. The parts of tragedy which must be treated as elements of the whole have been already mentioned. The quantitative parts—the separate parts into which it is divided—are here enumerated.

XIII

As the sequel to what has already been said, we must proceed to consider what the poet should aim at and what he should avoid in constructing his plots, and by what means the specific effect of tragedy will be produced.

A perfect tragedy should, as we have seen, be arranged not on the simple but on the complex plan. It should, moreover, imitate actions which excite pity and fear, this being the distinctive mark of tragic imitation. It follows plainly, in the first place, that the change of fortune presented must not be the spectacle of a virtuous man brought from prosperity to adversity, for this moves neither pity nor fear; it merely shocks us. Nor, again, that of a bad man passing from adversity to prosperity, for nothing can be more alien to the spirit of tragedy; it possesses no single tragic quality; it neither satisfies the moral sense nor calls forth pity or fear. Nor, again, should the downfall of the utter villain be exhibited. A plot of this kind would doubtless satisfy the moral sense, but it would inspire neither pity nor fear, for pity is aroused by unmerited misfortune, fear by the misfortune of a man like ourselves. Such an event, therefore, will be neither pitiful nor terrible. There remains then the character between these two extremes, that of a man who is not eminently good and just, yet whose misfortune is brought about not by vice or depravity but by some error or frailty. He must be one who is highly renowned and prosperous, a personage like Oedipus, Thyestes, or other illustrious men of such families.

A well constructed plot should therefore be single in its issue, rather than double as some maintain. The change of fortune should be not from bad to good, but, reversely, from good to bad. It should come about as the result not of vice, but of some great error or frailty in a character either such as we have described or better rather than worse. The practice of the stage bears out our view. At first the poets recounted any legend that came in their way. Now, the best tragedies are founded on the story of a few houses, on the fortunes of Alcmaeon, Oedipus, Orestes, Meleager, Thyestes, Telephus, and those others who have done or suffered something terrible. A tragedy, then, to be perfect according to the rules of art should be of this construction. Hence they are in error who censure Euripides just because he follows this principle in his plays, many of which end unhappily. It is, as we have said, the right ending. The best proof is that on the stage and in dramatic competition such plays, if well worked out, are the most tragic in effect, and Euripides, faulty though he may be in the general management of his subject, yet is felt to be the most tragic of the poets.

In the second rank comes the kind of tragedy which some place first. Like the *Odyssey,* it has a double thread of plot and also an opposite catastrophe for the good and for the bad. It is accounted the best because of the weakness of the spectators, for the poet is guided in what he writes by the wishes of his audience. The pleasure, however, thence derived is not the true tragic pleasure. It is proper rather to comedy, where those who in the piece are the deadliest enemies —like Orestes and Aegisthus—quit the stage as friends at the close, and no one slays or is slain.

XIV

Fear and pity may be aroused by spectacular means, but they may also result from the inner structure of the piece, which is the better way and indicates a superior poet. For the plot ought to be so constructed that, even without the aid of the eye, he who hears the tale told will thrill with horror and melt to pity at what takes place. This is the impression we should receive from hearing the story of the *Oedipus.* But to produce this effect by the mere spectacle is a less artistic method and dependent on extraneous aids. Those who employ spectacular means to create a sense not of the terrible but only of the monstrous are strangers to the purpose of tragedy, for we must not demand of tragedy any and every kind of pleasure, but only that which is proper to it. And since the pleasure which the poet should afford is that which comes from pity and fear through imitation, it is evident that this quality must be impressed upon the incidents.

Let us then determine what are the circumstances which strike us as terrible or pitiful.

Actions capable of this effect must happen between persons who are either friends or enemies or indifferent to one another. If an enemy kills an enemy, there is nothing to excite pity either in the act or the intention, except so far as the suffering in itself is pitiful. So again with indifferent persons. But when the tragic incident occurs between those who are near or dear to one another—if, for example, a brother kills or intends to kill a brother, a son his father, a mother her son, a son his mother, or any other deed of the kind is done—these are the situations to be looked for by the poet. He may not indeed destroy the framework of the received legends—the fact, for instance, that Clytemnestra was slain by Orestes and Eriphyle by Alcmaeon—but he ought to show invention of his own and skillfully handle the traditional material. Let us explain more clearly what is meant by skillful handling.

The action may be done consciously and with knowledge of the persons, in the manner of the older poets. It is thus too that Euripides makes Medea slay her children. Or, again, the deed of horror may be done, but done in ignorance, and the tie of kinship or friendship be discovered afterwards. The *Oedipus* of Sophocles is an example. Here indeed the incident is outside the drama proper, but cases occur where it falls within the action of the play: one may cite the *Alcmaeon* of Astydamas, or Telegonus in the *Wounded Odysseus*. Again, there is a third case, to be about to act with knowledge of the persons and then not to act. The fourth case is when someone is about to do an irreparable deed through ignorance and makes the discovery before it is done. These are the only possible ways. For the deed must either be done or not done, and that wittingly or unwittingly. But of all these ways, to be about to act knowing the persons, and then not to act, is the worst. It is shocking without being tragic, for no disaster follows. It is therefore never, or very rarely, found in poetry. One instance, however, is in the *Antigone*, where Haemon threatens to kill Creon. The next and better way is that the deed should be perpetrated. Still better, that it should be perpetrated in ignorance and the discovery made afterwards. There is then nothing to shock us, while the discovery produces a startling effect. The last case is the best, as when in the *Cresphontes* Merope is about to slay her son but, recognizing who he is, spares his life. So in the *Iphigenia* the sister recognizes the brother just in time. Again in the *Helle*, the son recognizes the mother when on the point of giving her up. This then is why a few families only, as has been already observed, furnish the subjects of tragedy. It was not art but happy chance that led poets to look for such situations and so impress the tragic quality upon their plots. They are compelled, therefore, to have recourse to those houses whose history contains moving incidents like these.

Enough has now been said concerning the structure of the incidents, and the proper constitution of the plot.

XV

In respect of character there are four things to be aimed at. First and most important, it must be good. Now any speech or action that manifests moral purpose of any kind will be expressive of character: the character will be good if the purpose is good. This rule is relative to each class. Even a woman may be good, and also a slave, though the woman may be said to be an inferior being and the slave quite worthless. The second thing to aim at is propriety. There is a type of manly valor, but valor in a woman, or unscrupulous cleverness, is inappropriate. Thirdly, character must be true to life, for this is a distinct thing from goodness and propriety as here described. The fourth point is consistency, for though the subject of the imitation, who suggested the type, be inconsistent, still he must be consistently inconsistent. As an example of motiveless degradation of character, we have Menelaus in the *Orestes;* of character indecorous and inappropriate, the lament of Odysseus in the *Scylla,* and the speech of Melanippe; of inconsistency, the *Iphigenia at Aulis,* for Iphigenia the suppliant in no way resembles her later self.

As in the structure of the plot, so too in the portraiture of character the poet should always aim either at the necessary or the probable. Thus a person of a given character should speak or act in a given way, by the rule either of necessity or of probability, just as this event should follow that by necessary or probable sequence. It is therefore evident that the unravelling of the plot, no less than the complication, must arise out of the plot itself; it must not be brought about by the *Deus ex Machina*—as in the *Medea* or in the return of the Greeks in the *Iliad*. The *Deus ex Machina* should be employed only for events external to the drama, for antecedent or subsequent events which lie beyond the range of human knowledge and which require to be reported or foretold, for to the gods we ascribe the power of seeing all things. Within the action there must be nothing irrational. If the irrational cannot be excluded, it should be outside the scope of the tragedy. Such is the irrational element in the *Oedipus* of Sophocles.

Again, since tragedy is an imitation of persons who are above the common level, the example of good portrait painters should be followed. They, while reproducing the distinctive form of the original, make a likeness which is true to life and yet more beautiful. So too the poet, in representing men who are irascible or indolent or have other defects of character, should preserve the type and yet ennoble it. In this way Achilles is portrayed by Agathon and Homer.

These then are rules the poet should observe. Nor should he neglect those appeals to the senses which, though not among the essentials, are the concomitants of poetry, for here too there is much room for error. But of this enough has been said in the published treatises.

XVI

What recognition is has been already explained. We will now enumerate its kinds.

First, the least artistic form, which, from poverty of wit, is most commonly employed—recognition by signs. Of these some are congenital, such as "the spear which the earth-born race bear on their bodies" or the stars introduced by Carcinus in his *Thyestes*. Others are acquired after birth, and of these some are bodily marks, as scars; some external tokens, as necklaces, or the little ark in the *Tyro* by which the discovery is effected. Even these admit of more or less skillful treatment. Thus in the recognition of Odysseus by his scar, the discovery is made in one way by the nurse, in another by the herdsmen. The use of tokens for the express purpose of proof—and indeed any formal proof with or without tokens—is a less artistic mode of recognition. A better kind is that which comes about by a turn of incident, as in the bath scene in the *Odyssey*.

Next come the recognitions invented at will by the poet, and on that account wanting in art. For example, Orestes in the *Iphigenia* reveals the fact that he is Orestes. She, indeed, makes herself known by the letter, but he, by speaking himself and saying what the poet, not what the plot requires. This, therefore, is nearly allied to the fault above mentioned, for Orestes might as well have brought tokens with him. Another similar instance is the "voice of the shuttle" in the *Tereus* of Sophocles.

The third kind depends on memory when the sight of some object awakens a feeling, as in the *Cyprians* of Dicaeogenes, where the hero breaks into tears on seeing the picture, or again in the "Lay of Alcinous," where Odysseus, hearing the minstrel play the lyre, recalls the past and weeps; and hence the recognition.

The fourth kind is by process of reasoning. Thus in the *Choephori:* "Some one resembling me has come; no one resembles me but Orestes; therefore Orestes has come." Such too is the discovery made by Iphigenia in the play of Polyidus the sophist. It was a natural reflection for Orestes to make, "So I too must die at the altar like my sister." So, again, in the *Tydeus* of Theodectes, the father says, "I came to find my son, and I lose my own life." So too in the *Phineidae:* the women, on seeing the place, inferred their fate: "Here we are doomed to die, for here we were cast forth." Again, there is a composite kind of recognition involving false inference on the part of one of the characters, as in the *Odysseus Disguised as a Messenger.* A said that no one else was able to bend the bow; hence B (the disguised Odysseus) imagined that A would recognize the bow which in fact he had not seen; and to bring about a recognition by this means —the expectation that A would recognize the bow—is false inference.

But of all recognitions the best is that which arises from the incidents themselves, where the startling discovery is made by natural means. Such is that in the *Oedipus* of Sophocles and in the *Iphigenia,* for it was natural that Iphigenia should wish to dispatch a letter. These recognitions alone dispense with the artificial aid of tokens or amulets. Next come the recognitions by process of reasoning.

XVII

In constructing the plot and working it out with the proper diction, the poet should place the scene, as far as possible, before his eyes. In this way, seeing everything with the utmost vividness, as if he were a spectator of the action, he will discover what is in keeping with it and be most unlikely to overlook inconsistencies. The need of such a rule is shown by the fault found in Carcinus. Amphiaraus was on his way from the temple. This fact escaped the observation of one who did not see the situation. On the stage, however, the piece failed, the audience being offended at the oversight.

Again, the poet should work out his play, to the best of his power, with appropriate gestures, for those who feel emotion are most convincing through natural sympathy with the characters they represent, and one who is agitated storms, one who is angry rages, with the most lifelike reality. Hence poetry implies either a happy gift of nature or a strain of madness. In the one case a man can take the mold of any character; in the other, he is lifted out of his proper self.

As for the story, whether the poet takes it ready made or constructs it for himself, he should first sketch its general outline and then fill in the episodes and amplify in detail. The general plan may be illustrated by the *Iphigenia*. A young girl is sacrificed; she disappears mysteriously from the eyes of those who sacrificed her; she is transported to another country, where the custom is to offer up all strangers to the goddess. To this ministry she is appointed. Some time later her own brother chances to arrive. The fact that the oracle for some reason ordered him to go there is outside the general plan of the play. The purpose, again, of his coming is outside the action proper. However, he comes, he is seized, and, when on the point of being sacrificed, reveals who he is. The mode of recognition may be either that of Euripides or of Polyidus, in whose play he exclaims very naturally,

"So it was not my sister only, but I too, who was doomed to be sacrificed"; and by that remark he is saved.

After this, the names being once given, it remains to fill in the episodes. We must see that they are relevant to the action. In the case of Orestes, for example, there is the madness which led to his capture and his deliverance by means of the purificatory rite. In the drama, the episodes are short, but it is these that give extension to epic poetry. Thus the story of the *Odyssey* can be stated briefly. A certain man is absent from home for many years; he is jealously watched by Poseidon and left desolate. Meanwhile his home is in a wretched plight—suitors are wasting his substance and plotting against his son. At length, tempest-tossed, he himself arrives; he makes certain persons acquainted with him; he attacks the suitors with his own hand and is himself preserved while he destroys them. This is the essence of the plot; the rest is episode.

XVIII

Every tragedy falls into two parts, complication and unravelling or *dénouement*. Incidents extraneous to the action are frequently combined with a portion of the action proper to form the complication; the rest is the unravelling. By the complication I mean all that extends from the beginning of the action to the part which marks the turning-point to good or bad fortune. The unravelling is that which extends from the beginning of the change to the end. Thus, in the *Lynceus* of Theodectes, the complication consists of the incidents presupposed in the drama, the seizure of the child, and then again the unravelling extends from the accusation of murder to the end.

There are four kinds of tragedy: the complex, depending entirely on reversal and recognition; the pathetic (where the motive is passion), such as the tragedies on Ajax and Ixion; the ethical (where the motives are ethical), such as the *Phthiotides* and the *Peleus*. The fourth kind is the simple. We here exclude the purely spectacular element, exemplified by the *Phorcides*, the *Prometheus*, and scenes laid in Hades. The poet should endeavor, if possible, to combine all poetic merits or, failing that, the greatest number and those the most important, the more so, in face of the cavilling criticism of the day. For whereas there have hitherto been good poets, each in his own branch, the critics now expect one man to surpass all others in their several lines of excellence.

In speaking of a tragedy as the same or different, the best test to take is the plot. Identity exists where the complication and unravelling are the same. Many poets tie the knot well but unravel it ill. Both arts, however, should always be mastered.

Again, the poet should remember what has been often said and not make a tragedy into an epic structure. By an epic structure I mean one with a multiplicity of plots, as if, for instance, you were to make a tragedy out of the entire story of the *Iliad*. In the epic poem, owing to its length, each part assumes its proper magnitude. In the drama the result is far from answering to the poet's expectation. The proof is that the poets who have dramatized the whole story of the fall of Troy, instead of selecting portions, like Euripides, or who have taken the whole tale of Niobe and not a part of her story, like Aeschylus, either fail utterly or meet with poor success on the stage. Even Agathon has been known to fail from this one defect. In his reversals of intention, however, he shows a marvelous skill in the effort to hit the popular taste, to produce a tragic effect that satisfies the moral sense. This effect is produced when the clever rogue, like Sisyphus, is outwitted or the brave villain defeated. Such an event is probable in Agathon's sense of the word: "It is probable," he says, "that many things should happen contrary to probability."

The chorus too should be regarded as one of the actors; it should be an integral part of the whole and share in the action in the manner not of Euripides but of Sophocles. As for the later poets, their choral songs pertain as little to the subject of the piece as to that of any other tragedy. They are therefore sung as mere interludes, a practice first begun by Agathon. Yet what difference is there between introducing such choral interludes and transferring a speech, or even a whole act, from one play to another?

XIX

It remains to speak of diction and thought, the other parts of tragedy having been already discussed. Concerning thought, we may assume what is said in the *Rhetoric,* to which inquiry the subject more strictly belongs. Under thought is included every effect which has to be produced by speech, the subdivisions being proof and refutation; the excitation of the feelings, such as pity, fear, anger, and the like; the suggestion of importance or its opposite. Now it is evident that the dramatic incidents must be treated from the same points of view as the dramatic speeches when the object is to evoke the sense of pity, fear, importance, or probability. The only difference is that the incidents should speak for themselves without verbal exposition, while the effects aimed at in speech should be produced by the speaker and as a result of the speech. For what were the business of a speaker if the thought were revealed quite apart from what he says?

Next, as regards diction. One branch of the inquiry treats of the modes of expression. But this province of knowledge belongs to the art of delivery and to the masters of that science. It includes, for instance, what is a command, a prayer, a narrative, a threat, a question, an answer, and so forth. To know or not to know these things involves no serious censure upon the poet's art. For who can admit the fault imputed to Homer by Protagoras, that in the words, "Sing, goddess, of the wrath," he gives a command under the idea that he utters a prayer? For to tell some one to do a thing or not to do it is, he says, a command. We may therefore pass this over as an inquiry that belongs to another art, not to poetry.

XX

Language in general includes the following parts: letter, syllable, connecting word, noun, verb, inflection or case, sentence or phrase.

A letter is an indivisible sound, yet not every such sound, but only one which can form part of a group of sounds. For even brutes utter indivisible sounds, none of which I call a letter. The sound I mean may be either a vowel, a semivowel, or a mute. A vowel is that which without impact of tongue or lip has an audible sound. A semivowel, that which with such impact has an audible sound, as *s* and *r*. A mute, that which with such impact has by itself no sound, but joined to a vowel sound becomes audible, as *g* and *d*. These are distinguished according to the form assumed by the mouth and the place where they are produced, according as they are aspirated or smooth, long or short; as they are acute, grave, or of an intermediate tone—which inquiry belongs in detail to a treatise on meter.

A syllable is a nonsignificant sound, composed of a mute and a vowel, for *gr* without *a* is a syllable, as also with *a, gra*. But the investigation of these differences belongs also to metrical science.

A connecting word is a nonsignificant sound, which neither causes nor hinders the union of many sounds into one significant sound; it may be placed at either end or in the middle of a sentence. Or a nonsignificant sound, which out of several sounds, each of them significant, is capable of forming one significant sound, as *amphi, peri*, and the like. Or a nonsignificant sound which marks the beginning, end, or division of a sentence, such, however, that it cannot correctly stand by itself at the beginning of a sentence, as *meu, etoi, de.*

A noun is a composite significant sound, not marking time, of which no part is in itself significant, for in double or compound words we do not employ the separate parts as if each were in itself significant. Thus in Theodorus, "god-given," the *dōrus* or "gift" is not in itself significant.

A verb is a composite significant sound, marking time, in which, as in the noun, no part is in itself significant. For "man" or "white" does not express the idea of "when," but "he walks" or "he has walked" does connote time, present or past.

Inflection belongs both to the noun and verb and expresses either the relation "of," "to," or the like; or that of number, whether one or many, as "man" or "men"; or the modes or tones in actual delivery, *e.g.*, a question or a command. "Did he go?" and "go" are verbal inflections of this kind.

A sentence or phrase is a composite significant sound, some at least of whose parts are in themselves significant, for not every such group of words consists of verbs and nouns—"the definition of man,"

for example—but it may dispense even with the verb. Still, it will
always have some significant part, as "in walking" or "Cleon son of
Cleon." A sentence or phrase may form a unity in two ways, either as
signifying one thing or as consisting of several parts linked together.
Thus the *Iliad* is one by the linking together of parts, the definition
of man by the unity of the thing signified.

XXI

Words are of two kinds, simple and double. By simple I mean
those composed of nonsignificant elements, such as *gē* ["earth"]. By
double or compound, those composed either of a significant and
nonsignificant element (though within the whole word no element is
significant), or of elements that are both significant. A word may likewise be triple, quadruple, or multiple in form, like so many Massilian
expressions, *e.g.*, *Hermo-caico-xanthus*, "who prayed to Father Zeus."

Every word is either current or strange or metaphorical or ornamental or newly-coined or lengthened or contracted or altered.

By a current or proper word I mean one which is in general use
among a people; by a strange word, one which is in use in another
country. Plainly, therefore, the same word may be at once strange and
current, but not in relation to the same people. The word *sigynon*,
"lance," is to the Cyprians a current term but to us a strange one.

Metaphor is the application of an alien name by transference either
from genus to species, or from species to genus, or from species to
species, or by analogy, that is, proportion. Thus from genus to species,
as, "There lies my ship," for lying at anchor is a species of lying. From
species to genus, as "Verily ten thousand noble deeds hath Odysseus wrought," for ten thousand is a species of large number and is
here used for a large number generally. From species to species, as,
"With blade of bronze drew away the life," and "Cleft the water with
the vessel of unyielding bronze." Here *arysai*, "to draw away," is
used for *tamein*, "to cleave," and *tamein* again for *arysai*—each being
a species of taking away. Analogy or proportion is when the second
term is to the first as the fourth to the third. We may then use the
fourth for the second, or the second for the fourth. Sometimes too we

qualify the metaphor by adding the term to which the proper word is relative. Thus the cup is to Dionysus as the shield to Ares. The cup may, therefore, be called "the shield of Dionysus," and the shield "the cup of Ares." Or again as old age is to life, so is evening to day. Evening may therefore be called "the old age of the day," and old age "the evening of life" or, in the phrases of Empedocles, "life's setting sun." For some of the terms of the proportion there is at times no word in existence; still the metaphor may be used. For instance, to scatter seed is called sowing, but the action of the sun in scattering his rays is nameless. Still this process bears to the sun the same relation as sowing to the seed. Hence the expression of the poet "sowing the god-created light." There is another way in which this kind of metaphor may be employed. We may apply an alien term and then deny of that term one of its proper attributes, as if we were to call the shield, not "the cup of Ares" but "the wineless cup."

An ornamental word . . . .

A newly-coined word is one which has never been even in local use, but is adopted by the poet himself. Some such words there appear to be, as *ernyges*, "sprouters," for *kerata*, "horns," and *arētēr*, "supplicator," for *hiereys*, "priest."

A word is lengthened when its own vowel is exchanged for a longer one or when a syllable is inserted. A word is contracted when some part of it is removed. . . .

An altered word is one in which part of the ordinary form is left unchanged and part is recast. . . .

Nouns in themselves are either masculine, feminine, or neuter. Masculine are such as end in *n, r, s,* or in some letter compounded with *s*—these being two, *Psi* and *Xi*. Feminine, such as end in vowels that are always long, namely *e* and *o* and—of vowels that admit of lengthening—those in *a*. Thus the number of letters in which nouns masculine and feminine end is the same, for *Psi* and *Xi* are equivalent to endings in *s* [*Sigma*]. No noun ends in a mute or vowel short by nature. Three only end in *i: meli, kommi, peperi;* five end in *u.* Neuter nouns end in these two latter vowels, also in *n* and *s.*

XXII

The perfection of style is to be clear without being mean. The clearest style is that which uses only current or proper words; at the same time it is mean—witness the poetry of Cleophon and of Sthenelus. That diction, on the other hand, is lofty and raised above the commonplace which employs unusual words. By unusual, I mean strange (or rare) words, metaphorical, lengthened—anything, in short, that differs from the normal idiom. Yet a style wholly composed of such words is either a riddle or a jargon: a riddle if it consists of metaphors, a jargon if it consists of strange (or rare) words. For the essence of a riddle is to express true facts under impossible combinations. Now this cannot be done by any arrangement of ordinary words, but by the use of metaphor it can. Such is the riddle: "A man I saw who on another man had glued the bronze by aid of fire," and others of the same kind. A diction that is made up of strange (or rare) terms is a jargon. A certain infusion, therefore, of these elements is necessary to style, for the strange (or rare) word, the metaphorical, the ornamental, and the other kinds above mentioned will raise it above the commonplace and mean, while the use of proper words will make it perspicuous. But nothing contributes more to produce a clearness of diction that is remote from commonness than the lengthening, contraction, and alteration of words. For by deviating in exceptional cases from the normal idiom, the language will gain distinction, while, at the same time, the partial conformity with usage will give perspicuity. The critics, therefore, are in error who censure these licenses of speech and hold the author up to ridicule. Thus Eucleides the elder declared that it would be an easy matter to be a poet if you might lengthen syllables at will. . . .

To employ such license at all obtrusively is no doubt grotesque, but in any mode of poetic diction there must be moderation. Even metaphors, strange (or rare) words, or any similar forms of speech would produce the like effect if used without propriety and with the express purpose of being ludicrous. How great a difference is made by the appropriate use of lengthening may be seen in epic poetry by the insertion of ordinary forms in the verse. So, again, if we take a strange (or rare) word, a metaphor, or any similar mode of expression and replace it by the current or proper term, the truth of our observation will be manifest. For example, Aeschylus and Euripides each composed the same iambic line. But the alteration of a single word by Euripides, who employed the rarer term instead of the ordinary one, makes one verse appear beautiful and the other trivial. Aeschylus in his *Philoctetes* says, "The cancer, which feeds upon the flesh of his foot." Euripides substitutes "feasts on" for "feeds on." Again, in the line, "But now being of slight consequence, and a weakling, and in disgrace," the difference will be felt if we substitute the common words, "And now being little, and feeble, and shamed." Or, if for the line, "Having placed a simple chair and a small table," we read "Having placed an ugly chair and a tiny table." Or, for "Shores roar," "Shores scream."

Again, Ariphrades ridiculed the tragedians for using phrases which no one would employ in ordinary speech. . . . It is precisely because such phrases are not part of the current idiom that they give distinction to the style. This, however, he failed to see.

It is a great matter to observe propriety in these several modes of expression—compound words, strange (or rare) words, and so forth. But the greatest thing by far is to have a command of metaphor. This alone cannot be imparted by another; it is the mark of genius, for to make good metaphors implies an eye for resemblances.

Of the various kinds of words, the compound are best adapted to dithyrambs, rare words to heroic poetry, metaphors to iambic. In heroic poetry, indeed, all these varieties are serviceable. But in iambic verse, which reproduces, as far as may be, familiar speech, the most appropriate words are those which are found even in prose. These are the current or proper, the metaphorical, the ornamental.

Concerning tragedy and imitation by means of action this may suffice.

XXIII

As to that poetic imitation which is narrative in form and employs a single meter, the plot manifestly ought, as in a tragedy, to be constructed on dramatic principles. It should have for its subject a single action, whole and complete, with a beginning, a middle, and an end. It will thus resemble a single and coherent picture of a living being and produce the pleasure proper to it. It will differ in structure from historical compositions, which of necessity present not a single action but a single period and all that happened within that period to one person or to many, little connected together as the events may be. For as the sea fight at Salamis and the battle with the Carthaginians in Sicily took place at the same time but did not tend to any one result, so in the sequence of events one thing sometimes follows another, and yet no single result is thereby produced. Such is the practice, we may say, of most poets. Here again, then, as has been already observed, the transcendent excellence of Homer is manifest. He never attempts to make the whole war of Troy the subject of his poem, though the war had a beginning and an end. It would have been too vast a theme and not easily embraced in a single view. If, again, he had kept it within moderate limits, it must have been overcomplicated by the variety of the incidents. As it is, he detaches a single portion and admits as episodes many events from the general story of the war—such as the catalogue of the ships and others—thus diversifying the poem. All other poets take a single hero, a single period, or an action single indeed, but with a multiplicity of parts. Thus did the author of the *Cypria* and of the *Little Iliad*. For this reason the *Iliad* and the *Odyssey* each furnish the subject of one tragedy, or, at most, of two, while the *Cypria* supplies materials for many and the *Little Iliad* for eight—the *Award of the Arms*, the *Philoctetes*, the *Neoptolemus*, the *Eurypylus*, *the Mendicant Odysseus*, the *Trojan Women*, the *Fall of Ilium*, the *Departure of the Fleet*.[2]

XXIV

Again, epic poetry must have as many kinds as tragedy: it must be simple or complex or ethical or pathetic. The parts also, with the exception of song and scenery, are the same, for it requires re-

[2] Of these plays only the *Trojan Women* of Euripides and the *Philoctetes* of Sophocles have survived.

versals of intention, recognitions, and tragic incidents. Moreover, the thoughts and the diction must be artistic. In all these respects Homer is our earliest and sufficient model. Indeed, each of his poems has a twofold character. The *Iliad* is at once simple and pathetic, and the *Odyssey* complex (for recognition scenes run through it) and at the same time ethical. Moreover, in diction and thought he is supreme.

Epic poetry differs from tragedy in the scale on which it is constructed and in its meter. As regards scale or length, we have already laid down an adequate limit: the beginning and the end must be capable of being brought within a single view. This condition will be satisfied by poems on a smaller scale than the old epics and answering in length to the group of tragedies presented at a single sitting.

Epic poetry has, however, a great—a special—capacity for enlarging its dimensions, and we can see the reason. In tragedy we cannot imitate several lines of actions carried on at one and the same time; we must confine ourselves to the action on the stage and the part taken by the players. But in epic poetry, owing to the narrative form, many events simultaneously transacted can be presented, and these, if relevant to the subject, add mass and dignity to the poem. The epic has here an advantage, and one that conduces to grandeur of effect, to diverting the mind of the hearer, and relieving the story with varying episodes. For sameness of incident soon produces satiety and makes tragedies fail on the stage.

As for the meter, the heroic measure has proved its fitness by the test of experience. If a narrative poem in any other meter or in many meters were now composed, it would be found incongruous. For of all measures the heroic is the stateliest and the most massive, and hence it most readily admits rare words and metaphors, which is another point in which the narrative form of imitation stands alone. On the other hand, the iambic and the trochaic tetrameter are stirring measures, the latter being akin to dancing, the former expressive of action. Still more absurd would it be to mix together different meters, as was done by Chaeremon. Hence no one has ever composed a poem on a great scale in any other than heroic verse. Nature herself, as we have said, teaches the choice of the proper measure.

Homer, admirable in all respects, has the special merit of being the only poet who rightly appreciates the part he should take him-self. The poet should speak as little as possible in his own person, for it is not this that makes him an imitator. Other poets appear them-selves upon the scene throughout and imitate but little and rarely. Homer, after a few prefatory words, at once brings in a man or woman or other personage, none of them wanting in characteristic qualities but each with a character of his own.

The element of the wonderful is admitted in tragedy. The ir-rational, on which the wonderful depends for its chief effects, has wider scope in epic poetry because there the person acting is not seen. Thus, the pursuit of Hector would be ludicrous if placed upon the stage—the Greeks standing still and not joining in the pur-suit, and Achilles waving them back. But in the epic poem the absurdity passes unnoticed. Now the wonderful is pleasing, as may be inferred from the fact that, in telling a story, everyone adds something startling of his own, knowing that his hearers like it. It is Homer who has chiefly taught other poets the art of telling lies skillfully. The secret of it lies in a fallacy. For, assuming that if one thing is or becomes, a second is or becomes, men imagine that, if the second is, the first likewise is or becomes. But this is a false inference. Hence, where the first thing is untrue, it is quite unnecessary, pro-vided the second be true, to add that the first is or has become. For the mind, knowing the second to be true, falsely infers the truth of the first. There is an example of this in the bath scene of the *Odyssey*.

Accordingly, the poet should prefer probable impossibilities to im-probable possibilities. The tragic plot must not be composed of irrational parts. Everything irrational should, if possible, be excluded; or, at all events, it should lie outside the action of the play (as, in the *Oedipus,* the hero's ignorance as to the manner of Laius' death); not within the drama, as in the *Electra,* the messenger's account of the Pythian games; or, as in the *Mysians,* the man who comes from Tegea to Mysia without speaking. The plea that otherwise the plot would have been ruined is ridiculous; such a plot should not in the first instance be constructed. But once the irrational has been intro-duced and an air of likelihood imparted to it, we must accept it in spite of the absurdity. Take even the irrational incidents in the *Odys-sey,* where Odysseus is left upon the shore of Ithaca. How intolerable even these might have been would be apparent if an inferior poet were to treat the subject. As it is, the absurdity is veiled by the poetic charm with which the poet invests it.

The diction should be elaborated in the pauses of the action, where there is no expression of character or thought. For, conversely, character and thought are merely obscured by a diction that is over brilliant.

XXV

With respect to critical difficulties and their solutions, the number and nature of the sources from which they may be drawn may be thus exhibited.

The poet being an imitator, like a painter or any other artist, must of necessity imitate one of the three objects—things as they were or are, things as they are said or thought to be, or things as they ought to be. The vehicle of expression is language, either current terms or, it may be, rare words or metaphors. There are also many modifications of language which we concede to the poets. Add to this, that the standard of correctness is not the same in poetry and politics, any more than in poetry and any other art. Within the art of poetry itself there are two kinds of faults, those which touch its essence and those which are accidental. If a poet has chosen to imitate something, but has imitated it incorrectly through want of capacity, the error is inherent in the poetry. But if the failure is due to a wrong choice —if he has represented a horse as throwing out both his off legs at once, or introduced technical inaccuracies in medicine, for example, or in any other art—the error is not essential to the poetry. These are the points of view from which we should consider and answer the objections raised by the critics.

First as to matters which concern the poet's own art. If he describes the impossible, he is guilty of an error, but the error may be justified if the end of the art be thereby attained (the end being that already mentioned)—if, that is, the effect of this or any other part of the poem is thus rendered more striking. A case in point is the pursuit of Hector. If, however, the end might have been as well or better attained without violating the special rules of the poetic art, the error is not justified, for every kind of error should, if possible, be avoided.

Again, does the error touch the essentials of the poetic art or some accident of it? For example, not to know that a hind has no horns is a less serious matter than to paint it inartistically.

Further, if it be objected that the description is not true to fact, the poet may perhaps reply, "But the objects are as they ought to be," just as Sophocles said that he drew men as they ought to be, Euripides as they are. In this way the objection may be met. If, however, the representation be of neither kind, the poet may answer, "This is how men say the thing is." This applies to tales about the gods. It may well be that these stories are not higher than fact nor yet true to fact; they are very possibly what Xenophanes says of them. But anyhow, "this is what is said." Again, a description may be no better than the fact: "still, it was the fact," as in the passage about the arms: "Upright upon their butt-ends stood the spears." This was the custom then, as it now is among the Illyrians.

Again, in examining whether what has been said or done by someone is poetically right or not, we must not look merely to the particular act or saying and ask whether it is poetically good or bad. We must also consider by whom it is said or done, to whom, when, in whose interest, or for what end—whether, for instance, it be to secure a greater good or avert a greater evil.

Other difficulties may be resolved by due regard to the usage of language. We may note a rare word, as in *oyreas men prōton,* where the poet perhaps employs *oyreas* not in the sense of mules, but of sentinels. So, again, of Dolon: "ill-favored indeed he was to look upon." It is not meant that his body was ill-shaped, but that his face was ugly, for the Cretans use the word *eueides,* "well-favored," to denote a fair face. Again, *zōroteron de keraie,* "mix the drink livelier," does not mean "mix it stronger," as for hard drinkers, but "mix it quicker."

Sometimes an expression is metaphorical, as "Now all gods and men were sleeping through the night," while at the same time the poet says, "Often indeed as he turned his gaze to the Trojan plain, he marvelled at the sound of flutes and pipes." "All" is here used

metaphorically for "many," all being a species of many. So in the
verse, "alone she hath no part," "alone" is metaphorical, for the best
known may be called the only one.

Again, the solution may depend upon accent or breathing [in pro-
nunciation]. Thus Hippias of Thasos solved the difficulties in the
line, "We grant he will obtain the thing prayed for," as "Allow him to
obtain the thing prayed for" [—a change determined by the accent
of a single word].

Or again, the question may be solved by punctuation, as in
Empedocles: "Of a sudden things became mortal that before had
learnt to be immortal, and things unmixed before mixed."

Or again, by ambiguity of construction, as in "more than two thirds
of the night had gone, and a third of it was left," where "more
than" is ambiguous.

Or by the usage of language. Thus any mixed drink is called
"wine." Hence Ganymede is said "to pour the wine to Zeus," though
the gods do not drink wine. So too workers in iron are called workers
in bronze. This, however, may also be taken as a metaphor.

Again, when a word seems to involve some inconsistency of meaning, we should consider how many senses it may bear in the
particular passage. For example: "there was stayed the spear of
bronze"—we should ask in how many ways we may take "being
checked there." The true mode of interpretation is the precise opposite of what Glaucon mentions. Critics, he says, jump at certain
groundless conclusions; they pass adverse judgment and then proceed
to reason on it; and, assuming that the poet has said whatever they
happen to think, find fault if a thing is inconsistent with their own
fancy. The question about Icarius has been treated in this fashion.
The critics imagine he was a Lacedaemonian. They think it strange,
therefore, that Telemachus should not have met him when he went
to Lacedaemon. But the Cephallenian story may perhaps be the true
one. They allege that Odysseus took a wife from among themselves
and that her father was Icadius, not Icarius. It is merely a mistake,
then, that gives plausibility to the objection.

In general, the impossible must be justified by reference to artistic
requirements or to the higher reality or to received opinion. With
respect to the requirements of art, a probable impossibility is to be
preferred to a thing improbable and yet possible. Again, it may be

impossible that there should be men such as Zeuxis painted. "Yes," we say, "but the impossible is the higher thing, for the ideal type must surpass the reality." To justify the irrational, we appeal to what is commonly said to be. In addition to which, we urge that the irrational sometimes does not violate reason, just as "it is probable that a thing may happen contrary to probability."

Things that sound contradictory should be examined by the same rules as in dialectical refutation—whether the same thing is meant in the same relation and in the same sense. We should therefore solve the question by reference to what the poet says himself or to what is tacitly assumed by a person of intelligence.

The element of the irrational and, similarly, depravity of character are justly censured when there is no inner necessity for introducing them. Such is the irrational element in the *Aegeus* of Euripides and the badness of Menelaus in the *Orestes*.

Thus there are five sources from which critical objections are drawn. Things are censured either as impossible or irrational or morally hurtful or contradictory or contrary to artistic correctness. The answers should be sought under the twelve heads above mentioned.

XXVI

The question may be raised whether the epic or tragic mode of imitation is the higher. If the more refined art is the higher, and the more refined in every case is that which appeals to the better sort of audience, the art which imitates anything and everything is manifestly most unrefined. The audience is supposed to be too dull to comprehend unless something of their own is thrown in by the performers, who therefore indulge in restless movements. Bad flute-players twist and twirl if they have to represent "the quoit-throw" or hustle the coryphaeus when they perform the "Scylla." Tragedy, it is said, has this same defect. We may compare the opinion that the older actors entertained of their successors. Mynniscus used to call Callippides "ape" on account of the extravagance of his action, and the same view was held of Pindarus. Tragic art, then, as a whole, stands to epic in the same relation as the younger to the older actors. So we are told that epic poetry is addressed to a cultivated audience, who

do not need gesture; tragedy, to an inferior public. Being then unrefined, it is evidently the lower of the two.

Now, in the first place, this censure attaches not to the poetic but
to the histrionic art, for gesticulation may be equally overdone in
epic recitation, as by Sosistratus, or in lyrical competition, as by
Mnasitheus the Opuntian. Next, all action is not to be condemned
—any more than all dancing—but only that of bad performers. Such
was the fault found in Callippides, as also in others of our own day,
who are censured for representing degraded women. Again, tragedy,
like epic poetry, produces its effect even without action; it reveals
its power by mere reading. If, then, in all other respects it is superior, this fault, we say, is not inherent in it.

And superior it is, because it has all the epic elements—it may
even use the epic meter—with the music and scenic effects as important accessories, and these produce the most vivid of pleasures.
Further, it has vividness of impression in reading as well as in representation. Moreover, the art attains its end within narrower limits,
for the concentrated effect is more pleasurable than one which is
spread over a long time and so diluted. What, for example, would be
the effect of the *Oedipus* of Sophocles if it were cast into a form
as long as the *Iliad?* Once more, the epic imitation has less unity,
as is shown by this, that any epic poem will furnish subjects for several
tragedies. Thus, if the story adopted by the poet has a strict unity, it
must either be concisely told and appear truncated; or, if it conform to the epic canon of length, it must seem weak and watery.
Such length implies some loss of unity if, I mean, the poem is constructed out of several actions, like the *Iliad* and the *Odyssey,* which
have many such parts, each with a certain magnitude of its own.
Yet these poems are as perfect as possible in structure; each is, in
the highest degree attainable, an imitation of a single action.

If, then, tragedy is superior to epic poetry in all these respects,
and, moreover, fulfills its specific function better as an art—for each art
ought to produce, not any chance pleasure, but the pleasure proper
to it, as already stated—it plainly follows that tragedy is the higher
art, as attaining its end more perfectly.

Thus much may suffice concerning tragic and epic poetry in general; their several kinds and parts, with the number of each and
their differences; the causes that make a poem good or bad; the objections of the critics and the answers to these objections.

Horace

(65–8 B.C.)

Son of a Roman freeman, Quintus Horatius Flaccus studied at Rome
and Athens and won early recognition as a poet. His patron Maecenas
gave him the Sabine farm on which he lived the life of a leisured
man of letters. *The Art of Poetry* (given its title by Quintilian) is
not a systematic treatise but an epistle addressed to the father and
two sons of the Piso family. The poem discusses the problems of writing poetry and drama and the qualities of the successful poet from
the point of view of an older experienced writer and friend of
the family. It is not possible to know how much the nature of the
epistle was influenced by its occasion, but Horace's warnings against
mediocrity and premature publication suggest that he may have had
misgivings about the literary qualifications of his young friends. Despite its practical cast, *The Art of Poetry* has been admired as a
summary statement of the principles of Horace's late classical age.
Besides formulating his famous statement of the function of poetry as
profit and delight, Horace endorses the standards of smoothness,
propriety of subject, simplicity and unity in composition, and moderation in all things. Rejecting the idea of poetic madness or irrational
inspiration, Horace sees natural genius and disciplined judgment as
interdependent, each ineffective without the other. His satirical treatment of the business spirit of Roman society and of the Bohemian
pseudopoets of the age has a fine contemporary ring. But he is less
concerned with questioning and rethinking the problems raised by

Plato, Aristotle, and other forerunners than with the graceful refor-
mulation of generally accepted ideas. With all his breadth and urbanity, there is in Horace a limiting aristocratic bias and willingness
to accept conventional rules and enforce them without question: "If
you would like your play to have appeal and to be repeatedly performed, let it have five acts, neither more nor less."

The best known verse translations of *The Art of Poetry* are those
of Ben Jonson, in heroic couplets, and Wentworth Dillon, Earl of
Roscommon, in blank verse. Of numerous prose translations, the most
closely literal is that of Christopher Smart, the eighteenth century poet.

THE ART OF POETRY

(*Ad Pisones*)

If a painter should wish to join a horse's neck to a human head
and spread a varicolored plumage over limbs of different animals
taken from here and there, so that what is a beautiful woman above
ends in an ugly fish below, could you, my friends, keep from laughing if given a private view? Believe me, Pisos, a book may be just
like such a picture, the ideas of which, like a sick man's dreams,
are all vain and fictitious, so that neither head nor foot can be
assigned to any one form. But painters and poets, you will say,
have always had the right of daring to do anything. We know this,
and this license we demand for ourselves and allow others, but not
to the degree that tame animals should be united to savage, nor that
serpents should be coupled with birds, lambs with tigers.

In pompous beginnings that promise a great deal, it often happens
that one or two verses of purple patchwork that make a great show
are tacked on, as when the grove and the altar of Diana and the

The translation by the present editors is based on the literal prose translation by Christopher Smart (1756).

meandering of a current hastening through pleasant fields, or the river Rhine, or the rainbow is described. But here there is no place for these things. Perhaps you know how to draw a cypress tree, but what good is that if you have been paid to paint a sailor swimming hopeless out of a shipwreck? A large amphora or wine jar was intended; why, as the wheel revolves, is a little pitcher turned out? In short, be your subject what it will, let it be simple and unified.

The great majority of us poets, father and sons worthy of such a father, are misled by our idea of what is correct. I labor to be concise, and I become obscure. Nerves and spirit fail him who aims at smoothness. One, striving for grandeur, falls into bombast; another, too cautious and fearful of the storm, crawls along the ground. He who wants to vary his subject in a marvelous manner paints the dolphin in the woods, the boar in the sea. The attempt to avoid error leads to faults if skill is lacking.

The humblest bronze-smith near the Aemilian school for gladiators can represent fingernails and imitate wavy hair in brass, but his work is unhappy because he does not know how to achieve a unified whole. I would no more wish to be like him, if I wanted to compose anything, than to live with a hideous nose while admired for my dark eyes and jet-black hair.

You who write, take a subject equal to your powers, and consider carefully just how much your shoulders can bear. Neither choice words nor lucid order will be wanting in the writer who selects his subject with care. If I am not mistaken, the excellence and beauty of the arrangement consists in the poet's ability to say no more than should be said just now and to put off most of his thoughts, waiving them for the present—to proceed by embracing one and rejecting another.

In the choice of words, too, the poet must be delicate and careful. You will express yourself most effectively if a skillful combination of terms gives an air of novelty to a well-known word. If new terms are needed to explain abstruse subjects, you can coin words never heard of by the old-fashioned Cethegi, who wear loincloths rather than tunics. Such license will be allowed if modestly used, and new and lately formed words will carry authority if they descend from a Greek source. Why should the Romans now deny to Virgil and Varius the privilege granted to Plautus and Caecilius? Why should I be

begrudged the power of adding a few words when the language of
Cato and Ennius has enriched our native tongue and provided new
names for things? It has been and ever will be allowable to coin
words bearing the stamp of the present day. As leaves in the woods
are changed with the fleeting years, the earliest fall off first. In the
same way words die of old age, and those lately formed flourish like
men in the days of their youth. We and all our works are doomed to
death: whether a harbor built to defend our fleets from the north
winds—a regal work; or a marsh, long barren and fit only for oars,
that now bears the plow and supports nearby cities; or a river, once
ruinous to crops, that has been taught to run in a better channel.
All mortal works must perish; much less can the honor and elegance
of language endure. Many words will revive that have fallen off, and
many now in high regard will lapse, according to the will of custom
or usage, within whose power lie the judgment, rule, and standard
of language.

Homer has taught us in what measure the deeds of kings and chiefs
and dire war should be written.

Verses of unequal lengths were first used for elegies, later for love
and fulfilled desires. But it has still not been determined what author
first used these common elegiac verses.

Rage armed Archilochus, the Greek satirist, with his own invention,
iambic verse. Both comedy and tragedy adopted the measure as
most suitable for dialogue, for overcoming the noise of the audience,
and for the action of the stage.

The Muse has allotted to the lyre the celebration of gods and the
sons of gods, the champion wrestler, the winning horse, the desire of
lovers, and the carefree joys of wine.

If I am not able to observe these genre distinctions and the differing
styles of works of genius, why should I be called a poet? Why,
out of false modesty, should I prefer ignorance to learning?

A comic subject resists treatment in tragic verse. In the same way
the banquet of Thyestes will not bear telling in the commonplace
verse suitable for comedy. Let each peculiar species of writing keep
its proper place. At times, however, even comedy exalts its voice,
and a character like Terence's Chremes rants in swelling strains. And
a tragic writer often expresses grief in prosaic language. When Tele-

phus and Peleus are in poverty and exile, they must throw aside their ranting and their sesquipedalian words if they wish to move the heart of the viewer with their grief.

It is not enough that poems be beautiful. They should be tender and affecting and lead the heart of the listener where they will. Just as people smile on those who smile, so they sympathize with those who weep. If you wish me to weep, you must first express the emotion of grief. Then, Telephus or Peleus, your misfortunes will really pain me. But if your words do not suit the parts assigned you, I shall laugh or fall asleep. Sad words suit a melancholy face; menacing words, an angry one; playful words, a merry look; serious words, an austere one. For nature first frames us from within to every change of fortune: she delights or angers us, or burdens us to the ground with heavy sorrow, and then expresses those emotions through her interpreter the tongue. If the words are not suited to the situation of the speaker, the Roman audience, from knights to plebeians, will simply guffaw. It makes a considerable difference whether it is a god or a hero who speaks, a man stricken in years or a young buck in the heat of youth, a gracious lady or a meddlesome nurse, a traveling merchant or a provincial farmer, a Colchian or an Assyrian, one brought up at Thebes or at Argos.

You who write, either follow tradition or make your invention consistent. If you have to represent the renowned Achilles, let him be indefatigable, wrathful, inexorable, and violent. He must deny that laws were made for him; he will arrogate everything to the force of arms. In the same way let Medea be bold and unconquerable, Ino pitiable, Ixion treacherous, Io wandering, Orestes sorrowful. If you try anything before unattempted on the stage and boldly create a new character, see that it remains to the end what it was in the beginning so that it is consistent. It is hard to treat a hackneyed subject with originality. You will be wiser to dramatize the *Iliad* by reducing it to acts than to introduce incidents and arguments never before treated. You can make a public story your own property if you do not dwell upon the whole circle of events, which makes for pettiness. Nor should you be so faithful a translator as to render the original word for word, like a mere copyist—nor so close an imitator as to fall into a rut from which you cannot escape.

method for writing

Nor should you begin like the epic bard of old: "I will sing the fate of Priam and the noble war." What will this boaster produce? The mountains are in labor, and a ridiculous mouse will be brought forth. How much more to the purpose is he who attempts nothing improperly: "Sing me, my Muse, that man who, after the fall of Troy, saw the manners and cities of many people." He does not wish to make smoke from a flash, but to bring light out of smoke so that he may enhance his marvelous stories of Antiphates, Scylla, the Cyclops, and Charybdis. Nor does he date Diomed's return from Meleager's death, nor trace the rise of the Trojan war from the twin eggs of Leda and the swanlike Zeus. He always hastens to the climax and projects his reader into the middle of things as if they were already known. That which he is afraid he cannot heighten with his touch, he leaves out; and in forming his fictions he so intermingles the false with the true that the middle remains consistent with the beginning, and the end with the middle.

Now listen to what I and the general public expect. If you want an appreciative audience who will wait for the final curtain and the chorus's call for plaudits, you must mark the manners of every age and period of life and represent what is fitting to varying natures and ages. The boy who has just learned to talk and to walk with a firm tread likes to play with his friends, becomes angry and then forgets his wrath, and changes every hour. The beardless youth, freed from his guardian, enjoys horses, dogs, and the sunlit fields; he is as soft as wax in yielding to vice, rude to advisers, slow to provide for his best interests, free with his money, high spirited and lusty, but quick to give up the objects of his passion. With changing interests the mature man seeks wealth and social connections; sensitive to points of honor, he is cautious about doing anything he might later wish undone. Many difficulties encompass the old man either because he neglects what he has gotten in his search for gain or because he approaches every transaction in a timorous and listless manner. Peevish and querulous, he glorifies the good old days when he was young and damns without mercy the youth of today. Our advancing years bring many benefits; our declining ones take many away. To avoid giving the qualities of age to youth and those of a man to a boy, we must stress the characteristics appropriate to each person's age.

An action is either represented on the stage or related there as done somewhere else. Events reported to the ear excite the mind less than those placed before the eyes of the spectator. You must not, however, show upon the stage things that ought to be done only behind the scenes, and you must also withhold from view many things that may more effectively be described by an actor after the event. Medea should not murder her sons before the audience, nor the nefarious Atreus prepare a banquet of human flesh; Procne should not be metamorphosed into a bird, Cadmus into a serpent. Whatever you show me in this manner inspires only disgust and incredulity.

If you would like your play to have appeal and to be repeatedly performed, let it have five acts, neither more nor less. And do not have a god intervene unless there is a problem requiring a god for its solution; nor should you let a fourth person be too eager to speak.

Let the chorus fill the role of an actor with vigor; it should not sing anything between the acts which is not consistent with the main design of the play. It should support the good characters with friendly advice, check the passionate, and cherish those who fear to do evil. It should praise the simple meal, the benefits of just laws, and the open gates of peaceful cities. It should respect what is told in confidence and implore the gods that prosperity may be taken from the haughty and returned to the wretched. Originally the slender and simple flute with a few stops (not as it is now, decked in brass like a trumpet) was used to accompany and assist the chorus; its sound could fill the rows that were not yet too crowded, where a sober, thrifty, and honest audience, small enough to be counted, gathered together. But when the Romans began to extend their territories and ampler walls spread around their city and when they began to indulge themselves by drinking wine in the daytime on feastdays, a greater freedom was taken in rhythm and music. For what taste could the unlettered clod just released from his labors have in common with the gentleman—the menial with the man of honor? Then the flutist added new movements and decoration to his ancient art and, strutting backward and forward, trailed his robe across the stage. New notes were added to the sober lyre. A hurried eloquence produced a new language, with wise sayings and prophecies of the future hardly to be distinguished from the wisdom of the Delphic oracles.

The poet who first tried his skill in tragic verse for the paltry prize of a goat soon began to bring wild satyrs naked to the stage. He was able to introduce crude jokes without loss of dignity because the spectators, riotous and drunk with festival wine, wished to be amused by sensation and novelty. But in presenting the banter and jokes of the satyrs, as serious subjects are turned to jest, it is important that no god or hero who has displayed himself in purple and gold should be allowed to sink to the level of tavern-talk, or—at the other extreme —while attempting to avoid the commonplace, speak cloudy and empty jargon. Disdaining to gush forth empty verses, tragedy will assume an air of modesty even among wanton satyrs—like a lady who is asked to dance on festival days.

As a writer of satyr plays, Pisos, I should not like unornamented common words, such as the vulgar speak, nor should I strain to depart so far from the language of tragedy as to make no distinction whether Davus is speaking, or the bold Pythias, who got a talent by gulling Simo, or Silenus, the guardian and attendant of the god Bacchus. I would so carefully develop a fiction taken from a well-known story that anyone hoping to do the same thing might sweat and labor in vain. Such power has a just arrangement and interconnection of the parts; such grace may be added to common subjects. In my judgment the fauns, which belong to the woods, should not comport themselves as though they were educated in the city, almost at the bar; nor, on the other hand, should they blunder out their obscene and scandalous speeches. These are offensive to all who have a horse, a father, or an estate. Such could never approve or offer the laurel crown to the kind of thing that delights the buyers of roasted peas and chestnuts.

A long syllable following a short one is called an "iambus," a lively measure. The term "trimeter" was given to rapid iambic lines yielding six beats in double time. Recently, however, so that it might come more slowly and majestically to the ear, the iambic line obligingly admitted the grave spondee, or foot with two long stresses, with the understanding, however, that the iambic was always to keep its place in the second and fourth of the six feet. But this kind of measure rarely appears in what some like to call the "noble" trimeters of Accius; nor can it be seen in the dramatic verse of Ennius, with its clumsy weight of spondees, which suggests either careless haste or ignorance of the art of poetry.

Since not every critic can judge inharmonious meter, Roman poets have enjoyed an undeserved indulgence. But should I for this reason run riot and write without discipline and control? Or, assuming that my faults will be noticed, should I feel reassured by the hope of being pardoned? If I am reasonably cautious, I might escape censure but I should hardly deserve praise.

Night and day, you should study the Greek masterpieces as models. Although our ancestors admired both the meter and the wit of Plautus, they did so too tolerantly (I will not say stupidly), as you and I can see if we know the difference between a crude joke and witty repartee and can tell true rhythm by using our ears and fingers.

Thespis is said to have invented tragedy, a type before unknown, and to have carried his plays around in carts, to be performed by actors whose faces were smeared with the dregs of wine. After him came Aeschylus, who introduced the tragic mask and robe; he designed a stage built of small planks and taught the players to speak in a grand theatrical tone and to strut with buskined feet. Then came the Old Comedy, which won popular praise, but the freedom it took degenerated into excess and violence that had to be restrained by law. Denied the "right" of character abuse, the chorus lapsed into shamed silence.

Our own poets have left no style unattempted. Nor do those merit the least honor who dared to forsake the footsteps of the Greeks and celebrate the deeds of their own country, whether in tragedy or comedy. Rome would have risen as high through her language as through her valor and arms if her poets, one and all, had not found the necessary use of the file to revise and polish their work so objectionable. You Pisos, who are of the blood of Pompilius, should reject that poem that many days and many a blot have not ten times smoothed to perfection.

Just because Democritus believes that native genius is more important than wretched art and bars all poets in their right minds from Helicon, many do not like to cut their fingernails or their beards. They live in solitude and shun the baths, thinking that they will gain the reputation and the name of poet if they never bow their lousy heads to Licinius the barber. It is stupid of me to take a purge for bile in the springtime; otherwise no one could write better poems. But the cost would be too much. Therefore I will serve as a whetstone, which can sharpen steel even though it is itself unable to cut: even though I am unable to write poetry myself, I will teach the duty and business of the poet—show where his materials can be found; what improves and develops him; what lends grace, what does not; where excellence can lead, and where error.

Wisdom is the first principle and source of all good writing. The philosophy of Socrates will guide you in your choice of subject; when it is well in mind, the words will follow spontaneously. He who has learned what he owes to his country and to his friends, with what affection a parent, a brother, and a stranger are to be loved, what is the duty of a senator, a judge, a general sent to war, will certainly know how to assign suitable attributes to each character. I should advise the skilled imitator to observe actual life and manners and to draw from them a language true to life. Sometimes a play glittering with commonplaces and having well defined characters (even though it is without real artistic power) will give more pleasure and hold an audience better than empty verses or tuneful trifles.

To the Greeks, who coveted nothing but glory, the Muse gave genius and the power of eloquence. Our Roman youth learn computation in order to divide the *as* or pound into twelve ounces or multiply it into a hundred *asses*.[1] Let the son of Albinus the usurer tell me, if from five ounces one be subtracted, what remains? He will say, "A third of a pound." Bravely done, my boy! You'll get ahead all right. Add an ounce, and what will that be? "Half a pound." Splendid. Once this sordid commercial lust has corroded their minds, how can we expect to get books of verses worth rubbing with cedar oil and preserving in cypress cases?

Poets wish either to profit or delight, or to combine enjoyment and usefulness in what they write. Be brief in whatever precepts you give so that impressionable minds will be able to comprehend and faithfully retain them. Superfluous verbiage spills out of minds already filled. For the sake of enjoyment, see that whatever fictions you invent have the virtue of verisimilitude. Don't let your play demand a belief in impossible absurdities: it will not do to take out of the belly of

---

[1] The *as*, the Roman monetary unit, was divided into twelve *unciae* or ounces; its multiples were called *asses*.

Lamia the witch a living child that she has just had for lunch. The senior citizens attack anything that is not didactic; the aristocratic young bloods turn their backs on poetry that is too austere. He who combines teaching with enjoyment carries the day by delighting and at the same time admonishing the reader. Such work makes money for the publisher, crosses the sea, and wins its author a lasting fame.

Yet there are faults that we should be willing to pardon. The musician's string will not always give the sound intended by the performer's hand and mind but often returns a sharp when a flat is called for; nor will the archer's arrow always hit the mark it threatens. When the beauties of a poem predominate, I shall not be offended by a few blemishes caused by inattention or human limitations. What shall we decide, then? Just as the copyist who repeats an error for which he has been reproved is without excuse and the harpist who always blunders on the same string is sure to be laughed at, so the slovenly writer is like Choerilus, the poet Aristotle ridiculed. I laugh in surprise when I find him tolerable in two or three places; yet I am displeased when great Homer nods. But then, when a work is long, it is natural that sleep should steal upon it.

As in painting, so in poetry: Some pieces will strike you more if you stand near and some at a greater distance. One loves the dark; another, which is not afraid of the critic's close scrutiny, chooses to be seen in the light. One has pleased once; the other will give pleasure through ten viewings. O you elder of the youths, although your judgment has benefited from your father's instruction and although you have native intelligence, take this truth to heart and remember it: In certain things mediocrity is allowable. A counselor and pleader at the bar of middling abilities is a long way from having the eloquence of Messalla or the legal knowledge of Cascellius; yet there is a demand for his services. But neither gods nor men nor booksellers have any use for a mediocre poet. Discordant music, heavy perfume, and poppies mixed with bitter Sardinian honey are offensive at a fine banquet, where the dinner could have done better without them. In the same way poetry, invented for the delight of our souls, must sink to the bottom if it fails to hit the summit of excellence.

He who does not know the games does not try to use the weapons of the Campus Martius, and he who lacks skill with the ball, the quoit, and the hoop holds back lest the crowd should laugh at him. Yet he who knows nothing about poetry will presume to compose. Why not? He is freeborn and of a good family; moreover, he has the income of a knight and is without vices. You, I am sure, would not do or say anything unwise, if I know your judgment and character. But if you should ever write anything, please show it to Maecius the critic and your father and me, and then put the manuscript back among your papers and withhold it for nine years. You have the power to blot out what you have not yet published, but a word sent abroad can never be recalled.

When men still lived in the forests, Orpheus, the priest and interpreter of the gods, deterred them from savage slaughter and bestial living; he is therefore said to have tamed tigers and fierce lions. Amphion, the builder of the Theban wall, is said to have moved the stones by the sound of his lyre and to have led them persuasively wherever he wished them to go. In days of old it was the wisdom of the poet that distinguished public from private welfare, things sacred from things profane, that prohibited sexual promiscuity and established rules for married people, that planned cities and engraved laws on wooden tablets. Thus honor came to divine poets and their songs. Then great Homer and the Spartan Tyrtaeus inspired men to warlike deeds with their verses. Oracles were delivered in poetry and a way of life taught; the favor of monarchs was courted in Pierian strains, and the establishment of plays and festivals brought relief from tiresome labor. Therefore you need not feel ashamed of the lyric Muse and Apollo, the god of song.

It has been asked whether praiseworthy poetry is the product of nature or art. For myself, I cannot imagine what study could accomplish without a rich natural vein or what raw genius could do by itself, so much does one require the help of the other and so amiably do they work together. The athlete who yearned to reach a goal has endured and accomplished much as a boy: he has sweated and shivered with cold; he has abstained from women and wine. The flutist at the Pythian games was first a pupil and feared his teacher. But nowadays it seems enough for a man to say of himself: "I make admirable poems. A plague on the hindmost; it is unthinkable that I should be outstripped and have to acknowledge that I am ignorant of that which I never learned."

Like a huckster who calls a crowd together to buy his wares, a wealthy poet, rich in land and money put out at interest, invites flatterers to come for a reward. But even though he may be able to set an elegant table, put up security for a poor man, and rescue him from the snares of the law, I wonder whether, for all his wealth, he can tell a true from a false friend. If you are giving someone a present, do not then show him your verses while he is still full of grateful joy, for he will cry out, "Charming! Excellent! Perfect!" He will turn pale. Tears will bedew his friendly eyes. He will leap about and beat the ground in ecstasy. Just as the professional mourners at a funeral are louder in their laments than those with grief in their hearts, the false admirer seems to be more moved than the true one. Certain kings have been known to ply a man with wine, in a kind of trial by drunkenness, to find out whether he is really worthy of their friendship. So, if you compose poems, don't let yourself be taken in by the hidden spirit of the fox.

If you should read anything to Quintilius, he would say, "Please improve this and that." If you answered that you could do no better, having tried two or three times in vain, he would order you to blot out and recast your ill-formed verses. If you should choose to defend rather than correct a fault, he would waste no more words or fruitless effort but leave you to love your own work without a rival. A good and sensible man will censure weak lines and condemn rough ones. He will draw a black line through those that lack art. He will lop off overambitious ornaments. He will make you clarify that which is obscure. He will challenge ambiguous expressions. He will mark what should be changed. In short, he will be as conscientious as the great Alexandrian critic, Aristarchus. He will not say, "Why should I give a friend offense over mere trifles." These trifles can lead the friend into serious trouble once he is ridiculed and badly received.

Just as people shun someone afflicted with the itch, jaundice, delirium, or insanity, those who are wise will have nothing to do with a mad poet. Boys chase after him, and fools attend him. Belching out verses he staggers about with his head held high, like a drunken fowler intent upon his prey. If he should fall into a well or ditch and call out, "Help, fellow citizens!" no one would care to pull him out. If someone should go to the trouble of throwing down a rope, I should say, "How do you know that he didn't throw himself in on purpose?" The Sicilian poet Empedocles, wishing to be thought an immortal god, coolly leapt into burning Aetna. Poets must be granted the right to kill themselves, if they wish. Saving a man against his will is as good as murdering him. This is not the first time he has behaved this way. Pull him back now and he will not be a man and give up his lust for a spectacular death. It is not clear why he writes poetry: it may be that he pissed on his father's ashes or polluted a sacred enclosure. What is clear is that he is mad; and, like a bear that has burst the bars of its cage, this ruthless reciter of his own work pursues the learned and ignorant alike. He fastens himself upon anyone he catches and reads him to death—like a leech that will not quit the skin till it is gorged with blood.

Longinus

(First Century A.D.)

On the Sublime, once attributed to Cassius Longinus, a third century
rhetorician, is now thought to have been the work of a Greek rhetorician in Rome during the first century A.D. The English title, first
used in 1739, is misleading because the treatise is not concerned with
"sublimity" in the most common eighteenth century sense of the term.
Rather, as its Greek manuscript title *Peri Hypsous* suggests, it is a discourse on the qualities of "elevation" or "greatness" in literature. Especially attractive to readers in the eighteenth century, when the forces
of the romantic revolution were gathering momentum, the treatise
combines a regard for the classical values of decorum, proportion, and
wholeness with appreciation of natural genius and the subjective
appeals of sensation and emotion (and even transport or ecstasy) in
literature. But the author also analyzes the qualities that especially
distinguish imaginative or poetic language from a viewpoint like
that of Ezra Pound when (in *How to Read*) he defines great literature
as simply "language charged with meaning to the utmost possible
degree." "Longinus," who prizes intensity, explores the ways in which
great literature has been charged with thought and feeling through
the writer's control of sound, syntax, imagery, figurative language,
and other rhetorical effects. The twentieth century reader finds unexpected ties with modern criticism in his discussions of imagery and
metaphor, of composition and formal arrangement, and of literary form
as an organic synthesis. In *Peri Hypsous* "Longinus" is ostensibly

[85]

composing a formal rhetorical treatise, organized according to the sources of sublimity defined in Chapter Eight, but he is actually more interested in analyzing literary effects through examples than in a pedantic definition and classification of rhetorical devices for their own sake.

The earliest surviving manuscript of *Peri Hypsous* dates from the tenth century. First published in 1554, the treatise became widely known through translations in the seventeenth century and reached the height of its influence in the eighteenth century. The incomplete surviving text, which breaks off in Chapter Forty-four, represents an estimated three-fifths of the original work. Among numerous translations in English, the most fully annotated is that of W. R. Roberts, ed., *Longinus on the Sublime* (1899; 1935). The influence of the treatise is discussed in T. R. Henn, *Longinus and English Criticism* (1934) and S. H. Monk, *The Sublime: A Study of Critical Theories in Eighteenth Century England* (1935).

FROM ON THE SUBLIME

(*Peri Hypsous*)

I

The treatise of Cæcilius on the Sublime, when, as you remember, my dear Terentian, we examined it together,[1] seemed to us to be beneath the dignity of the whole subject, to fail entirely in seizing the salient points, and to offer little profit (which should be

The text is based on the translation by H. L. Havell (1890). Breaks in the original manuscript are designated by bracketed references; the editors' omissions are indicated by ellipses.

[1] Caecilius of Calacte, a Sicilian rhetorician. The identity of Terentian, like that of Longinus, is unknown.

the principal aim of every writer) for the trouble of its perusal. There are two things essential to a technical treatise: the first is to define the subject; the second (I mean second in order, as it is by much the first in importance) to point out how and by what methods we may become masters of it ourselves. And yet Cæcilius, while wasting his efforts in a thousand illustrations of the nature of the sublime, as though here we were quite in the dark, somehow passes by as immaterial the question how we might be able to exalt our own genius to a certain degree of progress in sublimity. However, perhaps it would be fairer to commend this writer's intelligence and zeal in themselves, instead of blaming him for his omissions. And since you have bidden me also to put together, if only for your entertainment, a few notes on the subject of the sublime, let me see if there is anything in my speculations which promises advantage to men of affairs. In you, dear friend—such is my confidence in your abilities, and such the part which becomes you—I look for a sympathizing and discerning critic of the several parts of my treatise. For that was a just remark of his who pronounced that the points in which we resemble the divine nature are benevolence and love of truth.

As I am addressing a person so accomplished in literature, I need only state, without enlarging further on the matter, that the sublime, wherever it occurs, consists in a certain loftiness and excellence of language, and that it is by this, and this only, that the greatest poets and prose-writers have gained eminence, and won themselves a lasting place in the Temple of Fame. A lofty passage does not convince the reason of the reader, but takes him out of himself [in a transport or ecstasy]. That which is admirable ever confounds our judgment and eclipses that which is merely reasonable or agreeable. To believe or not is usually in our own power; but the sublime, acting with an imperious and irresistible force, sways every reader whether he will or no. Skill in invention, lucid arrangement and disposition of facts, are appreciated not by one passage, or by two, but gradually manifest themselves in the general structure of a work; but a sublime thought, if happily timed, illumines an entire subject with the vividness of a lightning-flash and exhibits the whole power of the writer in a moment of time.[2] Your own experience, I am sure, my dearest Terentian, would enable you to illustrate these and similar points of doctrine.

II

The first question which presents itself for solution is whether there is any art which can teach sublimity or loftiness in writing. For some hold generally that there is mere delusion in attempting to reduce such subjects to technical rules. The sublime, they tell us, is born in a man and not to be acquired by instruction; genius is the only master who can teach it. The vigorous products of nature (such is their view) are weakened and in every respect debased, when robbed of their flesh and blood by frigid technicalities. But I maintain that the truth can be shown to stand otherwise in this matter. Let us look at the matter in this way: nature in her loftier and more passionate moods, while detesting all appearance of restraint, is not wont to show herself utterly wayward and reckless; and though in all cases the vital informing principle is derived from her, yet to determine the right degree and the right moment and to contribute the precision of practice and experience is the peculiar province of scientific method. The great passions, when left to their own blind and rash impulses without the control of reason, are in the same danger as a ship let drive at random without ballast. Often they need the spur, but sometimes also the curb. The remark of Demosthenes with regard to human life in general—that the greatest of all blessings is to be fortunate, but next to that and equal in importance is to be well advised, for good fortune is utterly ruined by the absence of good counsel—may be applied to literature, if we substitute genius for fortune and art for counsel. Then, again (and this is the most impor-

[2] Pound's well-known definition of the *image* as "that which presents an intellectual and emotional complex in an instant of time" shows much the same regard for intensity and presentational immediacy in poetic expression.

tant point of all), a writer can only learn from art when he is to abandon himself to the direction of his genius.[3]

These are the considerations which I submit to the unfavorable critic of such useful studies. Perhaps they may induce him to alter his opinion as to the vanity and idleness of our present investigations. [Ms. break.]

III

> . . . And let them check the stove's long tongues of fire:
> For if I see one tenant of the hearth,
> I'll thrust within one curling torrent flame,
> And bring that roof in ashes to the ground:
> But now not yet is sung my noble lay.[4]

Such phrases cease to be tragic and become burlesque—I mean phrases like "curling torrent flames" and "vomiting to heaven" and representing Boreas as a piper and so on. Such expressions and such images produce an effect of confusion and obscurity, not of energy; and if each separately be examined under the light of criticism, what seemed terrible gradually sinks into absurdity. Since then, even in tragedy, where the natural dignity of the subject makes a swelling diction allowable, we cannot pardon a tasteless grandiloquence, how much more incongruous must it seem in sober prose! Hence we laugh at those fine words of Gorgias of Leontini, such as "Xerxes the Persian Zeus" and "vultures, those living tombs" and at certain conceits of Callisthenes which are high-flown rather than sublime and at some in Cleitarchus more ludicrous still—a writer whose frothy style tempts us to travesty Sophocles and say, "He blows a little pipe and blows it ill." The same faults may be observed in Amphicrates and Hegesias and Matris, who in their frequent moments (as they think) of inspiration, instead of playing the genius are simply playing the fool.

Speaking generally, it would seem that bombast is one of the

---

[3] Literally: "But the most important point of all is that the actual fact that there are some parts of literature which are in the power of natural genius alone, must be learnt from no other source than from art."

[4] Aeschylus in his lost *Orithyia*.

hardest things to avoid in writing. For all those writers who are ambitious of a lofty style, through dread of being convicted of feebleness and poverty of language, slide by a natural gradation into the opposite extreme. "Who fails in great endeavor, nobly fails" is their creed. Now bulk, when hollow and affected, is always objectionable, whether in material bodies or in writings, and in danger of producing on us an impression of littleness: "Nothing," it is said, "is drier than a man with the dropsy."

The characteristic, then, of bombast is that it transcends the sublime, but there is another fault diametrically opposed to grandeur: that is called puerility, and it is the failing of feeble and narrow minds —indeed, the most ignoble of all vices in writing. By puerility we mean a pedantic habit of mind which by over-elaboration ends in frigidity. Slips of this sort are made by those who, aiming at brilliancy, polish, and especially attractiveness, are landed in paltriness and silly affectation. Closely associated with it is a third sort of vice, in dealing with the passions, which Theodorus used to call false sentiment, meaning by that an ill-timed and empty display of emotion, where no emotion is called for, or of greater emotion than the situation warrants. Thus we often see an author hurried by the tumult of his mind into tedious displays of mere personal feeling which has no connection with the subject. Yet how justly ridiculous must an author appear whose most violent transports leave his readers quite cold! However, I will dismiss this subject, as I intend to devote a separate work to the treatment of the pathetic in writing.

IV

The last of the faults which I mentioned is frequently observed in Timæus[5]—I mean the fault of frigidity. In other respects he is an able writer and sometimes not unsuccessful in the loftier style, a man of wide knowledge, and full of ingenuity, a most bitter critic of the failings of others—but unhappily blind to his own. In his eagerness to be always striking out new thoughts he frequently falls into the most

[5] A Sicilian historian of the fourth century B.C.

childish absurdities. I will instance only one or two passages, as most of them have been pointed out by Cæcilius. Wishing to say something very fine about Alexander the Great, he speaks of him as a man "who annexed the whole of Asia in fewer years than Isocrates spent in writing his panegyric oration in which he urges the Greeks to make war on Persia." How strange is the comparison of the "great Emathian conqueror" with an Athenian rhetorician! By this mode of reasoning it is plain that the Spartans were very inferior to Isocrates in courage, since it took them thirty years to conquer Messene, while he finished the composition of this harangue in ten. Observe, too, his language on the Athenians taken in Sicily. "They paid the penalty for their impious outrage on Hermes in mutilating his statues; and the chief agent in their destruction was one who was descended on his father's side from the injured deity—Hermocrates, son of Hermon." I wonder, my dearest Terentian, how he omitted to say of the tyrant Dionysius that for his impiety towards Zeus and Herakles he was deprived of his power by Dion and Herakleides. Yet why speak of Timæus, when even men like Xenophon and Plato—the very demigods of literature— though they had sat at the feet of Socrates, sometimes forgot themselves in the pursuit of such paltry conceits. The former, in his account of the Spartan Polity, has these words: "Their voice you would no more hear than if they were of marble; their gaze is as immovable as if they were cast in bronze; you would deem them more modest than the very maidens in their eyes." To speak of the pupils of the eye as "modest maidens" was a piece of absurdity becoming Amphicrates rather than Xenophon. And then what a strange delusion to suppose that modesty is always without exception expressed in the eye! whereas it is commonly said that there is nothing by which an impudent fellow betrays his character so much as by the expression of his eyes. Thus Achilles addresses Agamemnon in the *Iliad* [I, 225] as "drunkard, with eye of dog." Timæus, however, with that want of judgment which characterizes plagiarists, could not leave to Xenophon the possession of even this piece of frigidity. In relating how Agathocles carried off his cousin, who was wedded to another man from the festival of the unveiling, he asks, "Who could have done such a deed, unless he had harlots instead of maidens in his eyes?" And Plato himself, elsewhere so supreme a master of style, meaning to describe certain recording tablets, says [in *Laws*], "They shall write, and deposit in the temples memorials of cypress wood"; and again, "Then concerning walls, Megillus, I give my vote with Sparta that we should let them lie asleep within the ground, and not awaken them." And Herodotus falls pretty much under the same censure, when he speaks of beautiful women as "tortures to the eye," though here there is some excuse, as the speakers in this passage are drunken barbarians. Still, even from dramatic motives, such errors in taste should not be permitted to deface the pages of an immortal work.

V

Now all these glaring improprieties of language may be traced to one common root—the pursuit of novelty in thought. It is this that has turned the brain of nearly all the learned world of today. Human blessings and human ills commonly flow from the same source; and, to apply this principle to literature, those ornaments of style, those sublime and delightful images which contribute to success, are the foundation and the origin, not only of excellence, but also of failure. It is thus with the figures called transitions and hyperboles and the use of plurals for singulars. I shall show presently the dangers which they seem to involve. Our next task, therefore, must be to propose and to settle the question how we may avoid the faults of style related to sublimity.

VI

Our best hope of doing this will be first of all to grasp some definite theory and criterion of the true sublime. Nevertheless, this is a hard matter; for a just judgment of style is the final fruit of long experience; still, I believe that the way I shall indicate will enable us to distinguish between the true and false sublime, so far is it can be done by rule.

VII

It is proper to observe that in human life nothing is truly great which is despised by all elevated minds. For example, no man of sense can regard wealth, honor, glory, and power, or any of those things which are surrounded by a great external parade of pomp and circumstance as the highest blessings, seeing that merely to despise such things is a blessing of no common order: certainly those who possess them are admired much less than those who, having the opportunity to acquire them, through greatness of soul neglect it. Now let us apply this principle to the sublime in poetry or in prose; let us ask in all cases, is it merely a specious sublimity? Is this gorgeous exterior a mere false and clumsy pageant, which if laid open will be found to conceal nothing but emptiness? If so, a noble mind will scorn instead of admiring it. It is natural to us to feel our souls lifted up by the true sublime and in a sort of generous exultation to be filled with joy and pride, as though we had ourselves originated the ideas which we read. If then any work, on being repeatedly submitted to the judgment of an acute and cultivated critic, fails to dispose his mind to lofty ideas, if the thoughts which it suggests do not extend beyond what is actually expressed, and if, the longer you read it, the less you think of it, there can be here no true sublimity, when the effect is not sustained beyond the mere act of perusal. But when a passage is pregnant in suggestion, when it is hard, nay impossible, to distract the attention from it, and when it takes a strong and lasting hold on the memory, then we may be sure that we have lighted on the true sublime. In general, we may regard those words as truly noble and sublime which always please and please all readers; for when the same book always produces the same impression on all who read it, whatever be the difference in their pursuits, their manner of life, their aspirations, their ages, or their language, such a harmony of opposites gives irresistible authority to their favorable verdict.

VIII

I shall enumerate the five principal sources, as we may call them, from which almost all sublimity is derived, assuming, of course, the preliminary gift on which all these five sources depend, namely, command of language. The first and the most important is strength and greatness of thought, as I have pointed out elsewhere in my work on Xenophon. The second is a vigorous and spirited treatment of the passions. These two conditions of sublimity depend mainly on natural endowments, whereas those which follow derive assistance from art. The third is a certain artifice in the employment of figures, which are of two kinds, figures of thought and figures of speech. The fourth is dignified expression, which is subdivided into (*a*) the proper choice of words and (*b*) the use of metaphors and other ornaments of diction. The fifth cause of sublimity, which embraces all those preceding, is dignity and elevation of structure.[6] Let us consider what is involved in each of these five forms separately.

I must first, however, remark that some of these five divisions are omitted by Cæcilius; for instance, he says nothing about the passions. Now if he made this omission from a belief that the sublime and the pathetic are one and the same thing, holding them to be always coexistent and interdependent, he is in error. Some passions are found which, far from being lofty, are actually low, such as pity, grief, fear. Conversely, sublimity is often not in the least affecting, as we may see (among innumerable other instances) in those bold expressions of our great poet on the sons of Aloëus:

> Highly they raged
> To pile huge Ossa on the Olympian peak,
> And Pelion with all his waving trees
> On Ossa's crest to raise, and climb the sky;

and the yet more tremendous climax:

> And now had they accomplished it.

[6] Translators' terms for this important fifth source include (besides "structure") "word arrangement," "general" or "total effect," and "composition"—all emphasizing the textual unity of the literary work.

And in orators, in all passages dealing with panegyric, and in all the more imposing and declamatory places, dignity and sublimity play an indispensable part; but pathos is mostly absent. Hence the most pathetic orators have usually but little skill in panegyric, and conversely those who are powerful in panegyric generally fail in pathos. If, on the other hand, Cæcilius supposed that pathos never contributes to sublimity, and this is why he thought it alien to the subject, he is entirely deceived. For I would confidently pronounce that nothing is so conducive to sublimity as an appropriate display of genuine passion which bursts out with a kind of "fine madness" and divine inspiration and falls on our ears like the voice of a god.

IX

I have already said that of all these five conditions of the sublime the most important is the first, that is, a certain lofty cast of mind [or natural genius]. Therefore, although this is a faculty rather natural than acquired, nevertheless it will be well for us in this instance also to train up our souls to sublimity and make them as it were ever big with noble thoughts. How, it may be asked, is this to be done? I have hinted elsewhere in my writings that sublimity is, so to say, the image of greatness of soul. Hence a thought in its naked simplicity, even though unuttered, is sometimes admirable by the sheer force of its sublimity; for instance, the silence of Ajax in the *Odyssey* [IX, 543] is great and grander than anything he could have said. It is absolutely essential, then, first of all to settle the question whence this grandeur of conception arises; and the answer is that true eloquence can be found only in those whose spirit is generous and aspiring. For those whose whole lives are wasted in paltry and illiberal thoughts and habits cannot possibly produce any work worthy of the lasting reverence of mankind. It is only natural that their words should be full of sublimity whose thoughts are full of majesty. Hence sublime thoughts belong properly to the loftiest minds. . . . Far to be preferred to Homer's description of the Battle of the Gods are those passages which exhibit the divine nature in its true light, as something spotless, great, and pure, as, for instance, the lines on Poseidon in the *Iliad:*

Mountain and wood and solitary peak,
The ships Achaian, and the towers of Troy,
Trembled beneath the god's immortal feet.
Over the waves he rode, and round him played,
Lured from the deeps, the ocean's monstrous brood,
With uncouth gambols welcoming their lord:
The charmèd billows parted: on they flew. [XIII, 18–27, XX, 60.]

And thus also the lawgiver of the Jews, no ordinary man, having formed an adequate conception of the Supreme Being, gave it adequate expression in the opening words of his "Laws": "God said"— what?—"let there be light, and there was light; let there be land, and there was."

I trust you will not think me tedious if I quote yet one more passage from our great poet (referring this time to human characters) in illustration of the manner in which he leads us with him to heroic heights. A sudden and baffling darkness as of night has overspread the ranks of his warring Greeks. Then Ajax in sore perplexity cries aloud:

Almighty Sire,
Only from darkness save Achaia's sons;
No more I ask, but give us back the day;
Grant but our sight, and slay us, if thou wilt. [XVII, 645.]

The feelings are just what we should look for in Ajax. He does not, you observe, ask for his life—such a request would have been unworthy of his heroic soul—but finding himself paralyzed by darkness and prohibited from employing his valor in any noble action, he chafes because his arms are idle and prays for a speedy return of light. "At least," he thinks, "I shall find a warrior's grave, even though Zeus himself should fight against me." In such passages the mind of the poet is swept along in the whirlwind of the struggle, and, in his own words, he

Like the fierce war-god, raves, or wasting fire
Through the deep thickets on a mountain-side;
His lips drop foam. [XV, 605.]

But there is another and a very interesting aspect of Homer's mind. When we turn to the *Odyssey*, we find occasion to observe that a great poetical genius in the decline of power which comes with old age naturally leans towards the fabulous; for it is evident that this work was composed after the *Iliad*, in proof of which we may mention, among many other indications, the introduction in the *Odyssey* of the sequel of the story of his heroes' adventures at Troy, as so many additional episodes in the Trojan war, and especially the tribute of sorrow and mourning which is paid in that poem to departed heroes, as if in fulfillment of some previous design. The *Odyssey* is, in fact, a sort of epilogue to the *Iliad*.

And for the same reason, I imagine, whereas in the *Iliad*, which was written when his genius was in its prime, the whole structure of the poem is founded on action and struggle, in the *Odyssey* he generally prefers the narrative style, which is proper to old age. Hence Homer in his *Odyssey* may be compared to the setting sun: he is still as great as ever, but he has lost his fervent heat. The strain is now pitched to a lower key than in the "tale of Troy divine": we begin to miss that high and equable sublimity which never flags or sinks, that continuous current of moving incidents, those rapid transitions, that force of eloquence, that opulence of imagery which is ever true to nature. Like the sea when it retires upon itself and leaves its shores waste and bare, henceforth the tide of sublimity begins to ebb and draws us away into the dim region of myth and legend. In saying this I am not forgetting the fine storm pieces in the *Odyssey*, the story of the Cyclops, and other striking passages. It is Homer grown old I am discussing, but still it is Homer. Yet in every one of these passages the mythical predominates over the real. . . .

X

Let us now consider whether there is anything further which conduces to the sublime in writing. It is a law of nature that in all things there are certain constituent parts, coexistent with their substance. It necessarily follows, therefore, that one cause of sublimity is the choice of the most striking circumstances involved in whatever we are describing and, further, the power of afterwards combining them into one animate whole. The reader is attracted partly by the selection of the incidents, partly by the skill which has welded them together. For instance, Sappho, in dealing with the passionate manifestations attending on the frenzy of lovers, always chooses her strokes from the signs which she has observed to be actually exhibited in such cases. But her peculiar excellence lies in the felicity with which she chooses and unites together the most striking and powerful features:

> Peer of the gods is that man, who
> face to face, sits listening
> to your sweet speech and lovely
> > laughter.
>
> It is this that rouses a tumult
> in my breast. At mere sight of you
> my voice falters, my tongue
> > is broken.
>
> Straightway, a delicate fire runs in
> my limbs; my eyes
> are blinded and my ears
> > thunder.
>
> Sweat pours out: a trembling hunts
> me down. I grow paler
> than dry grass and lack little
> > of dying.[7]

Is it not wonderful how at the same moment soul, body, ears, tongue, eyes, color, all fail her and are lost to her as completely as if they were not her own? Observe too how her sensations contradict one another—she freezes, she burns, she raves, she reasons, and all at the same instant. And this description is designed to show that she is assailed, not by any particular emotion, but by a tumult of different emotions. All these tokens belong to the passion of love; but it is in the choice, as I said, of the most striking features and in the combination of them into one picture that the perfection of this ode of Sappho's lies.

Similarly Homer in his descriptions of tempests always picks out

---

[7] Translation by William Carlos Williams. Reprinted by permission of Mrs. William Carlos Williams and New Directions.

the most terrific circumstances. . . . Moreover, by his bold and
forcible combination of prepositions of opposite meaning he tortures
his language to imitate the agony of the scene, the constraint which
is put on the words accurately reflecting the anxiety of the sailors'
minds and the diction being stamped, as it were, with the peculiar
terror of the situation. Similarly Archilochus in his description of the
shipwreck, and similarly Demosthenes when he describes how the
news came of the taking of Elatea. Each of these authors fastidiously
rejects whatever is not essential to the subject and in putting together
the most vivid features is careful to guard against the interposition
of anything frivolous, unbecoming, or tiresome. Such blemishes mar
the general effect and give a patched and gaping appearance to the
edifice of sublimity, which ought to be built up in a solid and uni-
form structure. . . .

XII

. . . I am not satisfied with the definition of amplification generally
given by authorities on rhetoric. They explain it to be a form of
language which invests the subject with a certain grandeur. Yes, but
this definition may be applied indifferently to sublimity, pathos, and
the use of figurative language since all these invest the discourse
with some sort of grandeur. The difference seems to me to lie in this,
that sublimity gives elevation to a subject, while amplification gives
extension as well. Thus the sublime is often conveyed in a single
thought, but amplification can subsist only with a certain prolixity
and diffusiveness. The most general definition of amplification would
explain it to consist in the gathering together of all the constituent
parts and topics of a subject, emphasizing the argument by repeated
insistence, herein differing from proof in that the object of proof
is logical demonstration. [Ms. break.]

Plato, like the sea, pours forth his riches in a copious and expansive
flood. Hence the style of the orator, who is the greater master of our
emotions, is often, as it were, red-hot and ablaze with passion,
whereas Plato, whose strength lay in a sort of weighty and sober
magnificence, though never frigid, does not rival the thunders of

Demosthenes. And, if a Greek may be allowed to express an opinion on the subject of Latin literature, I think the same difference may be discerned in the grandeur of Cicero as compared with that of his Grecian rival. The sublimity of Demosthenes is generally sudden and abrupt; that of Cicero is equally diffused. Demosthenes is vehement, rapid, vigorous, terrible: he burns and sweeps away all before him, and hence we may liken him to a whirlwind or a thunderbolt. Cicero is like a widespread conflagration, which rolls over and feeds on all around it, whose fire is extensive and burns long, breaking out successively in different places, and finding its fuel now here, now there. Such points, however, I resign to your more competent judgment. . . .

XIII

We may learn from Plato, if we would but observe his example, that there is yet another path besides those mentioned which leads to sublime heights. What path do I mean? The emulous imitation of the great poets and prose writers of the past. On this mark, dear friend, let us keep our eyes ever steadfastly fixed. Many gather the divine impulse from another's spirit, just as we are told that the Pythian priestess, when she takes her seat on the tripod, where there is said to be a rent in the ground breathing upwards a heavenly emanation, straightway conceives from that source the godlike gift of prophecy and utters her inspired oracles. So likewise from the mighty genius of the great writers of antiquity there is carried into the souls of their rivals, as from a fount of inspiration, an effluence which breathes upon them until, even though their natural temper be but cold, they share the sublime enthusiasm of others. Thus Homer's name is associated with a numerous band of illustrious disciples—not only Herodotus, but Stesichorus before him and the great Archilochus and above all Plato, who from the great fountainhead of Homer's genius drew into himself innumerable tributary streams. Perhaps it would have been necessary to illustrate this point, had not Ammonius and his school already classified and noted down the various examples. Now what I am speaking of is not plagiarism, but resembles the process of copying from fair forms or statues or works of skilled labor. Nor in my opinion would so many fair flowers of imagery have bloomed among the philosophical dogmas of Plato, nor would he have risen so often to the language and topics of poetry, had he not engaged heart and soul in a contest for precedence with Homer, like a young champion entering the lists against a veteran. It may be that he showed too ambitious a spirit in venturing on such a duel; but nevertheless it was not without advantage to him, "for strife like this," as Hesiod says, "is good for men." And where shall we find a more glorious arena or a nobler crown than here, where even defeat at the hands of our predecessors is not ignoble? . . .

XV

The dignity, grandeur, and energy of a style largely depend on a proper employment of images. The term *image* in its most general acceptance includes every thought, howsoever presented, which issues in speech. But the term is now generally confined to those cases when he who is speaking, by reason of the rapt and excited state of his feelings, imagines himself to see what he is talking about and produces a similar illusion in his hearers. Poets and orators both employ images, but with a very different object, as you are well aware. The poetical image is designed to astound; the oratorical image to give perspicuity. Both, however, seek to work on the emotions:

> Mother, I pray thee, set not thou upon me
> Those maids with bloody face and serpent hair:
> See, see, they come, they're here, they spring upon me!

And again:

> Ah, ah, she'll slay me! whither shall I fly?

The poet when he wrote like this saw the Erinyes with his own eyes, and he almost compels his readers to see them too. Euripides found his chief delight in the labor of giving tragic expression to these two passions of madness and love, showing here a real mastery which

I cannot think he exhibited elsewhere. Still, he is by no means diffident in venturing on other fields of the imagination. His genius was far from being of the highest order, but by taking pains he often raises himself to a tragic elevation. . . .

Wherein lies the force of an oratorical image? Doubtless in adding energy and passion in a hundred different ways to a speech, but especially in this, that when it is mingled with the practical, argumentative parts of an oration, it does not merely convince the hearer, but enthralls him. Such is the effect of those words of Demosthenes: "Supposing, now, at this moment a cry of alarm were heard outside the assize courts, and the news came that the prison was broken open and the prisoners escaped, is there any man here who is such a trifler that he would not run to the rescue at the top of his speed? But suppose someone came forward with the information that they had been set at liberty by the defendant, what then? Why, he would be lynched on the spot!" Compare also the way in which Hyperides excused himself, when he was proceeded against for bringing in a bill to liberate the slaves after Chæronea. "This measure," he said, "was not drawn up by any orator, but by the battle of Chæronea." This striking image, being thrown in by the speaker in the midst of his proofs, enables him by one bold stroke to carry all mere logical objection before him. In all such cases our nature is drawn towards that which affects it most powerfully. Hence an image lures us away from an argument: judgment is paralyzed, matters of fact disappear from view, eclipsed by the superior blaze. Nor is it surprising that we should be thus affected, for when two forces are thus placed in juxtaposition, the stronger must always absorb into itself the weaker. . . .

XIX

The removal of connecting particles gives a quick rush and "torrent rapture" to a passage, the writer appearing to be actually almost left behind by his own words. "Locking their shields," says Xenophon, "they thrust fought slew fell." And the words of Eurylochus in the *Odyssey* [X, 251]:

We passed at thy command the woodland's shade;
We found a stately hall built in a mountain glade.

Words thus severed from one another without the intervention of stops give a lively impression of one who through distress of mind at once halts and hurries in his speech. And this is what Homer has expressed by using the figure *Asyndeton*.[8]

XX

But nothing is so conducive to energy as a combination of different figures, when two or three uniting their resources mutually contribute to the vigor, the cogency, and the beauty of a speech. So Demosthenes in his speech against Meidias repeats the same words and breaks up his sentences in one lively descriptive passage: "He who receives a blow is hurt in many ways which he could not even describe to another, by gesture, by look, by tone." Then, to vary the movement of his speech and prevent it from standing still (for stillness produces rest, but passion requires a certain disorder of language, imitating the agitation and commotion of the soul), he at once dashes off in another direction, breaking up his words again, and repeating them in a different form, "by gesture, by look, by tone— when insult, when hatred, is added to violence, when he is struck with the fist, when he is struck as a slave!" By such means the orator imitates the action of Meidias, dealing blow upon blow on the minds of his judges. Immediately after, like a hurricane, he makes a fresh attack: "When he is struck with the fist, when he is struck in the face, this is what moves, this is what maddens a man, unless he is inured to outrage; no one could describe all this so as to bring home to his hearers its bitterness." You see how he preserves, by continual variation, the intrinsic force of these repetitions and broken clauses, so that his order seems irregular, and conversely his irregularity acquires a certain measure of order.

[8] Asyndeton, or the omission of connectives between clauses and sentences, is more striking in Greek, where connective particles are regularly employed. The preceding quotation from Xenophon (*Hellenica* IV, 3, 19) follows the translation of W. R. Roberts.

XXI

Supposing we add the conjunctions, after the practice of Isocrates and his school: "Moreover, I must not omit to mention that he who strikes a blow may hurt in many ways, in the first place by gesture, in the second place by look, in the third and last place by his tone." If you compare the words thus set down in logical sequence with the expressions of the *Meidias,* you will see that the rapidity and rugged abruptness of passion, when all is made regular by connecting links, will be smoothed away, and the whole point and fire of the passage will at once disappear. For as, if you were to bind two runners together, they will forthwith be deprived of all liberty of movement, even so passion rebels against the trammels of conjunctions and other particles, because they curb its free rush and destroy the impression of catapult impulse. . . .

XXXII

Concerning the number of metaphors to be employed together, Cæcilius seems to give his vote with those critics who make a law that not more than two, or at the utmost three, should be combined in the same place. The use, however, must be determined by the occasion. Those outbursts of passion which drive onwards like a winter torrent draw with them as an indispensable accessory whole masses of metaphor. It is thus in that passage of Demosthenes (who here also is our safest guide): "Those vile fawning wretches, each one of whom has lopped from his country her fairest members, who have toasted away their liberty, first to Philip, now to Alexander, who measure happiness by their bellies and their vilest appetites, who have overthrown the old landmarks and standards of felicity among Greeks —to be freemen, and to have no one for a master." Here the number of the metaphors is obscured by the orator's indignation against the betrayers of his country. And to effect this Aristotle and Theophrastus recommended the softening of harsh metaphors by the use of some such phrase as "So to say," "As it were," "If I may be permitted the expression," "If so bold a term is allowable." For thus to forestall criticism mitigates, they assert, the boldness of the metaphors. And I will not deny that these have their use. Nevertheless I must repeat the remark which I made in the case of figures and maintain that there are native antidotes to the number and boldness of metaphors, in well-timed displays of strong feeling and in unaffected sublimity, because these have an innate power by the dash of their movement of sweeping along and carrying all else before them. Or should we not rather say that they absolutely demand as indispensable the use of daring metaphors and will not allow the hearer to pause and criticize the number of them because he shares the passion of the speaker?

In the treatment, again, of familiar topics and in descriptive passages nothing gives such distinctness as a close and continuous series of metaphors. It is by this means that Xenophon has so finely delineated the anatomy of the human frame. And there is a still more brilliant and life-like picture in Plato's *Timaeus:* The human head he calls a *citadel;* the neck is an *isthmus* set to divide it from the chest; to support it beneath are the vertebræ, turning like *hinges;* pleasure he describes as a *bait* to tempt men to ill; the tongue is the *arbiter of tastes.* The heart is at once the *knot* of the veins and the *source* of the rapidly circulating blood and is stationed in the *guard-room* of the body. The ramifying blood vessels he calls *alleys.* "And casting about," he says, "for something to sustain the violent palpitation of the heart when it is alarmed by the approach of danger or agitated by passion, since at such times it is overheated, they (the gods) implanted in us the lungs, which are so fashioned that being soft and bloodless and having cavities within, they act like a buffer, and when the heart boils with inward passion by yielding to its throbbing save it from injury." He compares the seat of the desires to the *women's quarters,* the seat of the passions to the *men's quarters,* in a house. The spleen, again, is the *napkin* of the internal organs, by whose excretions it is saturated from time to time and swells to a great size with inward impurity. "After this," he continues, "they shrouded the whole with flesh, throwing it forward, like a cushion, as a barrier against injuries from without." The blood he terms the *pasture* of the flesh. "To assist the process of nutrition," he goes on, "they divided the body into ducts, cutting trenches like those in a garden, so that, the body being a system of narrow conduits, the current of the veins might flow as from a perennial fountainhead. And when the end is at hand," he says, "the soul is cast loose from her moorings like a ship and free to wander whither she will." These, and a hundred similar fancies, follow one another in quick succession. But those which I have pointed out are sufficient to demonstrate how great is the natural power of figurative language and how largely metaphors conduce to sublimity and to illustrate the important part which they play in all impassioned and descriptive passages.

That the use of figurative language, as of all other beauties of style, has a constant tendency towards excess is an obvious truth which I need not dwell upon. . . .

XXXIII

But supposing now that we assume the existence of a really un-blemished and irreproachable writer. It is not worth while to raise the whole question whether in poetry and prose we should prefer sublimity accompanied by some faults or a style which never rising above moderate excellence never stumbles and never requires correc-tion, and, further, whether the first place in literature is justly to be assigned to the more numerous or the loftier excellences? For these are questions proper to an inquiry on the sublime and urgently asking for settlement.

I know, then, that the largest intellects are far from being the most exact. A mind always intent on correctness is apt to be dissipated in trifles; but in great affluence of thought, as in vast material wealth, there must needs be an occasional neglect of detail. And is it not inevitably so? Is it not by risking nothing, by never aiming high, that a writer of low or middling powers keeps generally clear of faults and secure of blame? Whereas the loftier walks of literature are by their very loftiness perilous? I am well aware, again, that there is a law by which in all human productions the weak points catch the eye first, by which their faults remain indelibly stamped on the memory, while their beauties quickly fade away. Yet, though I have myself noted not a few faulty passages in Homer and in other authors of the highest rank and though I am far from being partial to their failings, nevertheless I would call them not so much willful blunders as oversights which were allowed to pass unregarded through that contempt of little things, that "brave disorder" which is natural to an exalted genius; and I still think that the greater excellences, though not everywhere equally sustained, ought always to be voted to the first place in literature, if for no other reason, for the mere grandeur of soul they evince. Let us take an instance: Apollonius in his *Argonautica* has given us a poem actually faultless; and in his pastoral poetry Theocritus is eminently happy, except when he occasionally attempts another style. And what then? Would you rather be a Homer or an Apollonius? Or take Eratosthenes and his *Erigone:* because that little work is without a flaw, is he therefore a greater poet than Archilochus, with all his disorderly profusion? greater than that impetuous, that god-gifted genius, which chafed against the restraints of law? or in lyric poetry would you choose to be a Bacchylides or a Pindar, in tragedy a Sophocles or (save the mark!) an Ion of Chios? Yet Ion and Bacchylides never stumble; their style is always neat, always pretty, while Pindar and Sophocles sometimes move onwards with a wide blaze of splendor, but often drop out of view in sudden and disastrous eclipse. Nevertheless no one in his sense would deny that a single play of Sophocles, the *Oedipus,* is of higher value than all the dramas of Ion put together. . . .

XXXIX

We have still left, my dear sir, the fifth of those sources which we set down at the outset as contributing to sublimity, that which consists in the mere arrangement of words in a certain order. Having already published two books dealing fully with the subject—so far at least as our investigations had carried us—it will be sufficient for the purpose of our present inquiry to add that harmony is an instrument which has a natural power, not only to win and to delight, but also in a remarkable degree to exalt the soul and sway the heart of man. When we see that a flute kindles certain emotions in its hearers, rendering them almost beside themselves and full of an orgiastic frenzy, and that by starting some kind of rhythmical beat it compels him who listens to move in time and assimilate his gestures to the tune, even though he has no taste whatever for music; when we know that the sounds of a harp, which in themselves have no meaning, by the change of key, by the mutual relation of the notes, and their arrangement in symphony, often lay a wonderful spell on an audience—though these are mere shadows and spurious imitations of persuasion, not, as I have said, genuine manifestations of human nature —can we doubt that composition (being a kind of harmony of that language which nature has taught us and which reaches, not our ears only, but our very souls), when it raises changing forms of words, of thoughts, of actions, of beauty, of melody, all of which are engrained in and akin to ourselves, and when by the blending of its manifold tones it brings home to the minds of those who stand by the feelings present to the speaker and ever disposes the hearer to sympathize with those feelings, adding word to word, until it has raised a majestic and harmonious structure—can we wonder if all this enchants us, wherever we meet with it, and filling us with the sense of pomp and dignity and sublimity and whatever else it embraces gains a complete mastery over our minds? It would be mere infatuation to join issue on truths so universally acknowledged and established by experience beyond dispute.

Now to give an instance: that is doubtless a sublime thought, indeed wonderfully fine, which Demosthenes applies to his decree: "This decree caused the danger which then hung round our city to pass away like a cloud." But the modulation is as perfect as the sentiment itself is weighty. It is uttered wholly in the dactylic measure, the noblest and most magnificent of all measures, and hence forming the chief constituent in the finest meter we know, the heroic. . . .

XL

There is another method very efficient in exalting a style. As the different members of the body, none of which, if severed from its connection, has any intrinsic excellence, unite by their mutual combination to form a complete and perfect organism, so also the elements of a fine passage, by whose separation from one another its high quality is simultaneously dissipated and evaporates, when joined in one organic whole, and still further compacted by the bond of harmony, by the mere rounding of the period gain power of tone. In fact, a clause may be said to derive its sublimity from the joint contributions of a number of particulars. And further (as we have shown at large elsewhere), many writers in prose and verse, though their natural powers were not high, were perhaps even low, and though the terms they employed were usually common and popular and conveying no impression of refinement, by the mere harmony of their composition have attained dignity and elevation and avoided the appearance of meanness. Such among many others are Philistus, Aristophanes occasionally, Euripides almost always. Thus when Heracles says, after the murder of his children, "I'm full of woes, I have no room for more," the words are quite common, but they are made sublime by being cast in a fine mold. By changing their position you will see that the poetical quality of Euripides depends more on his arrangement than on his thoughts. Compare his lines [from a lost play] on Dirce dragged by the bull:

> Whatever crossed his path,
> Caught in his victim's form, he seized, and dragging
> Oak, woman, rock, now here, now there, he flies.

The circumstance is noble in itself, but it gains in vigor because the language is disposed so as not to hurry the movement, not running, as it were, on wheels, because there is a distinct stress on each word, and the time is delayed, advancing slowly to a pitch of stately sublimity.

XLI

Nothing so much degrades the tone of a style as an effeminate and hurried movement in the language, such as is produced by pyrrhics and trochees and dichorees falling in time together into a regular dance measure. Such abuse of rhythm is sure to savor of coxcombry and petty affectation, and grows tiresome in the highest degree by a monotonous sameness of tone. But its worst effect is that, as those who listen to a ballad have their attention distracted from its subject and can think of nothing but the tune, so an over-rhythmical passage does not affect the hearer by the meaning of its words, but merely by their cadence, so that sometimes, knowing where the pause must come, they beat time with the speaker, striking the expected close like dancers before the stop is reached. Equally undignified is the splitting up of a sentence into a number of little words and short syllables crowded too closely together and forced into cohesion—hammered, as it were, successively together—after the manner of mortise and tenon.

XLII

Sublimity is further diminished by cramping the diction. Deformity instead of greatness ensues from over-compression. Here I am not referring to a judicious compactness of phrase, but to a style which is dwarfed and its force frittered away. To cut your words too short is to prune away their sense, but to be concise is to be direct. On the other hand, we know that a style becomes lifeless by over-extension, I mean by being relaxed to an unseasonable length.

XLIII

The use of trivial words has also a strong tendency to degrade a lofty passage. Thus in that description of the storm in Herodotus the matter is admirable, but some of the words admitted are beneath the dignity of the subject, such, perhaps, as "the seas having *seethed*," because the ill-sounding phrase "having seethed" detracts much from its impressiveness, or when he says, "the wind wore away," and "those who clung round the wreck met with an unwelcome end." "Wore away" is ignoble and vulgar, and "unwelcome" inadequate to the extent of the disaster. . . .

However, it is not incumbent on us to specify and enumerate whatever diminishes a style. We have now pointed out the various means of giving it nobility and loftiness. It is clear, then, that whatever is contrary to these will generally degrade and deform it.

XLIV

There is still another point which remains to be cleared up, my dear Terentian, and on which I shall not hesitate to add some remarks to gratify your inquiring spirit. It relates to a question which was recently put to me by a certain philosopher. "To me," he said, "in common, I may say, with many others, it is a matter of wonder that in the present age, which produces many highly skilled in the arts of popular persuasion, many of keen and active powers, many especially rich in every pleasing gift of language, the growth of highly exalted and wide-reaching genius has with a few rare exceptions almost entirely ceased. So universal is the dearth of eloquence which prevails throughout the world. Must we really," he asked, "give credit to that oft-repeated assertion that democracy is the kind nurse of genius and that high literary excellence has flourished with her prime and faded with her decay? Liberty, it is said, is all-powerful to feed the aspirations of high intellect, to hold out hope, and keep alive the flame of mutual rivalry and ambitious struggle for the highest place. Moreover, the prizes which are offered in every free state keep the spirits of her foremost orators whetted by perpetual exercise; they are, as it were, ignited by friction and naturally blaze forth freely because they are surrounded by freedom. But we of today," he continued, "seem to have learnt in our childhood the lessons of a benignant despotism, to have been cradled in her habits and customs from the time when our minds were still tender and never to have tasted the fairest and most fruitful fountain of eloquence, I mean liberty. Hence we develop nothing but a fine genius for flattery. This is the reason why, though all other faculties are consistent with the servile condition, no slave ever became an orator; because in him there is a dumb spirit which will not be kept down; his soul is chained; he is like one who has learnt to be ever expecting a blow. For, as Homer says [*Odyssey*, XVII, 322]:

The day of slavery
Takes half our manly worth away.

As, then (if what I have heard is credible), the cages in which those pygmies commonly called dwarfs are reared not only stop the growth of the imprisoned creature, but absolutely make him smaller by compressing every part of his body, so all despotism, however equitable, may be defined as a cage of the soul and a general prison."

My answer was as follows: "My dear friend, it is so easy and so characteristic of human nature always to find fault with the present. Consider, now, whether the corruption of genius is to be attributed not to a world-wide peace, but rather to the war within us which knows no limit, which engages all our desires, yes, and still further to the bad passions which lay siege to us today and make utter havoc and spoil of our lives. Are we not enslaved, nay, are not our careers completely shipwrecked by love of money, that fever which rages unappeased in us all, and love of pleasure—one the most debasing, the other the most ignoble of the mind's diseases? When I consider it, I can find no means by which we, who hold in such high honor or, to speak more correctly, who idolize boundless riches, can close the door of our souls against those evil spirits which grow up with them. For wealth unmeasured and unbridled is dogged by extravagance; she sticks close to him and treads in his footsteps, and as soon as he opens the gates of cities or of houses, she enters with him and makes her abode with him. And after a time they build their nests (to use a wise man's words) in our lives, and speedily set about breeding, and beget boastfulness, and vanity, and wantonness, no base-born children, but their very own. And if these also, the offspring of wealth, be allowed to come to their prime, quickly they engender in the soul those pitiless tyrants, violence, and lawlessness, and shame-lessness. Whenever a man takes to worshiping what is mortal and irrational in him and neglects to cherish what is immortal, these are the inevitable results. He never looks up again; he has lost all care for good report; by slow degrees the ruin of his life goes on, until it is consummated all round. All that is great in his soul fades, withers away, and is despised.

"If a judge who passes sentence for a bribe can never more give a free and sound decision on a point of justice or honor (for to him who takes a bribe honor and justice must be measured by his own interests), how can we of today expect, when the whole life of each one of us is controlled by bribery, while we lie in wait for other men's death and plan how to get a place in their wills, when we buy gain, from whatever source, each one of us, with our very souls in our slavish greed, how, I say, can we expect, in the midst of such a moral pestilence, that there is still left even one liberal and impartial critic whose verdict will not be biased by avarice in judging of those great works which live on through all time? I fear that for such men as we are it is better to serve than to be free. If our appetites were let loose altogether against our neighbors, they would be like wild beasts uncaged, and bring a deluge of calamity on the whole civilized world."

I ended by remarking generally that the genius of the present age is wasted by that indifference which with a few exceptions runs through the whole of life. If we ever shake off our apathy and apply ourselves to work, it is always with a view to pleasure or applause, not for that solid advantage which is worthy to be striven for and held in honor.

We had better then leave this generation to its fate and turn to what follows, which is the subject of the passions, to which we promised early in this treatise to devote a separate work. They play an important part in literature generally, and especially in relation to the sublime. [Ms. breaks off here.]

Dante Alighieri

(1265–1321)

Dante wrote his *Commedia* in the firm conviction that it is the function of poetry to express moral and philosophical truths. In a Latin letter to the General Can Grande della Scala of Verona, to whom he dedicated the *Paradiso,* the poet explains the structure of his work and his reason for calling it a comedy rather than a tragedy. Drawing upon the interpretive scheme developed by St. Thomas Aquinas, Dante points out that his poem presents four ascending levels of meaning: literal, allegorical, moral, and anagogical. But the fourfold scheme can also be reduced to an underlying dualism because, according to Dante, the last three levels are all in a general sense "allegorical" (or, in modern terms, "metaphorical") and as such distinguishable from the literal or plain sense meaning. A typical product of the rationalism of the Age of Faith, this medieval system of classifying literary meanings has attracted fresh attention in the twentieth century because of the modern critic's awareness of the complexity or, as Dante called it, the "polysemous" nature of poetic language. But for most readers the chief interest of the scheme lies in its pluralistic rather than its hierarchic character since it is hard for the modern intellectual to classify as confidently and neatly as the medieval writer could the ascending levels of meaning beyond the literal.

In addition to the *Commedia,* Dante's major works in his native

Italian tongue include the *Vita Nuova,* commemorating his love for Beatrice, and the *Convivio (Il Convito),* an unfinished book consisting of prose commentaries on a selection of his *canzoni.*

FROM LETTER TO
CAN GRANDE DELLA SCALA

For those who wish to give an introduction to a part of any work whatsoever, it is necessary to give some conception of the whole of which it is a part. Wishing to write something by way of introduction to the part of the comedy mentioned [the *Paradiso* of the *Commedia*], I think something should be said about the whole work, in order that there may be an easier and more perfect entrance to the part. There are six things to be considered at the beginning of any doctrinal work: the *subject,* the *agent,* the *form,* the *aim,* the *title of the book,* and the *kind of philosophy.* Of these there are three in which the part I have decided to dedicate to you [*Paradiso*] differs from the whole: namely, the *subject,* the *form,* and the *title.* In the others there is no variation, as will be apparent to whoever examines them. Therefore, for a consideration of the whole, these three things must be examined separately; and when this has been done, enough will be shown for an introduction to the part. Then we will examine the other three, not only in respect to the whole, but also in respect to the part I offer you.

For the clearness of what I say, it must be understood that the meaning of this work is not simple. Rather, it can be said to be polysemous, that is, of many meanings; for there is one meaning that is derived from the letter and another that is derived from the things indicated by the letter. The first is called *literal,* but the second *allegorical* or *moral* or *anagogical.* That this method of expounding

The text of this portion of the letter and of the brief following section from the *Convito* is based on that of C. S. Latham, *A Translation of Dante's Eleven Letters,* ed. G. R. Carpenter (Boston, 1891).

may be more clearly set forth, we can consider it in these lines: "When Israel went out of Egypt, the house of Jacob from a people of strange language, Judah was his sanctuary and Israel his dominion." If we consider the *letter* alone, the departure of the children of Israel from Egypt in the time of Moses is signified; if the *allegory,* our redemption accomplished in Christ is signified; if the *moral meaning,* the conversion of the soul from the sorrow and misery of sin to a state of grace is signified; if the *anagogical,* the departure of the sanctified soul from the slavery of this corruption to the liberty of everlasting glory is signified. And although these mystical meanings may be called by various names, they can in general all be said to be allegorical, since they differ from the literal or historical. For *allegory* is derived from the Greek *alleon,* which in Latin is *alienum* or *diversum*.[1]

Now that these things have been explained, it is evident that the *subject* around which the alternate meanings revolve must be double. Therefore the subject of this work must be understood as taken according to the letter and then as interpreted according to the allegorical meaning. The subject, then, of the whole work, taken according to the letter alone, is simply a consideration of the state of souls after death, for from and around this subject the action of the whole work turns. But, if the work is considered allegorically, the subject is man, liable to just reward or punishment, according as through the freedom of the will he is deserving or undeserving.

The *form* also is double: the form of the treatise, and the form of treating it. The form of the treatise is triple, according to its three-fold division. The first division is that of the whole work into three canticles; the second is that of each canticle into cantos; the third is that of each canto into rhythms. The form or method of treating is poetic, figurative, descriptive, digressive, transumptive, and, in addition, explanatory, divisive, probative, condemnatory, and explicit in examples.

The *title of the book* is: "Here begins the *Commedia* of Dante Alighieri, a Florentine by birth, but not by character." It must be

---

[1] *Allegory,* from the Greek *Allegoria,* from *allegorein,* to speak figuratively, probably from *alla* (neuter plural of *allos,* other) + *agorein,* to speak publicly (*Webster's Third New International Dictionary*).

understood that the word *comedy* is derived from *como*, village, and *oda*, which means song; hence comedy is, as it were, a village song.[2] Comedy is in truth a kind of poetic narrative that differs from all others. It differs from tragedy in its subject matter in that tragedy in its beginning is admirable and quiet, in its ending or catastrophe foul and horrible; accordingly, the word *tragedy* is derived from *tragos*, which means goat, and *oda*.[3] Tragedy is, then, a "goatish song," that is, foul like a goat as in the tragedies of Seneca. Comedy, however, begins with some adverse circumstances, but its theme has a happy ending, as in the comedies of Terence. Hence certain writers would say, in their salutation, in place of a greeting, "a tragic beginning and a comic ending." They differ also in their style of language, for tragedy is lofty and sublime, comedy mild and humble—as Horace says in his *Art of Poetry*, where he grants that sometimes comedians speak like tragedians and conversely: "At times, however, even comedy exalts its voice, and a character like Terence's Chremes rants in swelling strains. And a tragic writer often expresses grief in prosaic language."[4] From this, it should be clear why the present work is called a comedy. For, if we consider the theme, in its beginning it is horrible and foul, because it is Hell; in its ending, fortunate, desirable, and joyful, because it is Paradise; and, if we consider the style of language, the style is careless and humble, because it is the vulgar tongue, in which even housewives converse. There are also other kinds of poetic narration, such as the bucolic song, the elegy, the satire, and the votive hymn, as likewise can be seen in the poetics of Horace, but of these at present nothing need be said.

Now it must be evident in what manner the part offered you is to be assigned. For if the *subject* of the whole work, according to the letter, is the state of souls after death considered not in a special but in a general sense, it is obvious that in this part the subject is

[2] *Comedy*, from the Greek *komoidia*, from *komos*, revel or village festival (from *kome*, village) + *oidia*, song (*Webster's Third New International Dictionary*).

[3] *Tragedy*, from the Greek *tragos*, he goat + *oidia*, song (*ibid.*). One possible explanation of this obscure etymology may lie in tragedy's origin as a satyr-play; Peloponnesian satyrs were goat-like.

[4] See above, p. 74.

the same state treated in a special sense, namely, the state of the souls of the blessed after death. And if the subject of the whole work, allegorically considered, is man, liable to just reward or punishment according as through the freedom of the will he is deserving or undeserving, it is obvious that the subject in this part is restricted, and is man, liable to the reward of justice, according as he is deserving.

And thus the *form* of the part is evident in that assigned to the whole, for if the form of the whole treatise is triple, in this part it is only double, namely, the division of the canticle and the canto. The first division cannot apply to this, since this is a part of the first division.

The *title of the book* is also evident. For if the title of the whole book is "Here begins the *Commedia* . . . ," as above, the title of this part will be "Here begins the Third Canticle of the *Commedia* of Dante, which is called *Paradiso.*"

Now that these three things in which the part differs from the whole have been looked into, the other three in which there is no variation from the whole must be considered. The *agent,* then, of the whole and of the part is he who has been named and who throughout appears as the agent.[5]

The *aim* of the whole and of the part may be manifold—that is, both near and remote. But, omitting all subtle investigation, it can be briefly stated that the aim of the whole and of the part is to remove those living in this life from a state of misery and to guide them to a state of happiness.

Now the *kind of philosophy* under which we proceed in the whole and in the part is moral philosophy or ethics because the whole was undertaken not for speculation but for practial action. For although in some place or passage it may be handled in the manner of speculative philosophy, it is not for the sake of speculative philosophy but for the sake of practical needs, since, as Aristotle says in the second of the *Metaphysics,* "Practical men speculate somewhat now and then."

---

[5] That is, the poet himself, in his own person, as a prophet or agent through whom valuable and eternal truths were to be stated.

FROM IL CONVITO

Chapter I of the Second Treatise

I say that the explanation should be both literal and allegorical. . . . Books can be understood, and ought to be explained, in four principal senses. One is called *literal*, and it is this which goes no further than the letter, such as the simple narration of the thing of which you treat. . . .

The second is called *allegorical*, and this is the meaning hidden under the cloak of fables, truth concealed beneath a fair fiction—as when Ovid, saying that Orpheus with his lute tamed wild beasts and moved trees and rocks, means that the wise man, with the instrument of his voice, softens and humbles cruel hearts and moves at his will those who live neither for science nor for art and those who, having no rational life whatever, are almost like stones. . . . The theologians, however, take this meaning differently from the poets, but, because I intend to follow the method of the poets, I shall take the allegorical meaning according to their usage.

The third sense is called *moral*, and this readers should search for in all writings, for the benefit of themselves and their descendants. It is such as we can gather from the Gospel when Christ went up the mountain to be transfigured and of the twelve apostles took with him only three. From this fact we can understand in the moral sense that in most secret things we should have few companions.

The fourth sense is called *anagogical*, that is, beyond sense [or mystical]. It is when a book is spiritually expounded which, although a narration in its literal sense, by the things signified refers to the supernal things of eternal glory, as we may see in that psalm of the Prophet where he says that when Israel went out of Egypt Judea became holy and free. Although this is manifestly true according to the letter, it is also true in its spiritual meaning, which is that the soul, in forsaking its sins, becomes holy and free in its powers.

But in the demonstration of these meanings, the literal must always go first, as that in whose sense the others are included and without which it would be impossible and irrational to comprehend the others.

Sir Philip Sidney

(1554–86)

Not long before his soldier's death in Flanders, Sir Philip Sidney wrote the fullest English Renaissance statement of the nature and function of poetry. First published in 1595 in two editions with differing titles (*The Defence of Poesie; An Apologie for Poesie*), the essay is in part a reply to Puritan attacks like that of Stephen Gosson in *The School of Abuse* (1579). Sidney appeals to the classics as he argues for the antiquity and cultural importance of poetry, but he is not confined by their authority. He supports Aristotle's idea of poetry as imitation and Horace's stress on its didactic or educative value. In contending that poetry provides a fuller truth than either philosophy or history because it combines the precepts of one with the examples of the other (universals with particulars), Sidney anticipates the claims of some modern critics for poetry as the expression of a more complete knowledge than that provided by philosophy or history or science. As a Renaissance knight, Sidney is interested in poetry not only as the vehicle of truth, but even more as the "companion of camps," an essential moral guide to the intellectual who is also a man of action. Like later neoclassical critics, Sidney champions the unities of time and place and criticizes English drama for its mixture of comic and tragic modes, but he is not subservient to the past. With generous sympathy and high spirit (rare virtues in a critic), he celebrates English literature and the matchless poetic promise of his English tongue—a prophecy to be abundantly fulfilled by his younger Elizabethan contemporaries.

The most available source of Sidney's prose and poetry is Albert Feuillerat, *The Complete Works of Sir Philip Sidney* (4 volumes, 1922–26; reprinted 1962).

THE DEFENSE OF POESY

(1595)

When the right virtuous Edward Wotton and I were at the Emperor's court together, we gave ourselves to learn horsemanship of Jon Pietro Pugliano, one that, with great commendation, had the place of an esquire in his stable; and he, according to the fertileness of the Italian wit, did not only afford us the demonstration of his practice, but sought to enrich our minds with the contemplations therein which he thought most precious. But with none, I remember, mine ears were at any time more laden than when (either angered with slow payment, or moved with our learner-like admiration) he exercised his speech in the praise of his faculty.

He said soldiers were the noblest estate of mankind, and horsemen the noblest of soldiers. He said they were the masters of war and ornaments of peace, speedy goers and strong abiders, triumphers both in camps and courts; nay, to so unbelieved a point he proceeded, as that no earthly thing bred such wonder to a prince as to be a good horseman. Skill of government was but a *pedanteria* in comparison. Then would he add certain praises by telling what a peerless beast the horse was, the only serviceable courtier, without flattery, the beast of most beauty, faithfulness, courage, and such more, that if I had not been a piece of a logician before I came to

The text is based on that of the first edition of 1595, authorized by the Sidney family and published by William Ponsonby. Ellipses indicate the editors' omissions.

him, I think he would have persuaded me to have wished myself a horse. But thus much, at least, with his no few words, he drove into me, that self love is better than any gilding to make that seem gorgeous wherein ourselves be parties.

Wherein, if Pugliano's strong affection and weak arguments will not satisfy you, I will give you a nearer example of myself, who, I know not by what mischance, in these my not old years and idlest times, having slipped into the title of a poet, am provoked to say something unto you in the defense of that my unelected vocation, which if I handle with more good will than good reasons, bear with me, since the scholar is to be pardoned that followeth the steps of his master.

And yet I must say, that as I have more just cause to make a pitiful defense of poor poetry, which from almost the highest estimation of learning is fallen to be the laughingstock of children, so have I need to bring some more available proofs, since the former is by no man barred of his deserved credit, the silly latter hath had even the names of philosophers used to the defacing of it, with great danger of civil war among the Muses.

And first, truly, to all them that professing learning inveigh against poetry, [it] may justly be objected that they go ever near to ungratefulness to seek to deface that which, in the noblest nations and languages that are known, hath been the first light-giver to ignorance and first nurse, whose milk little [by] little enabled them to feed afterwards of tougher knowledges. And will they play the hedgehog, that being received into the den, drove out his host, or rather the vipers that with their birth kill their parents?

Let learned Greece, in any of her manifold sciences, be able to show me one book before Musaeus, Homer, and Hesiod, all three nothing else but poets. Nay, let any history be brought that can say any writers were there before them, if they were not men of the same skill, as Orpheus, Linus, and some others are named, who, having been the first of that country that made pens deliverers of their knowledge to posterity, may justly challenge to be called their fathers in learning. For not only in time they had this priority (although in itself antiquity be venerable), but went before them as causes to draw with their charming sweetness the wild untamed wits to an admiration of knowledge. So as Amphion was said to move stones with his poetry to build Thebes, and Orpheus to be listened to by beasts, indeed stony and beastly people. So among the Romans were Livius Andronicus and Ennius; so in the Italian language, the first that made it aspire to be a treasurehouse of science were the poets Dante, Boccaccio, and Petrarch; so in our English were Gower and Chaucer, after whom, encouraged and delighted with their excellent foregoing, others have followed to beautify our mother tongue, as well in the same kind as other arts.

This did so notably show itself that the philosophers of Greece durst not a long time appear to the world but under the masks of poets: so Thales, Empedocles, and Parmenides sang their natural philosophy in verses; so did Pythagoras and Phocylides their moral counsels; so did Tyrtaeus in war matters; and Solon in matters of policy; or rather they, being poets, did exercise their delightful vein in those points of highest knowledge which before them lay hidden to the world; for that wise Solon was directly a poet it is manifest, having written in verse the notable fable of the Atlantic Island, which was continued by Plato. And truly even Plato, whosoever well considereth shall find that in the body of his work, though the inside and strength were philosophy, the skin, as it were, and beauty depended most of poetry. For all stands upon dialogues, wherein he feigns many honest burgesses of Athens speak of such matters that if they had been set on the rack they would never have confessed them, besides his poetical describing the circumstances of their meetings, as the well-ordering of a banquet, the delicacy of a walk, with interlacing mere tales, as Gyges's Ring, and others, which who knows not to be flowers of poetry did never walk into Apollo's garden.

And even historiographers, although their lips sound of things done and verity be written in their foreheads, have been glad to borrow both fashion and perchance weight of the poets. So Herodotus entitled his history by the name of the nine Muses; and both he and all the rest that followed him either stole or usurped of poetry their passionate describing of passions, the many particularities of battles which no man could affirm, or, if that be denied me, long orations, put in the mouths of great kings and captains, which it is certain they never pronounced.

So that truly neither philosopher nor historiographer could at the first have entered into the gates of popular judgments if they had not taken a great passport of poetry, which in all nations, as this day, where learning flourisheth not, is plain to be seen, in all which they have some feeling of poetry. In Turkey, besides their lawgiving divines they have no other writers but poets. In our neighbor country Ireland, where truly learning goes very bare, yet are their poets held in a devout reverence. Even among the most barbarous and simple Indians, where no writing is, yet have they their poets who make and sing songs, which they call *areytos,* both of their ancestors' deeds and praises of their gods—a sufficient probability that if ever learning come among them, it must be by having their hard dull wits softened and sharpened with the sweet delights of poetry. For until they find a pleasure in the exercise of the mind, great promises of much knowledge will little persuade them that know not the fruits of knowledge. In Wales, the true remnant of the ancient Britons, as there are good authorities to show the long time they had poets, which they called bards, so through all the conquests of Romans, Saxons, Danes, and Normans, some of whom did seek to ruin all memory of learning from among them, yet do their poets, even to this day, last; so as it is not more notable in the soon beginning than in long continuing.

But since the authors of most of our sciences were the Romans, and before them the Greeks, let us a little stand upon their authorities, but even so far as to see what names they have given this now scorned skill. Among the Romans a poet was called *vates,* which is as much as a diviner, foreseer, or prophet, as by his conjoined words *vaticinium* and *vaticinari,* is manifest; so heavenly a title did that excellent people bestow upon this heart-ravishing knowledge. And so far were they carried into the admiration thereof that they thought in the chanceable hitting upon any such verses, great foretokens of their following fortunes were placed. Whereupon grew the word of *sortes Virgilianae,* when, by sudden opening Virgil's book, they lighted upon some verse of his, as it is reported by many. . . . Although it were a very vain and godless superstitition, as also it was to think spirits were commanded by such verses—whereupon this word *charms,* derived of *carmina,* cometh—so yet serveth it to show the great reverence those wits were held in; and altogether not without ground, since both the oracles of Delphos and Sibylla's prophecies were wholly delivered in verses; for that same exquisite observing of number and measure in the words and that high flying liberty of conceit proper to the poet did seem to have some divine force in it.

And may not I presume a little farther to show the reasonableness of this word *vates* and say that the holy David's psalms are a divine poem? If I do, I shall not do it without the testimony of great learned men, both ancient and modern. But even the name of "psalms" will speak for me, which, being interpreted, is nothing but "songs"; then, that it is fully written in meter, as all learned Hebricians agree, although the rules be not yet fully found; lastly, and principally, his handling his prophecy, which is merely poetical. For what else is the awaking his musical instruments, the often and free changing of persons, his notable *prosopopoeias*, when he maketh you, as it were, see God coming in his majesty, his telling of the beasts' joyfulness and hills leaping, but a heavenly poesy, wherein almost he showeth himself a passionate lover of that unspeakable and everlasting beauty to be seen by the eyes of the mind only, cleared by faith? But truly, now, having named him, I fear I seem to profane that holy name, applying it to poetry, which is among us thrown down to so ridiculous an estimation. But they that with quiet judgments will look a little deeper into it shall find the end and working of it such as, being rightly applied, deserveth not to be scourged out of the Church of God.

But now let us see how the Greeks have named it and how they deemed of it. The Greeks named him poet, which name hath, as the most excellent, gone through other languages. It cometh of this word *poiein*, which is "to make"; wherein, I know not whether by luck or wisdom, we Englishmen have met with the Greeks in calling him "a maker," which name, how high and incomparable a title it is, I had rather were known by marking the scope of other sciences than by any partial allegation.

There is no art delivered unto mankind that hath not the works of nature for his principal object, without which they could not consist and on which they so depend as they become actors and players, as it were, of what nature will have set forth. So doth the astronomer look upon the stars, and by that he seeth set down what order nature hath taken therein. So doth the geometrician and arithmetician in their diverse sorts of quantities. So doth the musician, in times, tell you which by nature agree, which not. The natural philosopher thereon hath his name, and the moral philosopher standeth upon the natural virtues, vices, or passions of man; and follow nature, saith he, therein, and thou shalt not err. The lawyer saith what men have determined, the historian, what men have done. The grammarian speaketh only of the rules of speech; and the rhetorician and logician, considering what in nature will soonest prove and persuade, thereon give artificial rules, which still are compassed within the circle of a question, according to the proposed matter. The physician weigheth the nature of man's body and the nature of things helpful and hurtful unto it. And the metaphysic, though it be in the second and abstract notions and therefore be counted supernatural, yet doth he, indeed, build upon the depth of nature. Only the poet, disdaining to be tied to any such subjection, lifted up with the vigor of his own invention, doth grow, in effect, into another nature, in making things either better than nature bringeth forth or quite anew, forms such as never were in nature, as the heroes, demigods, cyclops, chimeras, furies, and such like, so as he goeth hand in hand with nature, not enclosed within the narrow warrant of her gifts, but freely ranging within the zodiac of his own wit. Nature never set forth the earth in so rich tapestry as divers poets have done, neither with so pleasant rivers, fruitful trees, sweet smelling flowers, nor whatsoever else may make the too much loved earth more lovely. Her world is brazen, the poets only deliver a golden.

But let those things alone and go to man—for whom as the other things are, so it seemeth in him her uttermost cunning is employed—and know whether she have brought forth so true a lover as Theagenes, so constant a friend as Pylades, so valiant a man as Orlando, so right a prince as Xenophon's Cyrus, so excellent man every way as Virgil's Aeneas? Neither let this be jestingly conceived, because the works of the one be essential, the other in imitation or fiction; for every understanding knoweth the skill of each artificer standeth in that idea, or foreconceit of the work, and not in the work itself.

And that the poet hath that idea is manifest by delivering them forth in such excellency as he had imagined them. What delivering forth also is not wholly imaginative, as we are wont to say by them that build castles in the air, but so far substantially it worketh, not only to make a Cyrus, which had been but a particular excellency, as nature might have done, but to bestow a Cyrus upon the world to make many Cyruses, if they will learn aright why and how that maker made him. Neither let it be deemed too saucy a comparison to balance the highest point of man's wit with the efficacy of nature; but rather give right honor to the heavenly Maker of that maker, who, having made man to his own likeness, set him beyond and over all the works of that second nature; which in nothing he showeth so much as in poetry, when with the force of a divine breath he bringeth things forth far surpassing her doings, with no small arguments to the incredulous of that first accursed fall of Adam, since our erected wit maketh us know what perfection is, and yet our infected will keepeth us from reaching unto it. But these arguments will by few be understood and by fewer granted. Thus much I hope will be given me, that the Greeks, with some probability of reason, gave him the name above all names of learning.

Now let us go to a more ordinary opening of him that the truth may be the more palpable; and so, I hope, though we get not so unmatched a praise as the etymology of his names will grant, yet his very description, which no man will deny, shall not justly be barred from a principal commendation.

Poesy, therefore, is an art of imitation, for so Aristotle termeth it in the word *mimesis,* that is to say a representing, counterfeiting, or figuring forth—to speak metaphorically, a speaking picture, with this end, to teach and delight.

Of this have been three general kinds: the chief, both in antiquity and excellency, were they that did imitate the unconceivable excellencies of God. Such were David in his Psalms; Solomon in his Song of Songs, in his Ecclesiastes, and Proverbs; Moses and Deborah in their hymns; and the writer of Job which, beside other, the learned Emanuel Tremellius and Franciscus Junius do entitle the poetical part of the scripture. Against these none will speak that hath the Holy Ghost in due holy reverence. In this kind, though in a full

wrong divinity, were Orpheus, Amphion, Homer in his hymns, and
many other, both Greeks and Romans. And this poesy must be used
by whosoever will follow St. James's counsel in singing psalms when
they are merry and I know is used with the fruit of comfort by
some, when in sorrowful pangs of their death-bringing sins they
find the consolation of the never leaving goodness.

The second kind is of them that deal with matters philosophical:
either moral, as Tyrtaeus, Phocylides, Cato; or natural, as Lucretius,
and Virgil's *Georgics;* or astronomical, as Manilius and Pontanus; or
historical, as Lucan—which who mislike, the fault is in their judgment,
quite out of taste, and not in the sweet food of sweetly uttered
knowledge.

But because this second sort is wrapped within the fold of the
proposed subject and takes not the free course of his own invention,
whether they properly be poets or no, let grammarians dispute, and
go to the third, indeed right poets, of whom chiefly this question
ariseth, betwixt whom and these second is such a kind of difference
as betwixt the meaner sort of painters, who counterfeit only such
faces as are set before them, and the more excellent, who having
no law but wit, bestow that in colors upon you which is fittest for
the eye to see, as the constant though lamenting look of Lucretia,
when she punished in herself another's fault, wherein he painteth not
Lucretia, whom he never saw, but painteth the outward beauty of
such a virtue. For these third be they which most properly do
imitate to teach and delight, and to imitate borrow nothing of what
is, hath been, or shall be, but range, only reined with learned discretion, into the divine consideration of what may be and should be.
These be they that, as the first and most noble sort, may justly be
termed *vates,* so these are waited on in the excellentest languages
and best understandings with the foredescribed name of poets. For
these indeed do merely make to imitate and imitate both to delight
and teach and delight to move men to take that goodness in hand,
which without delight they would fly as from a stranger and teach to
make them know that goodness whereunto they are moved; which
being the noblest scope to which ever any learning was directed, yet
want there not idle tongues to bark at them.

These be subdivided into sundry more special denominations.

The most notable be the heroic, lyric, tragic, comic, satiric, iambic, elegiac, pastoral, and certain others, some of these being termed according to the matter they deal with, some by the sort of verse they like best to write in, for indeed the greatest part of poets have appareled their poetical inventions in that numbered kind of writing which is called verse—indeed but appareled, verse being but an ornament and no cause to poetry, since there have been many most excellent poets that never versified, and now swarm many versifiers that need never answer to the name of poets. For Xenophon, who did imitate so excellently as to give us *effigiem justi imperii,* the portraiture of a just empire, under the name of Cyrus, as Cicero saith of him, made therein an absolute heroical poem. So did Heliodorus in his sugared invention of that picture of love in Theagenes and Chariclea; and yet both these wrote in prose—which I speak to show that it is not rhyming and versing that maketh a poet (no more than a long gown maketh an advocate, who though he pleaded in armor should be an advocate and no soldier). But it is that feigning notable images of virtues, vices, or what else, with that delightful teaching, which must be the right describing note to know a poet by. Although, indeed, the senate of poets hath chosen verse as their fittest raiment, meaning as in matter they passed all in all, so in manner to go beyond them; not speaking table-talk fashion, or like men in a dream, words as they chanceably fall from the mouth, but peising [weighing] each syllable of each word by just proportion, according to the dignity of the subject.

Now therefore it shall not be amiss first to weigh this latter sort of poetry by his works and then by his parts, and if in neither of these anatomies he be condemnable, I hope we shall obtain a more favorable sentence. This purifying of wit, this enriching of memory, enabling of judgment, and enlarging of conceit, which commonly we call learning, under what name soever it come forth, or to what immediate end soever it be directed, the final end is to lead and draw us to as high a perfection as our degenerate souls, made worse by their clay lodgings, can be capable of. This, according to the inclination of the man, bred many formed impressions. For some that thought this felicity principally to be gotten by knowledge, and no knowledge to be so high or heavenly as to be acquainted with

the stars, gave themselves to astronomy; others, persuading themselves to be demigods if they knew the causes of things, became
natural and supernatural philosophers. Some an admirable delight
drew to music, and some the certainty of demonstration to the
mathematics. But all, one and other, having this scope—to know and
by knowledge to lift up the mind from the dungeon of the body to
the enjoying his own divine essence. But when by the balance of
experience it was found that the astronomer, looking to the stars,
might fall in a ditch, that the inquiring philosopher might be blind
in himself, and the mathematician might draw forth a straight
line with a crooked heart, then, lo, did proof, the overruler of opinions, make manifest that all these are but serving sciences, which,
as they have a private end in themselves, so yet are they all directed
to the highest end of the mistress knowledge, by the Greeks called
architectonikē, which stands, as I think, in the knowledge of a man's
self, in the ethic and politic consideration, with the end of well
doing and not of well knowing only—even as the saddler's next
end is to make a good saddle, but his further end to serve a nobler
faculty, which is horsemanship; so the horseman's to soldiery, and
the soldier not only to have the skill, but to perform the practice
of a soldier. So that the ending end of all earthly learning being
virtuous action, those skills that most serve to bring forth that, have
a most just title to be princes over all the rest. Wherein we can show
the poet is worthy to have it before any other competitors, among
whom principally to challenge it step forth the moral philosophers
[and historians]. . . .

Now whom shall we find, since the question standeth for the
highest form in the school of learning, to be moderator? Truly, as me
seemeth, the poet; and if not a moderator, even the man that ought
to carry the title from them both and much more from all other
serving sciences. Therefore compare we the poet with the historian and
with the moral philosopher; and, if he go beyond them both, no other
human skill can match him. For as for the divine, with all reverence
it is ever to be excepted, not only for having his scope as far beyond
any of these as eternity exceedeth a moment, but even for passing
each of these in themselves. And for the lawyer, though *Jus* be the
daughter of Justice, the chief of virtues, yet because he seeks to make

men good rather *formidine poenae* than *virtutis amore* [rather "by fear of punishment" than "by love of virtue"], or, to say righter, doth not endeavor to make men good, but that their evil hurt not others, having no care, so he be a good citizen, how bad a man he be. Therefore, as our wickedness maketh him necessary and necessity maketh him honorable, so is he not in the deepest truth to stand in rank with these, who all endeavor to take naughtiness away and plant goodness even in the secretest cabinet of our souls. And these four are all that any way deal in the consideration of men's manners, which being the supreme knowledge, they that best breed it deserve the best commendation.

The philosopher therefore and the historian are they which would win the goal, the one by precept, the other by example; but both, not having both, do both halt. . . . Now doth the peerless poet perform both; for whatsoever the philosopher saith should be done, he giveth a perfect picture of it in some one by whom he presupposeth it was done; so as he coupleth the general notion with the particular example. A perfect picture, I say, for he yieldeth to the powers of the mind an image of that whereof the philosopher bestoweth but a wordish description, which doth neither strike, pierce, nor possess the sight of the soul so much as that other doth. For as in outward things, to a man that had never seen an elephant or a rhinoceros, who should tell him most exquisitely all their shapes, color, bigness, and particular marks; or of a gorgeous palace, an architecture, who, declaring the full beauties, might well make the hearer able to repeat, as it were by rote, all he had heard, yet should never satisfy his inward conceit with being witness to itself of a true lively knowledge; but the same man, as soon as he might see those beasts well painted, or that house well in model, should straightway grow, without need of any description, to a judicial comprehending of them; so, no doubt, the philosopher, with his learned definitions—be it of virtues or vices, matters of public policy or private government—replenisheth the memory with many infallible grounds of wisdom, which, notwithstanding, lie dark before the imaginative and judging power, if they be not illuminated or figured forth by the speaking picture of poesy.

Tully taketh much pains, and many times not without poetical

helps, to make us know the force love of our country hath in us.
Let us but hear old Anchises speaking in the midst of Troy's
flames, or see Ulysses, in the fullness of all Calypso's delights, bewail
his absence from barren and beggarly Ithaca. Anger, the Stoics said,
was a short madness; let but Sophocles bring you Ajax on a stage,
killing and whipping sheep and oxen, thinking them the army of the
Greeks, with their chieftains Agamemnon and Menelaus, and tell me
if you have not a more familiar insight into anger than finding in
the schoolmen his genus and difference. See whether wisdom and
temperance in Ulysses and Diomedes, valor in Achilles, friendship in
Nisus and Euryalus, even to an ignorant man carry not an apparent
shining, and, contrarily, the remorse of conscience in Oedipus, the
soon-repenting pride in Agamemnon, the self-devouring cruelty in
his father Atreus, the violence of ambition in the two Theban
brothers, the sour sweetness of revenge in Medea, and, to fall lower,
the Terentian Gnatho and our Chaucer's Pandar so expressed that
we now use their names to signify their trades, and, finally, all virtues, vices, and passions so in their own natural states laid to the
view that we seem not to hear of them but clearly to see through
them.

But even in the most excellent determination of goodness, what
philosopher's counsel can so readily direct a prince as the feigned
Cyrus in Xenophon, or a virtuous man in all fortunes as Aeneas in
Virgil, or a whole commonwealth as the way of Sir Thomas More's
Utopia? I say the way because, where Sir Thomas More erred, it was
the fault of the man and not of the poet; for that way of patterning
a commonwealth was most absolute, though he perchance hath not
so absolutely performed it. . . .

For conclusion, I say the philosopher teacheth, but he teacheth
obscurely, so as the learned only can understand him; that is to say,
he teacheth them that are already taught. But the poet is the food
for the tenderest stomachs; the poet is, indeed, the right popular
philosopher. Whereof Aesop's tales give good proof, whose pretty
allegories, stealing under the formal tales of beasts, makes many,
more beastly than beasts, begin to hear the sound of virtue from those
dumb speakers.

But now may it be alleged, that if this imagining of matters be so fit for the imagination, then must the historian needs surpass, who brings you images of true matters, such as indeed were done and not such as fantastically or falsely may be suggested to have been done. Truly, Aristotle himself, in his discourse of poesy, plainly determineth this question, saying that poetry is *philosophōteron* and *spoudaioteron*, that is to say, it is more philosophical and more [studiously serious] than history. His reason is, because poesy dealeth with *katholou*, that is to say, with the universal consideration, and the history *kathekaston*, the particular. "Now," saith he, "the universal weighs what is fit to be said or done, either in likelihood or necessity, which the poesy considereth in his imposed names, and the particular only marketh, whether Alcibiades did or suffered this or that." Thus far Aristotle. Which reason of his, as all his, is most full reason. . . .

Now, to that which commonly is attributed to the praise of history, in respect of the notable learning is got by marking the success, as though therein a man should see virtue exalted and vice punished —truly, that commendation is peculiar to poetry and far off from history. For, indeed, poetry ever sets virtue so out in her best colors, making fortune her well-waiting handmaid, that one must needs be enamored of her. Well may you see Ulysses in a storm and in other hard plights, but they are but exercises of patience and magnanimity to make them shine the more in the near following prosperity. And of the contrary part, if evil men come to the stage, they ever go out (as the tragedy writer answered to one that misliked the show of such persons) so manacled as they little animate folks to follow them. But the history, being captived to the truth of a foolish world, is many times a terror from well-doing and an encouragement to unbridled wickedness. For see we not valiant Miltiades rot in his fetters, the just Phocion and the accomplished Socrates put to death like traitors, the cruel Severus live prosperously, the excellent Severus miserably murdered, Sulla and Marius dying in their beds, Pompey and Cicero slain then when they would have thought exile a happiness? See we not virtuous Cato driven to kill himself and rebel Caesar so advanced that his name yet, after sixteen hundred years, lasteth in the highest honor? . . .

For suppose it be granted, that which I suppose with great reason may be denied, that the philosopher in respect of his methodical proceeding doth teach more perfectly than the poet, yet do I think that no man is so much *philophilosophos* as to compare the philosopher, in moving, with the poet. And that moving is of a higher degree than teaching, it may by this appear, that it is well nigh both the cause and effect of teaching. For who will be taught, if he be not moved with desire to be taught? And what so much good doth that teaching bring forth (I speak still of moral doctrine) as that it moveth one to do that which it doth teach? . . .

Now therein of all sciences (I speak still of human and according to the human conceit) is our poet the monarch. For he doth not only show the way, but giveth so sweet a prospect into the way as will entice any man to enter into it. Nay, he doth, as if your journey should lie through a fair vineyard, at the very first give you a cluster of grapes, that full of that taste you may long to pass further. He beginneth not with obscure definitions, which must blur the margent with interpretations and load the memory with doubtfulness, but he cometh to you with words set in delightful proportion, either accompanied with, or prepared for, the well-enchanting skill of music; and with a tale, forsooth, he cometh unto you, with a tale which holdeth children from play and old men from the chimney corner, and, pretending no more, doth intend the winning of the mind from wickedness to virtue, even as the child is often brought to take most wholesome things by hiding them in such other as have a pleasant taste, which, if one should begin to tell them the nature of the aloes or rhubarb they should receive, would sooner take their physic at their ears than at their mouth. So is it in men (most of which are childish in the best things till they be cradled in their graves); glad they will be to hear the tales of Hercules, Achilles, Cyrus, Aeneas and, hearing them, must needs hear the right description of wisdom, valor, and justice, which, if they had been barely (that is to say, philosophically) set out, they would swear they be brought to school again. That imitation whereof poetry is hath the most conveniency to nature of all other, insomuch that, as Aristotle saith, those things which in themselves are horrible, as cruel battles, unnatural monsters, are made, in poetical imitation, delightful. . . .

By these, therefore, examples and reasons, I think it may be manifest that the poet, with that same hand of delight, doth draw the mind more effectually than any other art doth. And so a conclusion not unfitly ensueth, that, as virtue is the most excellent resting place for all worldly learning to make his end of, so poetry, being the most familiar to teach it and most princely to move towards it in the most excellent work is the most excellent workman.

But I am content not only to decipher him by his works (although works in commendation and dispraise must ever hold a high authority), but more narrowly will examine his parts, so that, as in a man, though all together may carry a presence full of majesty and beauty, perchance in some one defectious piece we may find a blemish.

Now, in his parts, kinds, or species, as you list to term them, it is to be noted that some poesies have coupled together two or three kinds, as the tragical and comical, whereupon is risen the tragicomical. Some, in the manner, have mingled prose and verse, as Sannazzaro and Boethius. Some have mingled matters heroical and pastoral. But that cometh all to one in this question, for, if severed they be good, the conjunction cannot be hurtful. Therefore, perchance forgetting some and leaving some as needless to be remembered, it shall not be amiss in a word to cite the special kinds to see what faults may be found in the right use of them.

Is it then the pastoral poem which is misliked? For, perchance, where the hedge is lowest, they will soonest leap over. Is the poor pipe disdained, which sometimes out of Melibaeus' mouth can show the misery of people under hard lords and ravening soldiers? And again, by Tityrus, what blessedness is derived to them that lie lowest, from the goodness of them that sit highest? . . .

Or is it the lamenting elegiac, which in a kind heart would move rather pity than blame, who bewaileth with the great philosopher Heraclitus the weakness of mankind and the wretchedness of the world, who surely is to be praised either for compassionately accompanying just causes of lamentations or for rightly pointing out how weak be the passions of woefulness?

Is it the bitter but wholesome iambic, which rubs the galled mind in making shame the trumpet of villainy with bold and open crying out against naughtiness?

Or the satiric, who . . . sportingly never leaveth till he make a man laugh at folly and at length, ashamed to laugh at himself, which

he cannot avoid without avoiding the folly, who . . . giveth us to
feel how many headaches a passionate life bringeth us to? . . .

No, perchance it is the comic, whom naughty play-makers and
stage-keepers have justly made odious. To the arguments of abuse I
will after answer. Only thus much now is to be said, that the
comedy is an imitation of the common errors of our life, which he
representeth in the most ridiculous and scornful sort that may be, so
as it is impossible that any beholder can be content to be such a
one. Now as in geometry the oblique must be known as well as the
right, and in arithmetic the odd as well as the even, so in the
actions of our life, who seeth not the filthiness of evil wanteth a
great foil to perceive the beauty of virtue. This doth the comedy
handle so, in our private and domestical matters, as with hearing it
we get, as it were, an experience of what is to be looked for of a
niggardly Demea, of a crafty Davus, of a flattering Gnatho, of a
vainglorious Thraso; and not only to know what effects are to be
expected, but to know who be such by the signifying badge given
them by the comedian. And little reason hath any man to say that
men learn evil by seeing it so set out, since, as I said before, there
is no man living but by the force truth hath in nature, no sooner
seeth these men play their parts but wisheth them in *pistrinum*
[treadmill] although, perchance, the sack of his own faults lie so
behind his back that he seeth not himself dance the same measure,
whereto yet nothing can more open his eyes than to see his own
actions contemptibly set forth. So that the right use of comedy will,
I think, by nobody be blamed.

And much less of the high and excellent tragedy, that openeth the
greatest wounds and showeth forth the ulcers that are covered with
tissue, that maketh kings fear to be tyrants and tyrants manifest
their tyrannical humors, that with stirring the effects of admiration
and commiseration teacheth the uncertainty of this world and upon
how weak foundations gilden roofs are builded. . . . But how
much it can move, Plutarch yieldeth a notable testimony of the
abominable tyrant Alexander Pheraeus, from whose eyes a tragedy,
well made and represented, drew abundance of tears, who without all
pity had murdered infinite numbers and some of his own blood, so
as he that was not ashamed to make matters for tragedies yet could

not resist the sweet violence of a tragedy. And if it wrought no further good in him, it was that he in despite of himself withdrew himself from harkening to that which might mollify his hardened heart. But it is not the tragedy they do mislike, for it were too absurd to cast out so excellent a representation of whatsoever is most worthy to be learned.

Is it the lyric that most displeaseth, who with his tuned lyre and well-accorded voice giveth praise, the reward of virtue, to virtuous acts, who giveth moral precepts and natural problems, who sometimes raiseth up his voice to the height of the heavens in singing the lauds of the immortal God? Certainly I must confess mine own barbarousness: I never heard the old song of Percy and Douglas that I found not my heart moved more than with a trumpet; and yet it is sung but by some blind crowder, with no rougher voice than rude style, which being so evil appareled in the dust and cobwebs of that uncivil age, what would it work trimmed in the gorgeous eloquence of Pindar? In Hungary I have seen it the manner at all feasts and other such like meetings to have songs of their ancestors' valor, which that right soldierlike nation think one of the chiefest kindlers of brave courage. The incomparable Lacedaemonians did not only carry that kind of music ever with them to the field, but even at home, as such songs were made, so were they all content to be singers of them, when the lusty men were to tell what they did, the old men what they had done, and the young men what they would do. And where a man may say that Pindar many times praiseth highly victories of small moment, rather matters of sport than virtue, as it may be answered, it was the fault of the poet and not of the poetry, so indeed the chief fault was in the time and custom of the Greeks, who set those toys at so high a price that Philip of Macedon reckoned a horse-race won at Olympus among his three fearful felicities. But as the inimitable Pindar often did, so is that kind most capable and most fit to awake the thoughts from the sleep of idleness to embrace honorable enterprises.

There rests the heroical, whose very name, I think, should daunt all backbiters. For by what conceit can a tongue be directed to speak evil of that which draweth with it no less champions than Achilles, Cyrus, Aeneas, Turnus, Tydeus, Rinaldo—who doth not only teach and move to truth, but teacheth and moveth to the most high and excellent truth, who maketh magnanimity and justice shine through all misty fearfulness and foggy desires, who, if the saying of Plato and Tully be true, that who could see virtue would be wonderfully ravished with the love of her beauty, this man setteth her out to make her more lovely in her holiday apparel to the eye of any that will deign not to disdain until they understand? But if anything be already said in the defense of sweet poetry, all concurreth to the maintaining the heroical, which is not only a kind, but the best and most accomplished kind of poetry. For, as the image of each action stirreth and instructeth the mind, so the lofty image of such worthies most inflameth the mind with desire to be worthy and informs with counsel how to be worthy. Only let Aeneas be worn in the tablet of your memory, how he governeth himself in the ruin of his country, in the preserving his old father and carrying away his religious ceremonies, in obeying the god's commandment to leave Dido, though not only all passionate kindness but even the human consideration of virtuous gratefulness would have craved other of him, how in storms, how in sports, how in war, how in peace, how a fugitive, how victorious, how besieged, how besieging, how to strangers, how to allies, how to enemies, how to his own, lastly, how in his inward self, and how in his outward government, and I think, in a mind most prejudiced with a prejudicating humor, he will be found in excellency fruitful. . . . But, truly, I imagine it falleth out with these poet-whippers as with some good women who often are sick, but in faith they cannot tell where. So the name of poetry is odious to them, but neither his cause nor effects, neither the sum that contains him nor the particularities descending from him, give any fast handle to their carping dispraise.

Since, then, poetry is of all human learnings the most ancient and of most fatherly antiquity, as from whence other learnings have taken their beginnings, since it is so universal that no learned nation doth despise it, nor barbarous nation is without it, since both Roman and Greek gave divine names unto it, the one of prophesying, the other of making, and that indeed that name of "making" is fit for him, considering that whereas other arts retain themselves within their subject and receive, as it were, their being from it, the poet only bringeth his own stuff and doth not learn a conceit out of a matter, but maketh matter for a conceit, since neither his description nor his end containeth any evil, the things described cannot be evil, since his effects be so good as to teach goodness and delight the learners of it, since therein (namely in moral doctrine, the chief of all knowledges) he doth not only far pass the historian, but, for instructing, is well nigh comparable to the philosopher, and for moving, leaveth him behind him, since the Holy Scripture (wherein there is no uncleanness) hath whole parts in it poetical, and that even our Savior Christ vouchsafed to use the flowers of it, since all his kinds are not only in their united forms but in their severed dissections fully commendable, I think, and think I think rightly, the laurel crown appointed for triumphant captains doth worthily, of all other learnings, honor the poet's triumph.

But because we have ears as well as tongues, and that the lightest reasons that may be will seem to weigh greatly if nothing be put in the counterbalance, let us hear and, as well as we can, ponder what objections be made against this art which may be worthy either of yielding or answering.

First, truly I note not only in these *misomousoi*, poet-haters, but in all that kind of people who seek a praise by dispraising others, that they do prodigally spend a great many wandering words in quips and scoffs, carping and taunting at each thing which, by stirring the spleen, may stay the brain from a thorough beholding the worthiness of the subject. . . .

But that which giveth greatest scope to their scorning humor is rhyming and versing. It is already said, and, as I think, truly said, it is not rhyming and versing that maketh poesy; one may be a poet without versing and a versifier without poetry. But yet presuppose it were inseparable, as indeed it seemeth Scaliger judgeth, truly it were an inseparable commendation. For if *oratio* next to *ratio,* speech next to reason, be the greatest gift bestowed upon mortality, that cannot be praiseless which doth most polish that blessing of speech—which considereth each word, not only as a man may say by his forcible quality, but by his best measured quantity, carrying even in themselves a harmony—without, perchance, number, measure, order, proportion be in our time grown odious.

But lay aside the just praise it hath by being the only fit speech for music—music, I say, the most divine striker of the senses—thus much is undoubtedly true, that if reading be foolish without remembering, memory being the only treasure of knowledge, those words which are fittest for memory are likewise most convenient for knowledge. Now that verse far exceedeth prose in the knitting up of the memory, the reason is manifest: the words, besides their delight, which hath a great affinity to memory, being so set as one cannot be lost but the whole work fails; which accusing itself calleth the remembrance back to itself and so most strongly confirmeth it. Besides, one word so, as it were, begetting another, as, be it in rhyme or measured verse, by the former a man shall have a near guess to the follower. Lastly, even they that have taught the art of memory have showed nothing so apt for it as a certain room divided into many places, well and thoroughly known. Now that hath the verse in effect perfectly, every word having his natural seat, which seat must needs make the word remembered. But what needs more in a thing so known to all men? Who is it that ever was scholar that doth not carry away some verses of Virgil, Horace, or Cato, which in his youth he learned and even to his old age serve him for hourly lessons? . . . But the fitness it hath for memory is notably proved by all delivery of arts, wherein, for the most part, from grammar to logic, mathematics, physic, and the rest, the rules chiefly necessary to be borne away are compiled in verses. So that verse being in itself sweet and orderly and being best for memory, the only handle of knowledge, it must be in jest that any man can speak against it.

Now then go we to the most important imputations laid to the poor poets. For aught I can yet learn, they are these:

First, that there being many other more fruitful knowledges, a man might better spend his time in them than in this.

Secondly, that it is the mother of lies.

Thirdly, that it is the nurse of abuse, infecting us with many pestilent desires, with a siren's sweetness drawing the mind to the serpent's tail of sinful fancies; and herein especially comedies give the largest field to ear, as Chaucer saith; how, both in other nations and ours, before poets did soften us, we were full of courage, given to martial exercises, the pillars of manlike liberty, and not lulled asleep in shady idleness with poets' pastimes.

And lastly and chiefly, they cry out with open mouth, as if they had overshot Robin Hood, that Plato banished them out of his commonwealth. Truly this is much, if there be much truth in it.

First, to the first, that a man might better spend his time is a reason indeed, but it doth, as they say, but *petere principium.* For if it be, as I affirm, that no learning is so good as that which teacheth and moveth to virtue and that none can both teach and move thereto so much as poesy, then is the conclusion manifest, that ink and paper cannot be to a more profitable purpose employed. And certainly, though a man should grant their first assumption, it should follow, methinks, very unwillingly, that good is not good because better is better. But I still and utterly deny that there is sprung out of earth a more fruiful knowledge.

To the second, therefore, that they should be the principal liars, I answer paradoxically, but truly, I think truly, that of all writers under the sun, the poet is the least liar and, though he would, as a poet can scarcely be a liar. The astronomer, with his cousin the geometrician, can hardly escape when they take upon them to measure the height of the stars. How often, think you, do the physicians lie, when they aver things good for sicknesses which afterwards send Charon a great number of souls drowned in a potion before they come to his ferry? And no less of the rest which take upon them to affirm. Now for the poet, he nothing affirmeth, and therefore never lieth, for, as I take it, to lie is to affirm that to be true which is false. So as the other artists, and especially the historian, affirming many things, can, in the cloudy knowledge of mankind, hardly escape from many lies. But the poet, as I said before, never affirmeth; the poet never maketh any circles about your imagination, to conjure you to believe for true what he writeth; he citeth not authorities of other histories, but even for his entry calleth the sweet Muses to inspire into him a good invention; in truth, not laboring to tell you what is or is not, but what should or should not be. And, therefore, though he recount things not true, yet because he telleth them not for true, he lieth not, without we will say that Nathan lied in his speech, before alleged, to David; which, as a wicked man durst scarce say, so think I none so simple would say that Aesop lied in the tales of his beasts, for who thinketh that Aesop wrote it for actually true were well worthy to have his name chronicled among the beasts he writeth of. . . .

Their third is how much it abuseth men's wit, training it to wanton sinfulness and lustful love. For, indeed, that is the principal if not only abuse I can hear alleged. They say the comedies rather teach than reprehend amorous conceits. They say the lyric is larded with passionate sonnets, the elegiac weeps the want of his mistress, and that even to the heroical Cupid hath ambitiously climbed. Alas, Love, I would thou couldst as well defend thyself as thou canst offend others! I would those on whom thou does attend could either put thee away or yield good reason why they keep thee! But grant love of beauty to be a beastly fault, although it be very hard, since only man, and no beast, hath that gift to discern beauty; grant that lovely name of love to deserve all hateful reproaches, although even some of my masters the philosophers spent a good deal of their lamp-oil in setting forth the excellency of it; grant, I say, what they will have granted, that not only love, but lust, but vanity, but, if they list, scurrility, possess many leaves of the poets' books; yet, think I, when this is granted, they will find their sentence may, with good manners, put the last words foremost and not say that poetry abuseth man's wit, but that man's wit abuseth poetry. For I will not deny but that man's wit may make poesy, which should be *eikastikē*, which some learned have defined, figuring forth good things, to be *phantastikē*, which doth contrariwise infect the fancy with unworthy objects, as the painter, that should give to the eye either some excellent perspective or some fine picture fit for building or fortification or containing in it some notable example, as Abraham sacrificing his son Isaac, Judith killing Holofernes, David fighting with Goliath, may leave those and please an ill-pleased eye with wanton shows of better hidden matters.

But, what! Shall the abuse of a thing make the right use odious? Nay, truly, though I yield that poesy may not only be abused, but that being abused, by the reason of his sweet charming force it can do more hurt than any other army of words, yet shall it be so far from concluding that the abuse should give reproach to the abused, that, contrariwise, it is a good reason that whatsoever being abused doth most harm, being rightly used (and upon the right use each thing receives his title) doth most good. Do we not see skill of physic, the best rampire to our often-assaulted bodies, being abused, teach poison, the most violent destroyer? Doth not knowledge of law, whose end is to even and right all things, being abused, grow the crooked fosterer of horrible injuries? Doth not (to go to the highest) God's word abused breed heresy, and his name abused become blasphemy? Truly, a needle cannot do much hurt, and as truly (with leave of ladies be it spoken) it cannot do much good. With a sword thou mayst kill thy father, and with a sword thou mayst defend thy prince and country. So that, as in their calling poets fathers of lies they said nothing, so in this their argument of abuse, they prove the commendation.

They allege herewith, that before poets began to be in price our nation had set their heart's delight upon action and not imagination, rather doing things worthy to be written than writing things fit to be done. What that before-time was, I think scarcely Sphinx can tell, since no memory is so ancient that gives not the precedence to poetry. And certain it is that, in our plainest homeliness, yet never was the Albion nation without poetry. Marry, this argument, though it be leveled against poetry, yet it is indeed a chain-shot against all learning—or bookishness, as they commonly term it. Of such mind were certain Goths, of whom it is written that, having in the spoil of a famous city taken a fair library, one hangman, belike fit to execute the fruits of their wits, who had murthered a great number of bodies, would have set fire on it. "No," said another very gravely, "take heed what you do, for while they are busy about those toys we shall with more leisure conquer their countries."

This indeed is the ordinary doctrine of ignorance, and many words sometimes I have heard spent in it; but, because this reason is generally against all learning, as well as poetry, or rather all learning but poetry; because it were too large a digression to handle it, or at least too superfluous, since it is manifest that all government of action is to be gotten by knowledge, and knowledge best by gathering many knowledges, which is reading, I only say with Horace, to him that is of that opinion, *Iubeo stultum esse libenter* ["I bid him to be a fool as much as he will"]; for as for poetry itself, it is the freest from this objection, for poetry is the companion of camps. I dare undertake *Orlando Furioso* or honest King Arthur will never displease a soldier, but the quiddity of *ens* and *prima materia* will hardly agree with a corselet. And, therefore, as I said in the beginning, even Turks and Tartars are delighted with poets. Homer, a Greek, flourished before Greece flourished. And, if to a slight conjecture a conjecture may be opposed, truly it may seem that as by him their learned men took almost their first light of knowledge, so their active men received their first motions of courage. Only Alexander's example may serve, who by Plutarch is accounted of such virtue that fortune was not his guide but his footstool, whose acts speak for him, though Plutarch did not—indeed the phoenix of warlike princes. This Alexander left his schoolmaster, living Aristotle, behind him, but took dead Homer with him. He put the philosopher Callisthenes to death for his seeming philosophical, indeed mutinous, stubbornness, but the chief thing he was ever heard to wish for was that Homer had been alive. He well found he received more bravery of mind by the pattern of Achilles than by hearing the definition of fortitude. . . .

But now, indeed, my burden is great, that Plato's name is laid upon me, whom, I must confess, of all philosophers I have ever esteemed most worthy of reverence, and with good reason, since of all philosophers he is the most poetical. Yet if he will defile the fountain out of which his flowing streams have proceeded, let us boldly examine with what reasons he did it.

First, truly, a man might maliciously object that Plato, being a philosopher, was a natural enemy of poets. For, indeed, after the philosophers had picked out of the sweet mysteries of poetry the right discerning of true points of knowledge, they forthwith, putting it in method and making a school art of that which the poets did only teach by a divine delightfulness, beginning to spurn at their guides, like ungrateful apprentices were not content to set up shop for themselves, but sought by all means to discredit their masters; which, by the force of delight being barred them, the less they could overthrow them the more they hated them. . . .

But I honor philosophical instructions and bless the wits which bred them so as they be not abused, which is likewise stretched to poetry. Saint Paul himself sets a watchword upon philosophy, indeed upon the abuse. So doth Plato upon the abuse, not upon poetry. Plato found fault that the poets of his time filled the world with wrong opinions of the gods, making light tales of that unspotted essence, and therefore would not have the youth depraved with such opinions. Herein may much be said; let this suffice: the poets did not induce such opinions but did imitate those opinions already induced. . . .

Plato, therefore, whose authority I had much rather justly construe than unjustly resist, meant not in general of poets . . . but only meant to drive out those wrong opinions of the deity, whereof now, without further law, Christianity hath taken away all the hurtful belief, perchance, as he thought, nourished by the then esteemed poets. And a man need go no further than to Plato himself to know his meaning who in his dialogue called *Ion* giveth high and rightly divine commendation unto poetry. So as Plato, banishing the abuse, not the thing, not banishing it, but giving due honor to it, shall be our patron and not our adversary. For indeed, I had much rather, since truly I may do it, show their mistaking of Plato, under whose lion's skin they would make an ass-like braying against poesy, than go about to overthrow his authority, whom, the wiser a man is, the more just cause he shall find to have in admiration, especially since he attributeth unto poesy more than myself do, namely to be a very inspiring of a divine force, far above man's wit, as in the forenamed dialogue is apparent.

Of the other side, who would show the honors have been by the best sort of judgments granted them, a whole sea of examples would present themselves: Alexander's, Caesar's, Scipio's, all favorers of poets. . . . And even the Greek Socrates, whom Apollo confirmed to be the only wise man, is said to have spent part of his old time in putting Aesop's fables into verses, and, therefore, full evil should it become his scholar Plato to put such words in his master's mouth against poets. But what needs more? Aristotle writes the *Art of Poesy,* and why, if it should not be written? Plutarch teacheth the use to be gathered of them, and how, if they should not be read? And who reads Plutarch's either history or philosophy shall find he trimmeth both their garments with guards of poesy.

But I list not to defend poesy with the help of her underling historiography. Let it suffice to have showed it is a fit soil for praise to dwell upon, and what dispraise may be set upon it is either easily overcome or transformed into just commendation. So that, since the excellences of it may be so easily and so justly confirmed, and the low creeping objections so soon trodden down, it is not being an art of lies, but of true doctrine, not of effeminateness, but of notable stirring of courage, not of abusing man's wit, but of strengthening man's wit, not banished, but honored by Plato, let us rather plant more laurels for to engarland the poets' heads (which honor of being laureate, as besides them only triumphant captains were, is a sufficient authority to show the price they ought to be held in) than suffer the ill-savored breath of such wrong speakers once to blow upon the clear springs of poesy.

But since I have run so long a career in this matter, methinks, before I give my pen a full stop, it shall be but a little more lost time to inquire why England, the mother of excellent minds, should be grown so hard a stepmother to poets, who certainly in wit ought to pass all others, since all only proceeds from their wit, being, indeed, makers of themselves, not takers of others. . . . That poesy, thus embraced in all other places, should only find in our time a hard welcome in England, I think the very earth laments it and therefore decks our soil with fewer laurels than it was accustomed. For heretofore poets have in England also flourished . . . .

Chaucer undoubtedly did excellently in his *Troilus and Criseyde,* of whom, truly, I know not whether to marvel more, either that he in that misty time could see so clearly or that we in this clear age go so stumblingly after him. Yet had he great wants, fit to be forgiven in so reverend an antiquity. I account the *Mirror of Magistrates* meetly furnished of beautiful parts. And in the Earl of Surrey's lyrics, many things tasting of a noble birth and worthy of a noble mind. The *Shepherds' Calendar* hath much poesy in his eclogues, indeed worthy the reading, if I be not deceived. That same framing of his style to an old rustic language, I dare not allow, since neither Theocritus in Greek, Virgil in Latin, nor Sannazzaro in Italian did affect it. Besides these, I do not remember to have seen but few (to speak boldly) printed that have poetical sinews in them. For proof whereof, let but most of the verses be put in prose, and then ask the meaning, and it will be found that one verse did but beget another, without ordering at the first what should be at the last—which becomes a confused mass of words, with a tinkling sound of rhyme, barely accompanied with reason.

Our tragedies and comedies, not without cause cried out against, observing rules neither of honest civility nor skillful poetry. Excepting *Gorboduc* (again I say of those that I have seen), which notwithstanding as it is full of stately speeches and well-sounding phrases, climbing to the height of Seneca's style and as full of notable morality, which it doth most delightfully teach and so obtain the very end of poesy, yet in truth it is very defectious in the circumstances, which grieves me because it might not remain as an exact model of all tragedies. For it is faulty both in place and time, the two necessary companions of all corporal actions. For where the stage should always represent but one place, and the uttermost time presupposed in it should be, both by Aristotle's precept and common reason, but one day, there is both many days and many places inartificially imagined.

But if it be so in *Gorboduc*, how much more in all the rest, where you shall have Asia of the one side and Afric of the other, and so many other under kingdoms that the player, when he comes in, must ever begin with telling where he is, or else the tale will not be conceived? Now shall you have three ladies walk to gather flowers, and then we must believe the stage to be a garden. By and by, we hear news of shipwreck in the same place, then we are to blame if we accept it not for a rock. Upon the back of that comes out a hideous monster with fire and smoke, and then the miserable beholders are bound to take it for a cave. While, in the meantime, two armies fly in, represented with four swords and bucklers, and then what hard heart will not receive it for a pitched field?

Now of time they are much more liberal, for ordinary it is, that two young princes fall in love. After many traverses, she is got with child, delivered of a fair boy, he is lost, groweth a man, falleth in love, and is ready to get another child. And all this in two hours' space; which, how absurd it is in sense, even sense may imagine, and art hath taught, and all ancient examples justified, and at this day the ordinary players in Italy will not err in. . . .

But, besides these gross absurdities, how all their plays be neither right tragedies nor right comedies, mingling kings and clowns, not because the matter so carrieth it, but thrust in the clown by head and shoulders to play a part in majestical matters, with neither decency nor discretion, so as neither the admiration and commiseration, nor the right sportfulness, is by their mongrel tragicomedy obtained. I know Apuleius did somewhat so, but that is a thing recounted with space of time, not represented in one moment, and I know the ancients have one or two examples of tragicomedies, as Plautus hath *Amphytrio*. But, if we mark them well, we shall find that they never, or very daintily, match hornpipes and funerals. So falleth it out that, having indeed no right comedy in that comical part of our tragedy, we have nothing but scurrility, unworthy of any chaste ears, or some extreme show of doltishness, indeed fit to lift up a loud laughter and nothing else, where the whole tract of a comedy should be full of delight, as the tragedy should be still maintained in a well-raised admiration.

But our comedians think there is no delight without laughter, which is very wrong, for though laughter may come with delight, yet cometh it not of delight, as though delight should be the cause of laughter. But well may one thing breed both together. Nay, rather in themselves they have, as it were, a kind of contrariety. For delight we scarcely do, but in things that have a conveniency to ourselves or to the general nature; laughter almost ever cometh of things most disproportioned to ourselves and nature. Delight hath a joy in it either permanent or present; laughter hath only a scornful tickling. For example, we are ravished with delight to see a fair woman and yet are far from being moved to laughter. We laugh at deformed creatures, wherein certainly we cannot delight. We delight in good chances; we laugh at mischances. We delight to hear the happiness of our friends and country, at which he were worthy to be laughed at that would laugh. We shall, contrarily, sometimes laugh to find a matter quite mistaken and go down the hill against the bias in the mouth of some such men as, for the respect of them, one shall be heartily sorry he cannot choose but laugh and so is rather pained than delighted with laughter. Yet deny I not but that they may go well together. For as in Alexander's picture well set out we delight without laughter, and in twenty mad antics we laugh without delight, so in Hercules, painted with his great beard and furious countenance, in a woman's attire, spinning at Omphale's commandment, it breeds both delight and laughter, for the representing of so strange a power in love procures delight, and the scornfulness of the action stirreth laughter.

But I speak to this purpose, that all the end of the comical part be not upon such scornful matters as stir laughter only, but mix with it that delightful teaching which is the end of poesy. And the great fault, even in that point of laughter, and forbidden plainly by Aristotle, is that they stir laughter in sinful things, which are rather execrable than ridiculous; or in miserable, which are rather to be pitied than scorned. For what is it to make folks gape at a wretched beggar and a beggarly clown, or against law of hospitality, to jest at strangers because they speak not English so well as we do? . . .

Other sorts of poetry almost have we none but that lyrical kind of songs and sonnets, which, Lord if he gave us so good minds, how well it might be employed and with how heavenly fruits, both private and public, in singing the praises of the immortal beauty, the immortal goodness of that God who giveth us hands to write and wits to conceive, of which we might well want words, but never matter, of which we could turn our eyes to nothing but we should ever have new budding occasions.

But, truly, many of such writings as come under the banner of unresistible love, if I were a mistress, would never persuade me they were in love, so coldly they apply fiery speeches, as men that had rather read lovers' writings, and so caught up certain swelling phrases—which hang together like a man that once told me the wind was at northwest and by south because he would be sure to name winds enough—that in truth they feel those passions, which easily, as I think, may be betrayed by that same forcibleness, or *energia* (as the Greeks call it) of the writer. But let this be a sufficient though short note that we miss the right use of the material point of poesy.

Now for the outside of it, which is words, or (as I may term it) diction, it is even well worse. So is it that honey-flowing matron Eloquence appareled, or rather disguised, in a courtesan-like painted affectation, one time with so farfetched words, that many seem monsters, but must seem strangers to any poor Englishman, another time with coursing of a letter, as if they were bound to follow the method of a dictionary, another time with figures and flowers, extremely winter-starved.

But I would this fault were only peculiar to versifiers and had not as large possession among prose-printers and, which is to be marveled, among many scholars and, which is to be pitied, among some preachers. Truly, I could wish (if at least I might be so bold to wish in a thing beyond the reach of my capacity) the diligent imitators of Tully and Demosthenes (most worthy to be imitated) did not so much keep Nizolian paperbooks of their figures and phrases as by attentive translation (as it were) devour them whole and make them wholly theirs. For now they cast sugar and spice upon every dish that is served at the table, like those Indians, not content to wear earrings at the fit and natural place of the ears, but they will thrust jewels through their nose and lips because they will be sure to be fine. . . .

But what! Methinks I deserve to be pounded for straying from poetry to oratory, but both have such an affinity in the wordish consideration that I think this digression will make my meaning receive the fuller understanding—which is not to take upon me to teach poets how they should do, but only, finding myself sick among the rest, to show some one or two spots of the common infection grown among the most part of writers that, acknowledging ourselves somewhat awry, we may bend to the right use both of matter and manner, whereto our language giveth us great occasion, being indeed capable of any excellent exercising of it. I know some will say it is a mingled language. And why not so much the better, taking the best of both the other? Another will say it wanteth grammar. Nay, truly, it hath that praise, that it wants not grammar, for grammar it might have, but it needs it not, being so easy in itself and so void of those cumbersome differences of cases, genders, moods, and tenses, which, I think, was a piece of the tower of Babylon's curse that a man should be put to school to learn his mother tongue. But for the uttering sweetly and properly the conceit of the mind, which is the end of speech, that hath it equally with any other tongue in the world, and is particularly happy in compositions of two or three words together, near the Greek, far beyond the Latin, which is one of the greatest beauties can be in a language.

Now, of versifying there are two sorts, the one ancient, the other modern. The ancient marked the quantity of each syllable, and according to that framed his verse; the modern, observing only number, with some regard of the accent, the chief life of it standeth in that like sounding of the words which we call rhyme. Which of these be the more excellent would bear many speeches; the ancient no doubt more fit for music, both words and tune observing quantity, and more fit lively to express divers passions by the low or lofty sound of the well-weighed syllable. The latter, likewise, with his rhyme striketh a certain music to the ear; and, in fine, since it doth delight, though by another way, it obtaineth the same purpose, there being in either, sweetness, and wanting in neither, majesty. Truly the English, before any vulgar language I know, is fit for both sorts, for, for the ancient, the Italian is so full of vowels that it must ever be cumbered with elisions, the Dutch so, of the other side, with consonants that they cannot yield the sweet sliding fit for a verse. The French, in his whole language, hath not one word that hath his accent in the last syllable saving two, called antepenultima, and little more hath the Spanish, and therefore very gracelessly may they use dactyls. The English is subject to none of these defects.

Now for rhyme, though we do not observe quantity, we observe the accent very precisely, which other languages either cannot do or will not do so absolutely. That caesura, or breathing place in the midst of the verse, neither Italian nor Spanish have; the French and we never almost fail of. Lastly, even the very rhyme itself the Italian cannot put in the last syllable, by the French named the masculine rhyme, but still in the next to the last, which the French call the female, or the next before that, which the Italians term *sdrucciola*. The example of the former is *buono, suono;* of the *sdrucciola* is *femina, semina.* The French, of the other side, hath both the male, as *bon, son,* and the female as *plaise, taise,* but the *sdrucciola* he hath not. Where the English hath all three, as *due, true; father, rather; motion, potion,* with much more which might be said, but that already I find the triflingness of this discourse is much too much enlarged.

So that since the ever praiseworthy poesy is full of virtue-breeding

delightfulness and void of no gift that ought to be in the noble name
of learning, since the blames laid against it are either false or feeble,
since the cause why it is not esteemed in England is the fault of
poet-apes, not poets, since, lastly, our tongue is most fit to honor
poesy and to be honored by poesy, I conjure you all that have had
the evil luck to read this ink-wasting toy of mine, even in the name
of the Nine Muses, no more to scorn the sacred mysteries of poesy,
no more to laugh at the name of poets, as though they were next
inheritors to fools, no more to jest at the reverend title of a rhymer,
but to believe, with Aristotle, that they were the ancient treasurers
of the Grecians' divinity, to believe, with Bembus, that they were the
first bringers in of all civility, to believe, with Scaliger, that no
philosopher's precepts can sooner make you an honest man than the
reading of Virgil, to believe, with Clauserus, the translator of Cornu-
tus, that it pleased the heavenly deity by Hesiod and Homer, under
the veil of fables, to give us all knowledge, logic, rhetoric, philosophy
natural and moral, and *quid non,* to believe, with me, that there are
many mysteries contained in poetry, which of purpose were written
darkly, lest by profane wits it should be abused, to believe, with
Landin, that they are so beloved of the gods that whatsoever they
write proceeds of a divine fury. Lastly, to believe themselves, when
they tell you they will make you immortal by their verses.

Thus doing, your name shall flourish in the printers' shops. Thus
doing, you shall be of kin to many a poetical preface. Thus doing
you shall be most fair, most rich, most wise, most all; you shall dwell
upon superlatives. . . . Thus doing, your soul shall be placed with
Dante's Beatrix, or Virgil's Anchises.

But if (fie of such a but!) you be born so near the dull-making
cataract of Nilus that you cannot hear the planet-like music of poetry,
if you have so earth-creeping a mind that it cannot lift itself up to
look to the sky of poetry or rather, by a certain rustical disdain,
will become such a mome as to be a Momus of poetry, then, though
I will not wish unto you the ass's ears of Midas, nor to be driven by
a poet's verse, as Bubonax was, to hang himself, nor to be rhymed
to death, as is said to be done in Ireland, yet thus much curse I must
send you in the behalf of all poets: that while you live, you live
in love and never get favor for lacking skill of a sonnet, and, when
you die, your memory die from the earth for want of an epitaph.

Ben Jonson

(1572–1637)

Ben Jonson's critical principles and opinions are most fully set forth
in *Timber: or, Discoveries Made upon Men and Matter, as They
Have Flowed out of His Daily Readings or Had Their Refluxe to
His Peculiar Notion of the Times,* a random collection of notes and
papers gathered together after his death and published in the 1640–
41 folio edition of his *Works.* Many of the opinions and much of the
phrasing (even in the famous characterization of Shakespeare) can
be traced to classical or earlier Renaissance sources, where there is
also considerable precedent for Jonson's listing the requirements of
the poet as natural wit, exercise or practice, imitation of models, and
study. But Jonson places his own stamp and signature on anything
he borrows. What Dryden later said of his drama applies also to his
prose: "He invades authors like a monarch, and what would be
theft in other poets is only victory in him." Jonson advises the beginning writer to follow the model of an earlier poet, but he warns
against servile imitation. The Ancients are to be regarded as "guides,
not commanders"; and he will not have the poet confined within
"the narrow limits of laws which either the grammarians or philosophers prescribe." In style, Jonson characteristically favors conciseness, clarity, and directness. He is impatient of pretentious or obscure
diction, and he considers sentences most beautiful when they are not
too long; a good English sentence should have the functional strength
of "a pike or javelin." Jonson's remarks are the seasoned opinions of
a freeborn Renaissance Englishman.

The best text of *Timber, or Discoveries* is that of the Oxford edition, *Ben Jonson,* ed. C. H. Herford, Percy and Evelyn Simpson (1947). In *Ben Jonson's "Timber or Discoveries"* (1953), R. S. Walker presents a systematically rearranged modernized text.

FROM TIMBER, OR DISCOVERIES

(1640–41)

I know nothing can conduce more to letters than to examine the writings of the Ancients and not to rest in their sole authority or take all upon trust from them, provided the plagues of judging and pronouncing against them be away, such as are envy, bitterness, precipitation, impudence, and scurrile scoffing. For to all the observations of the Ancients we have our own experience, which, if we will use and apply, we have better means to pronounce. It is true they opened the gates and made the way, that went before us, but as guides, not commanders: *Non domini nostri, sed duces fuere.* Truth lies open to all; it is no man's several. . . .

I do hear them say often, "Some men are not witty because they are not everywhere witty"—than which nothing is more foolish. If an eye or a nose be an excellent part in the face, therefore be all eye or nose? I think the eyebrow, the forehead, the cheek, chin, lip, or any part else are as necessary and natural in the place. But now nothing is good that is natural: Right and natural language seems to have least of the wit in it; that which is writhed and tortured is counted the more exquisite. Cloth of bodkin or tissue must be embroidered, as if no face were fair that were not powdered or painted, no beauty to be had, but in wresting and writhing our own tongue.

The text is based on that of the first publication in the Folio of 1640–41. Spaces between lines represent breaks between the disconnected sections of the original collection; ellipses indicate the editors' omissions.

Nothing is fashionable till it be deformed, and this is to write like a gentleman. All must be as affected and preposterous as our gallants' clothes, sweet bags, and night dressings, in which you would think our men lay in like ladies, it is so curious.

Nothing in our age, I have observed, is more preposterous than the running judgments upon poetry and poets, when we shall hear those things commended and cried up for the best writings which a man would scarce vouchsafe to wrap any wholesome drug in; he would never light his tobacco with them. And those men almost named for miracles who yet are so vile that if a man should go about to examine and correct them, he must make all they have done but one blot. Their good is so entangled with their bad as forcibly one must draw on the other's death with it. . . .

Poetry in this latter age hath proved but a mean mistress to such as have wholly addicted themselves to her or given their names up to her family. They who have but saluted her on the by, and now and then tendered their visits, she hath done much for and advanced in the way of their own professions (both the law and the gospel) beyond all they could have hoped or done for themselves without her favor. . . .

Indeed, the multitude commend writers as they do fencers or wrestlers, who if they come in robustiously and put for it with a deal of violence are received for the braver fellows, when many times their own rudeness is a cause of their disgrace and a slight touch of their adversary gives all that boisterous force the foil. But in these things the unskillful are naturally deceived and, judging wholly by the bulk, think rude things greater than polished, and scattered more numerous than composed. Nor think this only to be true in the sordid multitude, but the neater sort of our gallants, for all are the multitude; only they differ in clothes, not in judgment or understanding.

I remember the players have often mentioned it as an honor to Shakespeare that in his writing, whatsoever he penned, he never blotted out line. My answer hath been, "Would he had blotted a thousand." Which they thought a malevolent speech. I had not told posterity this but for their ignorance who choose that circumstance to commend their friend by, wherein he most faulted. And to justify my own candor, for I loved the man and do honor his memory (on this side idolatry) as much as any. He was indeed honest and of an open and free nature, had an excellent fantasy, brave notions, and gentle expressions, wherein he flowed with that facility that sometimes it was necessary he should be stopped: *Sufflaminadus erat* ["He wanted checking"] as Augustus said of Haterius.[1] His wit was in his own power; would the rule of it had been so too. Many times he fell into those things, could not escape laughter: as when he said in the person of Caesar, one speaking to him, "Caesar, thou dost me wrong." He replied, "Caesar did never wrong, but with just cause," and such like, which were ridiculous. But he redeemed his vices with his virtues. There was ever more in him to be praised than to be pardoned.

. . . The true artificer will not run away from nature, as he were afraid of her, or depart from life and the likeness of truth, but speak to the capacity of his hearers. And though his language differ from the vulgar somewhat, it shall not fly from all humanity with the *Tamerlanes* and *Tamer-Chams* of the late age, which had nothing in them but the scenical strutting and furious vociferation to warrant them to the ignorant gapers. He knows it is his only art so to carry it as none but artificers perceive it. In the meantime perhaps he is called barren, dull, lean, a poor writer (or by what contumelious word can come in their cheeks) by these men who without labor, judgment, knowledge, or almost sense, are received or preferred before him. He gratulates them and their fortune. Another age or juster men will acknowledge the virtues of his studies: his wisdom in dividing; his subtlety in arguing; with what strength he doth inspire his readers; with what sweetness he strokes them; in inveighing, what sharpness; in jest, what urbanity he uses. How he doth reign in men's affections; how invade and break in upon them and makes their minds like the thing he writes. Then in his elocution to behold what word is proper,

---

[1] In characterizing Shakespeare Jonson makes extensive use of the source in Seneca the Elder of this reference to Haterius, a minor Latin poet.

which hath ornament, which height, what is beautifully translated, where figures are fit, which gentle, which strong to show the composition manly. And how he hath avoided faint, obscure, obscene, sordid, humble, improper, or effeminate phrase; which is not only praised of the most, but commended (which is worse) especially for that it is naught. . . .

Cicero is said to be the only wit that the people of Rome had equalled to their empire. *Ingenium par imperio.* We have had many, and in their several ages (to take in but the former *Seculum*): Sir Thomas More; the elder Wyatt; Henry, Earl of Surrey; [Sir Thomas] Chaloner; [Sir Thomas] Smith; [Sir Thomas] Eliot; B[ishop] Gardiner were for their times admirable, and the more, because they began eloquence with us. Sir Nicho[las] Bacon was singular, and almost alone, in the beginning of Queen Elizabeth's times. Sir Philip Sidney and Mr. [Richard] Hooker (in different matter) grew great masters of wit and language, and in whom all vigor of invention and strength of judgment met. The Earl of Essex, noble and high, and Sir Walter Raleigh, not to be contemned either for judgment or style. Sir Henry Savile, grave and truly lettered; Sir Edwin Sandys, excellent in both; Lo[rd] Egerton, the Chancellor, a grave and great orator, and best when he was provoked. But his learned and able (although unfortunate) successor [Sir Francis Bacon] is he who hath filled up all numbers and performed that in our tongue which may be compared or preferred either to insolent Greece or haughty Rome. In short, within his view and about his times were all the wits born that could honor a language or help study. Now things daily fall: wits grow downward and eloquence grows backward. So that he may be named and stand as the mark and acme of our language.

I have ever observed it to have been the office of a wise patriot, among the greatest affairs of the state, to take care of the commonwealth of learning. For schools they are the seminaries of state, and nothing is worthier the study of a statesman than that part of the republic which we call the advancement of letters. Witness the care of Julius Caesar, who, in the heat of the civil war, writ his books of *Analogy*[2] and dedicated them to Tully. This made the late Lord

[2] *De Analogia,* a work by Caesar that has not survived.

St. Albans entitle his work *Novum Organum*. Which though by the superficial of men, who cannot get beyond the title of *Nominals*, it is not penetrated nor understood, it really openeth all defects of learning whatsoever and is a book, *Qui longum noto scriptori porriget aevum* ["which extends the writer's fame into eternity"].

My conceit of his person was never increased toward him by his place or honors. But I have and do reverence him for the greatness that was only proper to himself in that he seemed to me ever, by his work, one of the greatest men and most worthy of admiration that had been in many ages. In his adversity I ever prayed that God would give him strength, for greatness he could not want. Neither could I condole in a word or syllable for him, as knowing no accident could do harm to virtue but rather help to make it manifest. . . .

A prince without letters is a pilot without eyes. All his government is groping. In sovereignty it is a most happy thing not to be compelled, but so it is the most miserable not to be counseled. And how can he be counseled that cannot see to read the best counselors, which are books, for they neither flatter us nor hide from us? He may hear, you will say. But how shall he always be sure to hear truth or be counseled the best things, not the sweetest? They say princes learn no art truly but the art of horsemanship. The reason is, the brave beast is no flatterer. He will throw a prince as soon as his groom. Which is an argument that good counselors to princes are the best instruments of a good age. For, though the prince himself be of prompt inclination to all virtue, yet the best pilots have need of mariners, beside sails, anchor, and other tackle. . . .

Poetry and picture are arts of a like nature, and both are busy about imitation. It was excellently said of Plutarch, poetry was a speaking picture and picture a mute poesy. For they both invent, feign, and devise many things and accommodate all they invent to the use and service of nature. Yet of the two the pen is more noble than the pencil. For that can speak to the understanding, the other but to the sense. They both behold pleasure and profit as their common object but should abstain from all base pleasures lest they should err from their end and, while they seek to better men's minds, destroy their manners. They both are born artificers, not made. Nature is more powerful in them than study. . . .

For a man to write well, there are required three necessaries: to read the best authors, observe the best speakers, and much exercise of his own style. In style, to consider what ought to be written and after what manner, he must first think and excogitate his matter, then choose his words and examine the weight of either, then take care in placing and ranking both matter and words, that the composition be comely, and to do this with diligence and often. No matter how slow the style be at first, so it be labored and accurate, seek the best and be not glad of the forward conceits or first words that offer themselves to us, but judge of what we invent, and order what we approve. Repeat often what we have formerly written, which, beside that it helps the consequence and makes the juncture better, it quickens the heat of imagination, that often cools in the time of setting down, and gives it new strength, as if it grew lustier by the going back. As we see in the contention of leaping, they jump farthest that fetch their race largest; or, as in throwing a dart or javelin, we force back our arms to make our loose the stronger. Yet if we have fair gale of wind, I forbid not the steering out of our sail, so the favor of the gale deceive us not. For all that we invent doth please us in the conception or birth; else we would never set it down. But the safest is to return to our judgment and handle over again those things the easiness of which might make them justly suspected. So did the best writers in their beginnings; they imposed upon themselves care and industry. They did nothing rashly. They obtained first to write well, and then custom made it easy and a habit. By little and little, their matter showed itself to them more plentifully; their words answered, their composition followed; and all, as in a well ordered family, presented itself in the place. So that the sum of all is: ready writing makes not good writing, but good writing brings on ready writing. Yet when we think we have got the faculty, it is even then good to resist it, as to give a horse a check sometimes with a bit, which doth not so much stop his course as stir his mettle. Again, whither a man's genius is best able to reach, thither

it should more and more contend, lift and dilate itself, as men of
low stature raise themselves on their toes and so ofttimes get even,
if not eminent. Besides, as it is fit for grown and able writers to stand
of themselves and work with their own strength, to trust and endeavor by their own faculties, so it is fit for the beginner and learner
to study others, and the best. For the mind and memory are more
sharply exercised in comprehending another man's things than our
own, and such as accustom themselves and are familiar with the
best authors shall ever and anon find somewhat of them in themselves
and in the expression of their minds, even when they feel it not, be
able to utter something like theirs, which hath an authority above
their own. Nay, sometimes it is the reward of a man's study, the praise
of quoting another man fitly. And though a man be more prone
and able for one kind of writing than another, yet he must exercise
all. For as in an instrument, so in style, there must be a harmony and
consent of parts.

I take this labor in teaching others, that they should not be always
to be taught, and I would bring my precepts into practice. For rules
are ever of lesser force and value than experiments. Yet with this
purpose, rather to show the right way to those that come after than
to detect any that have slipped before by error, and I hope it will be
more profitable. For men do more willingly listen, and with more
favor, to precept than reprehension. Among diverse opinions of an
art, and most of them contrary in themselves, it is hard to make
election, and therefore, though a man cannot invent new things after
so many, he may do a welcome work yet to help posterity to judge
rightly of the old. But arts and precepts avail nothing except nature
be beneficial and aiding. And therefore these things are no more
written to a dull disposition than rules of husbandry to a barren
soil. No precepts will profit a fool, no more than beauty will the
blind or music the deaf. As we should take care that our style in writing be neither dry nor empty, we should look again it be not winding,
or wanton with far-fetched descriptions; either is a vice. But that is
worse which proceeds out of want than that which riots out of plenty.
The remedy of fruitfulness is easy, but no labor will help the contrary.
I will like and praise some things in a young writer which, yet if he

continue in, I cannot but justly hate him for the same. There is a time to be given all things for maturity, and that even your country husbandman can teach, who to a young plant will not put the pruning knife because it seems to fear the iron, as not able to admit the scar. No more would I tell a green writer all his faults, lest I should make him grieve and faint and at last despair. For nothing doth more hurt than to make him so afraid of all things as he can endeavor nothing. Therefore youth ought to be instructed betimes, and in the best things, for we hold those longest we take soonest. . . . And as it is fit to read the best authors to youth first, so let them be of the openest and clearest. As Livy before Salust, Sidney before Donne, and beware of letting them taste Gower or Chaucer at first, lest, falling too much in love with antiquity and not apprehending the weight, they grow rough and barren in language only. When their judgments are firm and out of danger, let them read both the old and the new, but no less take heed that their new flowers and sweetness do not as much corrupt as the others' dryness and squalor, if they choose not carefully. Spenser, in affecting the Ancients, writ no language. Yet I would have him read for his matter, but as Virgil read Ennius. The reading of Homer and Virgil is counseled by Quintilian as the best way of informing youth and confirming man. For besides that the mind is raised with the height and sublimity of such a verse, it takes spirit from the greatness of the matter and is tincted with the best things. Tragic and lyric poetry is good too, and comic with the best, if the manners of the reader be once in safety. In the Greek poets, as also in Plautus, we shall see the economy and disposition of poems better observed than in Terence and the later, who thought the sole grace and virtue of their fable the sticking in of sentences, as ours do the forcing in of jests. . . .

Speech is the only benefit man hath to express his excellency of mind above other creatures. It is the instrument of society. . . . In all speech, words and sense are as the body and the soul. The sense is as the life and soul of language, without which all words are dead. Sense is wrought out of experience, the knowledge of human life and actions, or of the liberal arts, which the Greeks called *Egkyklopaideian*. Words are the people's; yet there is a choice of them to be made. . . . They are to be chosen according to the persons we make speak or the things we speak of. Some are of the camp, some of the council-board, some of the shop, some of the sheepcote, some of the pulpit, some of the bar, etc. And herein is seen their elegance and propriety, when we use them fitly and draw them forth to their just strength and nature by way of translation or metaphor. But in this translation we must only serve necessity . . . or commodity, which is a kind of necessity, that is, when we either absolutely want a word to express by, and that is necessity, or when we have not so fit a word, and that is commodity. . . . Metaphors farfetched hinder to be understood and, affected, lose their grace. Or when the person fetcheth his translations from a wrong place. As if a privy counselor should at the table take his metaphor from a dicing house or ordinary or vintner's vault, or a justice of the peace draw his similitudes from the mathematics, or a divine from a bawdyhouse or taverns. . . . Metaphors are thus many times deformed, as in him that said, *Castratum morte Africani Rempublicam* ["the republic is mutilated by the death of Africanus"]. . . . All attempts that are new in this kind are dangerous and somewhat hard before they be softened with use. A man coins not a new word without some peril, and less fruit, for, if it happen to be received, the praise is but moderate; if refused, the scorn is assured. Yet we must adventure, for things at first hard and rough are by use made tender and gentle. It is an honest error that is committed following great chiefs.

Custom is the most certain mistress of language, as the public stamp makes the current money. But we must not be too frequent with the mint, everyday coining. Nor fetch words from the extreme and utmost ages, since the chief virtue of a style is perspicuity, and nothing so vicious [faulty or corrupt] in it, as to need an interpreter. Words borrowed of antiquity do lend a kind of majesty to style and are not without their delight sometimes. For they have the authority of years and out of their intermission do win to themselves a kind of grace like newness. But the eldest of the present and newest of the past language is the best. For what was the ancient language, which some men so dote upon, but the ancient custom? Yet when I name custom, I understand not the vulgar custom. For that were a precept no less dangerous to language, than life, if we should speak or live after the manners of the vulgar. But that I call custom of speech which is the consent of the learned, as custom of life which is the consent of the good. . . .

A good man always profits by his endeavor; yea, when he is absent; nay, when he is dead, by his example and memory. So good authors in their style: A strict and succinct style is that where you can take away nothing without loss, and that loss to be manifest. The brief style is that which expresses much in little. The concise style, which expresses not enough, but leaves somewhat to be understood. The abrupt style, which hath many breaches and doth not seem to end, but fall. The congruent and harmonious fitting of parts in a sentence hath almost the fastening and force of knitting and connection, as in stones well squared, which will rise strong a great way without mortar.

Periods are beautiful when they are not too long, for so they have their strength too, as in a pike or javelin. As we must take the care that our words and sense be clear, so, if the obscurity happen through the hearer's or reader's want of understanding, I am not to answer for them, no more than for their not listening or marking; I must neither find them ears nor mind. But a man cannot put a word so in sense but something about it will illustrate it, if the writer understand himself. For order helps much to perspicuity as confusion hurts. . . . We should therefore speak what we can the nearest way so as we keep our gait, not leap, for too short may as well be not let into the memory as too long not kept in. Whatsoever loseth the grace and clearness converts into a riddle; the obscurity is marked, but not the value. That perisheth and is passed by, like the pearl in the fable. Our style should be like a skein of silk, to be carried and found by the right thread, not raveled and perplexed; then all is a knot, a heap. . . . Quintilian warns us that in no kind of translation or metaphor or allegory we make a turn from what we began: as if we fetch the original of our metaphor from sea and billows, we end not in flames and ashes; it is a most foul inconsequence. Neither must we draw out our allegory too long, lest either we make ourselves obscure or fall into affectation, which is childish. But why do men depart at all from the right and natural ways of speaking? Sometimes for necessity, when we are driven or think it fitter to speak that in obscure words, or by circumstance, which uttered plainly would offend the hearers. Or to avoid obsceneness, or sometimes for pleasure and variety, as travelers turn out of the highway, drawn either by the commodity of a footpath or the delicacy or freshness of the fields. And all this is called *eschematismenē*, or figured language.

Language most shows a man: speak that I may see thee. It springs out of the most retired and inmost parts of us and is the image of the parent of it, the mind. No glass renders a man's form or likeness so true as his speech. Nay, it is likened to a man, and, as we consider feature and composition in a man, so words in language, in the greatness, aptness, sound, structure, and harmony of it. Some men are tall and big; so some language is high and great. Then the words are chosen, their sound ample, the composition full, the absolution plenteous and poured out all grave, sinewy, and strong. Some are little and dwarfs; so of speech it is humble and low, the words poor and flat, the members and periods thin and weak, without knitting or number. The middle are of a just stature. There the language is plain and pleasing, even without stopping, round without swelling—all well turned, composed, elegant, and accurate. . . .

Now that I have informed you in the knowing these things, let me lead you by the hand a little farther in the direction of the use and make you an able writer by practice. The conceits of the mind are pictures of things, and the tongue is the interpreter of those pictures. The order of God's creatures in themselves is not only admirable and glorious, but eloquent. Then he who could apprehend the consequence of things in their truth, and utter his apprehensions as truly, were the best writer or speaker. . . . As the image of a king, in his seal ill-represented, is not so much a blemish to the wax or the signet that sealed it, as to the prince it representeth, so disordered speech is not so much injury to the lips that give it forth as to the disproportion and incoherence of things in themselves so negligently expressed. Neither can his mind be thought to be in tune, whose words do jar, nor his reason in frame, whose sentence is preposterous, nor his elocution clear and perfect, whose utterance breaks itself into fragments and uncertainties. Were it not a dishonor to a mighty prince to have the majesty of his embassy spoiled by a careless ambassador? And is it not as great an indignity that an excellent conceit and capacity by the indiligence of an idle tongue should be disgraced? Negligent speech doth not only discredit the person of the speaker, but it discrediteth the opinion of his reason and judgment; it discrediteth the force and uniformity of the matter and substance. If it be so then in words, which fly and escape censure and where one good phrase begs pardon for many incongruities and faults, how shall he then be thought wise, whose penning is thin and shallow? How shall you look for wit from him whose leisure and head, assisted with the examination of his eyes, yield you no life or sharpness in his writing? . . .

What is a poet?

A poet is that which by the Greeks is called *kat eōchen, ho poiëtes*, a maker, or feigner: His art, an art of imitation or feigning, expressing the life of man in fit measure, numbers, and harmony, according to Aristotle—from the word *poiein*, which signifies to make or feign. Hence, he is called a poet, not he which writeth in measure only, but that feigneth and formeth a fable and writes things like the truth. For the fable and fiction is, as it were, the form and soul of any poetical work, or poem.

What mean you by a poem?

A poem is not alone any work or composition of the poet's in many or few verses, but even one alone verse sometimes makes a perfect poem. As when Aeneas hangs up and consecrates the arms of Abas with this inscription, *Aeneas haec de Danais victoribus arma* ["Aeneas, these arms from Trojan victories"], and calls it a poem, or *carmen*. . . . And anciently all the oracles were called *carmina;* or, whatever sentence was expressed, were it much or little, it was called an epic, dramatic, lyric, elegiac, or epigrammatic poem.

But how differs a poem from what we call poesy?

A poem, as I have told you, is the work of the poet, the end and fruit of his labor and study. Poesy is his skill or craft of making—the very fiction itself, the reason or form of the work. And these three voices differ as the thing done, the doing, and the doer; the thing feigned, the feigning, and the feigner—so the poem, the poesy, and the poet. Now the poesy is the habit or art—nay, rather the queen of arts, which had her original from heaven, received thence from the Hebrews, and had in prime estimation with the Greeks, transmitted to the Latins and all nations that professed civility. The study of it, if we will trust Aristotle, offers to mankind a certain rule and pattern of living well and happily, disposing us to all civil offices of society. If we will believe Tully, it nourisheth and instructeth our youth, delights our age, adorns our prosperity, comforts our adversity, entertains us at home, keeps us company abroad, travels with us, watches, divides the times of our earnest and sports, shares in our country recesses and recreations, insomuch as the wisest and best learned have thought her the absolute mistress of manners and nearest of kin to virtue. And, whereas they entitle philosophy to be a rigid and austere poesy, they have on the contrary styled poesy a dulcet and gentle philosophy which leads on and guides us by the hand to action with a ravishing delight and incredible sweetness. But, before we handle the kinds of poems, with their special differences, or make court to the art itself, as a mistress, I would lead you to the knowledge of our poet by a perfect information, what he is or should be by nature, by exercise, by imitation, by study, and so bring him down through the disciplines of grammar, logic, rhetoric, and the ethics, adding somewhat, out of all, peculiar to himself and worthy of your admittance or reception.

First, we require in our poet or maker (for that title our language affords him elegantly, with the Greek) a goodness of natural wit. For, whereas all other arts consist of doctrine and precepts, the poet must be able by nature and instinct to pour out the treasure of his mind; and, as Seneca saith, *Aliquando secundus Anacreontem insanire, jucundum esse* ["It is pleasant, according to Anacreon, to be at times frenzied"], by which he understands the poetical rapture. And according to that of Plato: *Frustra poeticus fores sui compos pulsavit* ["Master of himself, he beat vainly on the doors of poetry"]. And of Aristotle: *Nullum magnum ingenium sine mixtura dementiae fuit. Nec potest grande aliquid, et supra caeteros loqui, nisi mota mens* ["No great genius existed without a mixture of madness. It is not possible to utter a great or noble thing unless the spirit be moved"]. Then it riseth higher, as by a divine instinct, when it contemns common and known conceptions. It utters somewhat above a mortal mouth. Then it gets aloft and flies away with his rider whither before it was doubtful to ascend. This the poets understood by their Helicon, Pegasus, or Parnassus. . . .

To this perfection of nature in our poet we require, [second,] exercise of those parts, and frequent. If his wit will not arrive suddenly at the dignity of the Ancients, let him not yet fall out with it, quarrel, or be over hastily angry, offer to turn it away from study, in a humor, but come to it again upon better cogitation, try another time, with labor. If then it succeed not, cast not away the quills yet, nor scratch the wainscot; beat not the poor desk, but bring all to the forge and file again; turn it anew. There is no statute law of the kingdom bids you be a poet against your will, or the first quarter. If it come in a year or two, it is well. . . . A rhymer and a poet are two things. It is said of the incomparable Virgil that he brought forth his verses like a bear and after formed them with licking. Scaliger, the father, writes it of him that he made a quantity of verses in the morning, which afore night he reduced to a less number. But that which Valerius Maximus hath left recorded of Euripides, the tragic poet, his answer to Alcestis, another poet, is as memorable as modest: who, when it was told to Alcestis that Euripides had in three days brought forth but three verses, and those with some difficulty and throes, Alcestis, glorying he could with ease have sent forth a hundred in the space, Euripides roundly replied, "Like enough. But here is the difference: Thy verses will not last those three days; mine will to all time." Which was as to tell him he could not write a verse. I have met many of these rattles that made a noise and buzzed. They had their hum, and no more. Indeed, things wrote with labor deserve to be so read and will last their age.

The third requisite in our poet or maker is imitation: to be able to convert the substance or riches of another poet to his own use. To make choice of one excellent man above the rest and so to follow him till he grow very *he*, or so like him as the copy may be mistaken for the principal. Not as a creature that swallows what it takes in crude, raw, or indigested, but that feeds with an appetite and hath a stomach to concoct, divide, and turn all into nourishment. Not to imitate servilely, as Horace saith, and catch at vices for virtue, but to draw forth out of the best and choicest flowers, with the bee, and turn all into honey, work it into one relish and savor, make our imitation sweet, observe how the best writers have imitated, and follow them. How Virgil and Statius have imitated Homer; how Horace, Archilochus; how Alcaes, and the other lyrics; and so of the rest.

But, [fourth,] that which we especially require in him is an exactness of study and multiplicity of reading, which maketh a full man, not alone enabling him to know the history or argument of a poem and to report it, but so to master the matter and style as to show he knows how to handle, place, or dispose of either, with elegancy, when need shall be. And not think he can leap forth suddenly a poet by dreaming he hath been in Parnassus or having washed his lips, as they say, in Helicon.

There goes more to his making than so. For to nature, exercise, imitation, and study, art must be added to make all these perfect. And though these challenge to themselves much in the making up of our maker, it is art only can lead him to perfection and leave him there in possession, as planted by her hand. It is the assertion of Tully, if to an excellent nature there happen an accession or confirmation of learning and discipline, there will then remain somewhat noble and singular. For . . . without art, nature can ne'er be perfect, and without nature, art can claim no being. But our poet must beware that his study be not only to learn of himself, for he that shall affect to do that confesseth his ever having a fool to his master. He must read many, but ever the best and choicest; those that can teach him anything he must ever account his masters and reverence, among whom Horace and (he that taught him) Aristotle deserve to be the first in estimation. Aristotle was the first accurate critic and truest judge—nay, the greatest philosopher the world ever had, for he noted

the vices of all knowledges in all creatures, and out of many men's perfections in a science he formed still one art. So he taught us two offices together: how we ought to judge rightly of others and what we ought to imitate specially in ourselves. But all this in vain, without a natural wit and a poetical nature in chief. For no man, so soon as he knows this or reads it, shall be able to write the better, but as he is adapted to it by nature, he shall grow the perfecter writer.
. . .

I am not of that opinion to conclude a poet's liberty within the narrow limits of laws which either the grammarians or philosophers prescribe. For, before they found out those laws, there were many excellent poets that fulfilled them. Amongst whom none more perfect than Sophocles, who lived a little before Aristotle. Which of the Greeklings durst ever give precepts to Demosthenes? Or to Pericles, whom the age surnamed "heavenly" because he seemed to thunder and lighten with his language? Or to Alcibiades, who had rather nature for his guide than art for his master?

But, whatsoever nature at any time dictated to the most happy, or long exercise to the most laborious, that the wisdom and learning of Aristotle hath brought into an art because he understood the causes of things, and what other men did by chance or custom, he doth by reason, and not only found out the way not to err but the short way we should take not to err. . . .

To judge of poets is only the faculty of poets, and not of all poets, but the best. . . . But some will say critics are a kind of tinkers that make more faults than they mend ordinarily. See their diseases and those of grammarians. It is true, many bodies are the worse for the meddling with, and the multitude of physicians hath destroyed many sound patients with their wrong practice. But the office of a true critic, or censor, is not to throw by a letter anywhere or damn an innocent syllable but lay the words together and amend them, judge sincerely of the author and his matter, which is the sign of solid and perfect learning in a man. Such was Horace, an author of much civility and (if anyone among the heathen can be) the best master both of virtue and wisdom, an excellent and true judge upon cause and reason, not because he thought so but because he knew so, out of use and experience. . . .

The parts of a comedy are the same with a tragedy, and the end is partly the same. For they both delight and teach: the comics are called *didaskaloi* of the Greeks, no less than the tragics.

Nor is the moving of laughter always the end of comedy, that is rather a fowling [fouling?] for the people's delight or their fooling. For, as Aristotle says rightly, the moving of laughter is a fault in comedy, a kind of turpitude that depraves some part of a man's nature without a disease. As a wry face without pain moves laughter, or a deformed vizard, or a rude clown dressed in a lady's habit and using her actions, we dislike and scorn such representations, which made the ancient philosophers ever think laughter unfitting in a wise man. And this induced Plato to esteem of Homer as a sacrilegious person because he presented the gods sometimes laughing. As, also, it is divinely said of Aristotle that to seem ridiculous is a part of dishonesty, and foolish.

So that what either in the words or sense of an author or in the language or actions of men is awry, or depraved, doth strangely stir mean affections and provoke for the most part to laughter. And therefore it was clear that all insolent and obscene speeches, jests upon the best men, injuries to particular persons, perverse and sinister sayings (and the rather unexpected) in the Old Comedy did move laughter, especially where it did imitate any dishonesty, and scurrility came forth in the place of wit, which who understands the nature and genius of laughter cannot but perfectly know. . . .

Of the magnitude and compass of any fable, epic or dramatic

To the resolving of this question we must first agree in the definition of the fable. The fable is called the imitation of one entire and perfect action whose parts are so joined and knit together as nothing in the structure can be changed or taken away without impairing or troubling the whole, of which there is a proportionable magnitude in the members. As, for example, if a man would build a house, he would first appoint a place to build it in which he would define within certain bounds. So in the constitution of a poem the action is aimed at by the poet which answers place in a building, and that action hath his largeness, compass, and proportion. But, as a court or king's palace requires other dimensions than a private house, so the epic asks a magnitude from other poems. Since what is place in the one is action in the other, the difference is in space. So that by this definition we conclude the fable to be the imitation of one perfect and entire action as one perfect and entire place is required to a building. By perfect we understand that to which nothing is wanting, as place to the building that is raised and action to the fable that is formed. It is perfect perhaps not for a court or king's palace, which requires a greater ground, but for the structure we would raise. So the space of the action may not prove large enough for the epic fable, yet be perfect for the dramatic, and whole.

Whole we call that, and perfect, which hath a beginning, a midst, and an end. So the place of any building may be whole and entire for that work, though too little for a palace. As to a tragedy or a comedy, the action may be convenient and perfect that would not fit an epic poem in magnitude. So a lion is a perfect creature in himself, though it be less than an elephant. . . . Therefore, as in every body, so in every action which is the subject of a just work there is required a certain proportionable greatness, neither too vast nor too minute. . . . Too vast oppresseth the eyes and exceeds the memory; too little scarce admits either.

Now in every action it behooves the poet to know which is his utmost bound, how far with fitness and a necessary proportion he may produce and determine it. That is, till either good fortune change into the worse, or the worse into the better. For as a body without porportion cannot be goodly, no more can the action, either in comedy or tragedy, without his fit bounds. And every bound, for the nature of the subject, is esteemed the best that is largest, till it can increase no more; so it behooves the action in tragedy or comedy to be let grow till the necessity ask a conclusion—wherein two things are to be considered: First, that it exceed not the compass of one day; next, that there be place left for digression and art. For the episodes and digressions in a fable are the same that household stuff and other furniture are in a house. And so far for the measure and extent of a fable dramatic.

Now, that it should be one and entire. One is considerable two

ways: either as it is only separate and by itself or, as being composed
of many parts, it begins to be one as those parts grow or are wrought
together. That it should be one the first way alone and by itself no
man that hath tasted letters ever would say, especially having required before a just magnitude and equal proportion of the parts in
themselves. Neither of which can possibly be if the action be single
and separate, not composed of parts which laid together in themselves with an equal and fitting proportion tend to the same end
—which things out of antiquity itself hath deceived many, and more
this day it doth deceive.

So many there be of old that have thought the action of one man
to be one—as of Hercules, Theseus, Achilles, Ulysses, and other heroes
—which is both foolish and false, since by one and the same person
many things may be severally done which cannot fitly be referred or
joined to the same end—which not only the excellent tragic poets
but the best masters of the epic, Homer and Virgil, saw. For though
the argument of an epic poem be far more diffused and poured out
than that of tragedy, yet Virgil, writing of Aeneas, hath pretermitted
many things. He neither tells how he was born, how brought up,
how he fought with Achilles, how he was snatched out of the battle
by Venus; but that one thing, how he came into Italy, he prosecutes
in twelve books. The rest of his journey, his error by sea, the sack of
Troy, are put not as the argument of the work but episodes of the
argument. So Homer laid by many things of Ulysses and handled
no more than he saw tended to one and the same end.

. . . As a house consisting of diverse materials becomes one structure and one dwelling, so an action composed of diverse parts may
become one fable epic or dramatic. For example, in a tragedy look
upon Sophocles' *Ajax:* Ajax, deprived of Achilles' armor, which he
hoped from the suffrage of the Greeks, disdains, and, growing impatient of the injury, rageth and turns mad. In that humor he doth
many senseless things and at last falls upon the Grecian flock and kills
a great ram for Ulysses. Returning to his sense, he grows ashamed
of the scorn and kills himself and is by the chiefs of the Greeks forbidden burial. These things agree and hang together, not as they were
done but as seeming to be done, which made the action whole,
entire, and absolute.

For the whole, as it consisteth of parts, so without all the parts is not the whole, and to make it absolute is required not only the parts, but such parts as are true. For a part of the whole was true which, if you take away, you either change the whole or it is not the whole. For if it be such a part as being present or absent nothing concerns the whole, it cannot be called a part of the whole; and such are the episodes, of which hereafter. For the present, here is one example: The single combat of Ajax with Hector, as it is described in Homer, nothing belongs to this *Ajax* of Sophocles.

John Dryden

(1631–1700)

First laureate of England's Augustan age, John Dryden might well
speak of the return of monarchy in 1660 as the "restoration of our
happiness," for the glittering years that followed brought him success as a poet, dramatist, and critic. His best known work in criticism
is *An Essay of Dramatic Poesy* (1668), cast in the form of a Platonic
dialogue among four persons including Neander, the spokesman for
the author, and three others who have been identified with historical
counterparts: Crites with Sir Robert Howard, Lisideius with Sir
Charles Sedley, and Eugenius with Dryden's patron Charles Sackville,
Lord Buckhurst. The four debate the relative merits of the Ancients
and the Moderns, of the "last generation" of Elizabethan and Ja-
cobean playwrights and the present age, and of the French and the
English drama. They also discuss the problem of the dramatic unities
and of the propriety of rhyme in drama, both questions of lively
interest in Dryden's time. In all cases Dryden's Neander acts as an
urbane Socrates, arbitrating opinions and resolving questions. He
mediates undogmatically between the claims of tradition and the
individual talent in a way that makes clear the attractiveness of
Dryden to T. S. Eliot and other modern defenders of classicism who
helped to revive his reputation in the twentieth century. Firmly
rejecting extremes, Neander respects models and rules but sees the
necessity of new forms of expression in later times. His measured
judgment of Shakespeare, recognizing limitations as well as genius,
helped to establish the playwright's modern reputation. Neander consistently supports the neoclassical principles of decorum in thought

and language and subordination of parts to a proportioned and unified whole—this formal integrity being dependent upon the power of
the writer's judgment (rather than imagination, as the romantic critic
would later insist). An unusual feature of the essay is a specimen
"examen" or critique—inspired by the example of Corneille—of Ben
Jonson's *Epicoene: or, The Silent Woman.* This critique is the first
extended close analysis of a single work in English criticism. The
Essay is typical of Dryden's criticism in its pragmatic rather than
theoretical bent. In an easy conversational style, described by Samuel
Johnson as "airy, animated, and vigorous," [1] the critic writes with
an awareness of the problems of the practical playwright who must
hold and please an audience.

A new scholarly edition of Dryden's works is being published by
the University of California Press. The best available text and com-
mentary for his criticism is still W. P. Ker, ed., *The Essays of John
Dryden: Selected and Edited* (2 volumes, 1926; reprinted 1961).

AN ESSAY OF DRAMATIC POESY

(1668)

It was that memorable day, in the first summer of the late war,
when our navy engaged the Dutch, a day wherein the two most

The text is based on that of the first edition of 1668. Ellipses indicate the
editors' omissions.

[1] Johnson's characterization of Dryden's style (in *Lives of the Poets*)
is a just and discerning statement by a quite different but equally distinguished master of English prose: "The clauses are never balanced, nor
the periods modelled: every word seems to drop by chance, though it
falls into its proper place. Nothing is cold or languid; the whole is airy,
animated, and vigorous; what is little is gay; what is great is splendid. He
may be thought to mention himself too frequently; but while he forces
himself upon our esteem, we cannot refuse him to stand high in his
own. Everything is excused by the play of images and the sprightliness
of expression. Though all is easy, nothing is feeble; though all seems
careless, there is nothing harsh; and though since his earlier works more
than a century has passed, they have nothing yet uncouth or obsolete."

mighty and best appointed fleets which any age had ever seen disputed the command of the greater half of the globe, the commerce of nations, and the riches of the universe. While these vast floating bodies, on either side, moved against each other in parallel lines, and our countrymen, under the happy conduct of his Royal Highness, went breaking, by little and little, into the line of the enemies, the noise of the cannon from both navies reached our ears about the city, so that all men being alarmed with it, and in a dreadful suspense of the event which we knew was then deciding, every one went following the sound as his fancy led him; and, leaving the town almost empty, some took towards the park, some cross the river, others down it—all seeking the noise in the depth of silence.

Among the rest, it was the fortune of Eugenius, Crites, Lisideius, and Neander to be in company together—three of them persons whom their wit and quality have made known to all the town and whom I have chose to hide under these borrowed names, that they may not suffer by so ill a relation as I am going to make of their discourse.

Taking then a barge which a servant of Lisideius had provided for them, they made haste to shoot the bridge and left behind them that great fall of waters which hindered them from hearing what they desired; after which, having disengaged themselves from many vessels which rode at anchor in the Thames and almost blocked up the passage towards Greenwich, they ordered the watermen to let fall their oars more gently; and then, every one favoring his own curiosity with a strict silence, it was not long ere they perceived the air break about them like the noise of distant thunder, or of swallows in a chimney—those little undulations of sound, though almost vanishing before they reached them, yet still seeming to retain somewhat of their first horror, which they had betwixt the fleets. After they had attentively listened till such time as the sound by little and little went from them, Eugenius, lifting up his head and taking notice of it, was the first who congratulated to the rest that happy omen of our nation's victory, adding we had but this to desire in confirmation of it, that we might hear no more of that noise which was now leaving the English coast. When the rest had concurred in the same opinion, Crites, a person of a sharp judgment and somewhat too delicate a taste in wit, which the world have mistaken in him for ill-nature, said, smiling to us, that if the concernment of this battle had not been so exceeding great, he could scarce have wished the victory at the price he knew he must pay for it, in being subject to the reading and hearing of so many ill verses as he was sure would be made upon it. . . . Crites . . . said the public magistrate ought to send betimes to forbid them. . . . "In my opinion," replied Eugenius, "you pursue your point too far, for as to my own particular I am so great a lover of poesy that I could wish them all rewarded who attempt but to do well. . . ." "There are so few who write well in this age," says Crites, "that methinks any praises should be welcome; they neither rise to the dignity of the last age nor to any of the Ancients . . . ."

"If your quarrel," said Eugenius, "to those who now write be grounded only on your reverence to antiquity, there is no man more ready to adore those great Greeks and Romans than I am; but, on the other side, I cannot think so contemptibly of the age I live in, or so dishonorably of my own country, as not to judge we equal the Ancients in most kinds of poesy and in some surpass them; neither know I any reason why I may not be as zealous for the reputation of our age as we find the Ancients themselves in reference to those who lived before them. . . .

"But I see I am engaging in a wide dispute, where the arguments are not like to reach close on either side, for poesy is of so large an extent, and so many both of the Ancients and Moderns have done well in all kinds of it, that in citing one against the other, we shall take up more time this evening than each man's occasions will allow him: therefore I would ask Crites to what part of poesy he would confine his arguments and whether he would defend the general cause of the Ancients against the Moderns, or oppose any age of the Moderns against this of ours?"

Crites . . . told Eugenius he approved his propositions, and if he pleased, he would limit their dispute to dramatic poesy, in which he thought it not difficult to prove either that the Ancients were superior to the Moderns or the last age to this of ours.

Eugenius was somewhat surprised when he heard Crites make choice of that subject. "For ought I see," said he, "I have undertaken a harder province than I imagined, for though I never judged the plays of the Greek or Roman poets comparable to ours, yet, on the other side, those we now see acted come short of many which were written in the last age. But my comfort is, if we are overcome, it will be only by our own countrymen, and if we yield to them in this one part of poesy, we more surpass them in all the other, for in the epic or lyric way, it will be hard for them to show us one such amongst them, as we have many now living, or who lately were so: they can produce nothing so courtly writ, or which expresses so much the conversation of a gentleman, as Sir John Suckling; nothing so even, sweet, and flowing, as Mr. Waller; nothing so majestic, so correct, as Sir John Denham; nothing so elevated, so copious, and full of spirit, as Mr. Cowley; as for the Italian, French, and Spanish plays, I can make it evident that those who now write surpass them and that the drama is wholly ours."

All of them were thus far of Eugenius's opinion that the sweetness of English verse was never understood or practiced by our fathers; even Crites himself did not much oppose it; and everyone was willing to acknowledge how much our poesy is improved by the happiness of some writers yet living, who first taught us to mold our thoughts into easy and significant words, to retrench the superfluities of expression, and to make our rhyme so properly a part of the verse that it should never mislead the sense, but itself be led and governed by it.

Eugenius was going to continue this discourse when Lisideius told him it was necessary, before they proceeded further, to take a standing measure of their controversy; for how was it possible to be decided who writ the best plays, before we know what a play should be? But, this once agreed on by both parties, each might have recourse to it, either to prove his own advantages or to discover the failings of his adversary.

He had no sooner said this, but all desired the favor of him to give the definition of a play; and they were the more importunate because neither Aristotle, nor Horace, nor any other who writ of that subject had ever done it.

Lisideius, after some modest denials, at last confessed he had a rude notion of it, indeed, rather a description than a definition, but which served to guide him in his private thoughts when he was to make a judgment of what others writ: <u>that he conceived a play</u> ought to be *a just and lively image of human nature, repesenting its passions and humors, and the changes of fortune to which it is subject, for the delight and instruction of mankind.*

This definition, though Crites raised a logical objection against it— that it was only *a genere et fine,* and so not altogether perfect—was yet well received by the rest; and after they had given order to the watermen to turn their barge and row softly that they might take the cool of the evening in their return, Crites, being desired by the company to begin, spoke on behalf of the Ancients in this manner:

"If confidence presage a victory, Eugenius, in his own opinion, has already triumphed over the Ancients: nothing seems more easy to him than to overcome those whom it is our greatest praise to have imitated well, for we do not only build upon their foundation, but by their models. Dramatic poesy had time enough, reckoning from Thespis (who first invented it) to Aristophanes, to be born, to grow up, and to flourish in maturity. It has been observed of arts and sciences, that in one and the same century they have arrived to a great perfection, and no wonder, since every age has a kind of universal genius, which inclines those that live in it to some particular studies: the work then being pushed on by many hands, must of necessity go forward.

"Is it not evident, in these last hundred years (when the study of philosophy has been the business of all the virtuosi in Christendom), that almost a new nature has been revealed to us? That more errors of the school have been detected, more useful experiments in philosophy have been made, more noble secrets in optics, medicine, anatomy, astronomy, discovered, than in all those credulous and doting ages from Aristotle to us? So true is it, that nothing spreads more fast than science, when rightly and generally cultivated.

"Add to this, the more than common emulation that was in those times of writing well, which though it be found in all ages and all persons that pretend to the same reputation, yet poesy, being then in more esteem than now it is, had greater honors decreed to the professors of it, and consequently the rivalship was more high between them; they had judges ordained to decide their merit, and prizes to reward it, and historians have been diligent to record of Aeschylus, Euripides, Sophocles, Lycophron, and the rest of them, both who they were that vanquished in these wars of the theater and how often they were crowned . . . .

"But now, since the rewards of honor are taken away, that virtuous emulation is turned into direct malice, yet so slothful that it contents itself to condemn and cry down others, without attempting to do better: 'tis a reputation too unprofitable to take the necessary pains for it; yet wishing they had it is incitement enough to hinder others from it. And this, in short, Eugenius, is the reason why you have now so few good poets and so many severe judges. Certainly, to imitate the Ancients well, much labor and long study is required, which pains, I have already shown, our poets would want encouragement to take, if yet they had ability to go through with it. Those Ancients have been faithful imitators and wise observers of that nature which is so torn and ill represented in our plays; they have handed down to us a perfect resemblance of her, which we, like ill copiers, neglecting to look on, have rendered monstrous and disfigured. But, that you may know how much you are indebted to those your masters and be ashamed to have so ill requited them, I must remember you that all the rules by which we practice the drama at this day (either such as relate to the justness and symmetry of the plot, or the episodical ornaments, such as descriptions, narrations, and other beauties, which are not essential to the play) were delivered to us from the observations which Aristotle made of those poets which either lived before him or were his contemporaries: we have added nothing of our own, except we have the confidence to say our wit is better; of which none boast in this our age but such as understand not theirs. Of that book which Aristotle has left us, the *Poetics,* Horace's *Art of Poetry* is an excellent comment and, I believe, restores to us that Second Book of his concerning *Comedy,* which is wanting in him.

"Out of these two have been extracted the famous rules, which the French call *Des Trois Unitez,* or The Three Unities, which ought to be observed in every regular play, namely, of Time, Place, and Action.

"The Unity of Time they comprehend in twenty-four hours, the compass of a natural day, or as near as it can be contrived, and the reason of it is obvious to everyone—that the time of the feigned action, or fable of the play, should be proportioned as near as can be to the duration of that time in which it is represented: since, therefore, all plays are acted on the theater in a space of time much within the compass of twenty-four hours, that play is to be thought the nearest imitation of nature, whose plot or action is confined within that time; and, by the same rule which concludes this general proportion of time, it follows that all the parts of it are to be equally subdivided; . . . 'tis therefore the poet's duty to take care that no act should be imagined to exceed the time in which it is represented on the stage and that the intervals and inequalities of time be supposed to fall out between the acts.

"This rule of time, how well it has been observed by the Ancients, most of their plays will witness; you see them in their tragedies (wherein to follow this rule is certainly most difficult) from the very beginning of their plays falling close into that part of the story which they intend for the action or principal object of it, leaving the former part to be delivered by narration; so that they set the audience, as it were, at the post where the race is to be concluded, and, saving them the tedious expectation of seeing the poet set out and ride the beginning of the course, you behold him not till he is in sight of the goal, and just upon you.

"For the second Unity, which is that of Place, the Ancients meant by it that the scene ought to be continued through the play in the same place where it was laid in the beginning, for, the stage on which it is represented being but one and the same place, it is unnatural to conceive it many, and those far distant from one another. I will not deny but, by the variation of painted scenes, the fancy, which in these cases will contribute to its own deceit, may sometimes imagine it several places, with some appearance of probability; yet it still carries the greater likelihood of truth if those places be supposed so near each other, as in the same town or city, which may all be comprehended under the larger denomination of one place, for a greater distance will bear no proportion to the shortness of time which is allotted in the acting to pass from one of them to another; for the observation of this, next to the Ancients, the French are to be most commended. They tie themselves so strictly to the Unity of Place that you never see, in any of their plays, a scene changed in the middle of an act: if the act begins in a garden, a street, or chamber, 'tis ended in the same place; and, that you may know it to be the same, the stage is so supplied with persons that it is never empty all the time: he that enters the second, has business with him who was on before, and, before the second quits the stage, a third appears who has business with him. This Corneille calls *la liaison des scenes*, the continuity or joining of the scenes, and 'tis a good mark of a well-contrived play when all the persons are known to each other, and every one of them has some affairs with all the rest.

"As for the third Unity, which is that of Action, the Ancients meant no other by it than what the logicians do by their *finis*, the end or scope of any action—that which is the first in intention and last in execution. Now the poet is to aim at one great and complete action, to the carrying on of which all things in his play, even the very obstacles, are to be subservient, and the reason of this is as evident as any of the former. For two actions, equally labored and driven on by the writer, would destroy the unity of the poem; it would be no longer one play, but two—not but that there may be many actions in a play, as Ben Jonson has observed in his *Discoveries*, but they must be all subservient to the great one, which our language happily expresses in the name of *underplots*: such as in Terence's *Eunuch* is the difference and reconcilement of Thais and Phædria, which is not the chief business of the play, but promotes the marriage of Chærea and Chremes's sister, principally intended by the poet. There ought to be but one action, says Corneille, that is, one complete action which leaves the mind of the audience in a full repose; but this cannot be brought to pass but by many other imperfect actions which conduce to it and hold the audience in a delightful suspense of what will be.

"If by these rules (to omit many other drawn from the precepts and practice of the Ancients) we should judge our modern plays, 'tis probable that few of them would endure the trial: that which should be the business of a day takes up in some of them an age; instead of one action, they are the epitomes of a man's life; and for one spot of ground (which the stage should represent) we are sometimes in more countries than the map can show us.

"But if we will allow the Ancients to have contrived well, we must acknowledge them to have writ better. Questionless we are deprived of a great stock of wit in the loss of Menander among the Greek poets, and of Cæcilius, Afranius, and Varius, among the Romans; . . . but so long as Aristophanes in the Old Comedy and Plautus in the new are extant, while the tragedies of Euripides, Sophocles, and Seneca are to be had, I can never see one of those plays which are now written but it increases my admiration of the Ancients. And yet I must acknowledge farther that, to admire them as we ought, we should understand them better than we do. Doubtless many things appear flat to us, whose wit depended on some custom or story which never came to our knowledge, or perhaps on some criticism in their language which being so long dead, and only remaining in their books, 'tis not possible they should make us know it perfectly. To read Macrobius explaining the propriety and elegancy of many words in Virgil which I had before passed over without consideration, as common things, is enough to assure me that I ought to think the same of Terence and that in the purity of his style (which Tully so much valued that he ever carried his works about him) there is yet left in him great room for admiration if I knew but where to place it. In the meantime I must desire you to take notice that the greatest man of the last age (Ben Jonson) was willing to give place to them in all things: he was not only a professed imitator of Horace but a learned plagiary of all the others. You track him everywhere in their snow: if Horace, Lucan, Petronius Arbiter, Seneca, and Juvenal had their own from him, there are few serious thoughts which are new in him; you will pardon me, therefore, if I presume he loved their fashion when he wore their clothes. But since I have otherwise a great veneration for him, and you, Eugenius, prefer him above all other poets, I will use no farther argument to you than his example: I will produce Father Ben to you, dressed in all the ornaments and colors of the Ancients; you will need no other guide to our party if you follow him; and, whether you consider the bad plays of our age or regard the good ones of the last, both the best and worst of the modern poets will equally instruct you to esteem the Ancients."

Crites had no sooner left speaking, but Eugenius, who had waited with some impatience for it, thus began:

"I have observed in your speech that the former part of it is convincing as to what the Moderns have profited by the rules of the Ancients, but in the latter you are careful to conceal how much they have excelled them. We own all the helps we have from them and want neither veneration nor gratitude while we acknowledge that to overcome them we must make use of the advantages we have received from them; but to these assistances we have joined our own industry, for, had we sat down with a dull imitation of them, we might then have lost somewhat of the old perfection but never acquired any that was new. We draw not therefore after their lines, but those of nature, and having the life before us, besides the experience of all they knew, it is no wonder if we hit some airs and features which they have missed. I deny not what you urge of arts and sciences, that they have flourished in some ages more than others, but your instance in philosophy makes for me: for if natural causes be more known now than in the time of Aristotle, because more studied, it follows that poesy and other arts may, with the same pains, arrive still nearer to perfection, and, that granted, it will rest for you to prove that they wrought more perfect images of human life than we; which, seeing in your discourse you have avoided to make good, it shall now be my task to show you some part of their defects and some few excellencies of the Moderns. . . .

"Be pleased then in the first place to take notice that the Greek poesy, which Crites has affirmed to have arrived to perfection in the reign of the Old Comedy, was so far from it that the distinction of it into acts was not known to them, or, if it were, it is yet so darkly delivered to us that we cannot make it out.

"All we know of it is from the singing of their chorus, and that too is so uncertain that in some of their plays we have reason to conjecture they sung more than five times. Aristotle indeed divides the integral parts of a play into four. First, the *Protasis,* or entrance, which gives light only to the characters of the persons and proceeds very little into any part of the action. Secondly, the *Epitasis,* or working up of the plot, where the play grows warmer, the design or action of it is drawing on, and you see something promising that it will come to pass. Thirdly, the *Catastasis,* or counterturn, which destroys that expectation, imbroils the action in new difficulties, and leaves you far distant from that hope in which it found you, as you may have observed in a violent stream resisted by a narrow passage —it runs round to an eddy and carries back the waters with more swiftness than it brought them on. Lastly, the *Catastrophe,* which the Grecians called *lysis,* the French *le dénouement,* and we the discovery or unravelling of the plot: there you see all things settling again upon their first foundations; and, the obstacles which hindered the design or action of the play once removed, it ends with that resemblance of truth and nature, that the audience are satisfied with the conduct of it. Thus this great man delivered to us the image of a play, and I must confess it is so lively that from thence much light has been derived to the forming it more perfectly into acts and scenes. But what poet first limited to five the number of the acts, I know not; only we see it so firmly established in the time of Horace, that he gives it for a rule in comedy: *Neu brevior quinto, neu sit productior actu* ["Let it be neither less nor more than five acts"]. So that you see the Grecians cannot be said to have consummated this art, writing rather by entrances than by acts and having rather a general indigested notion of a play than knowing how and where to bestow the particular graces of it.

"But since the Spaniards at this day allow but three acts, which they call *Jornadas,* to a play, and the Italians in many of theirs follow them, when I condemn the Ancients, I declare it is not altogether because they have not five acts to every play, but because they have not confined themselves to one certain number: it is building a house without a model, and, when they succeeded in such undertakings, they ought to have sacrificed to Fortune, not to the Muses.

"Next, for the plot, which Aristotle called *to mythos,* and often, *tōn pragmatōn synthesis,* and from him the Romans *fabula;* it has already been judiciously observed by a late writer that in their tragedies it was only some tale derived from Thebes or Troy, or at least something that happened in those two ages which was worn so threadbare by the pens of all the epic poets, and even by tradition itself of the talkative Greeklings (as Ben Jonson calls them), that before it came upon the stage it was already known to all the audience, and the people, so soon as ever they heard the name of Oedipus, knew as well as the poet that he had killed his father by a mistake and committed incest with his mother, before the play, that they were now to hear of a great plague, an oracle, and the ghost of Laius, so that they sat with a yawning kind of expectation, till he was to come with his eyes pulled out and speak a hundred or two of verses in a tragic tone, in complaint of his misfortunes. . . .

"But in the first place give me leave to tell you that the Unity of Place, however it might be practiced by them, was never any of their rules: we neither find it in Aristotle, Horace, or any who have written of it, till in our age the French poets first made it a precept of the stage. The Unity of Time, even Terence himself (who was the best and most regular of them) has neglected: his *Heauton-timorumenos,* or *Self-Punisher,* takes up visibly two days; therefore, says Scaliger, the two first acts concluding the first day were acted overnight, the three last on the ensuing day, and Euripides, in tying himself to one day, has committed an absurdity never to be forgiven him, for in one of his tragedies he has made Thesus go from Athens to Thebes, which was about forty English miles, under the walls of it to give battle, and appear victorious in the next act, and yet, from the time of his departure to the return of the Nuntius, who gives the relation of his victory, Aethra and the chorus have but thirty-six verses, that is, not for every mile a verse. . . .

"'Tis true, they have kept the continuity, or, as you called it, *liaison des scenes,* somewhat better: two do not perpetually come in together, talk, and go out together, and other two succeed them, and do the same throughout the act, which the English call by the name of single scenes; but the reason is because they have seldom above two or three scenes, properly so called, in every act; for it is to be accounted a new scene, not every time the stage is empty; but every person who enters, though to others, makes it so because he introduces a new business. Now the plots of their plays being narrow and the persons few, one of their acts was written in a less compass than one of our well-wrought scenes; and yet they are often deficient even in this. . . .

"But as they have failed both in laying of their plots, and managing of them, swerving from the rules of their own art by misrepresenting nature to us, in which they have ill satisfied one intention of a play, which was delight, so in the instructive part they have erred worse:

instead of punishing vice and rewarding virtue, they have often shown a prosperous wickedness and an unhappy piety. They have set before us a bloody image of revenge in Medea and given her dragons to convey her safe from punishment; a Priam and Astyanax murdered, and Cassandra ravished, and the lust and murder ending in the victory of him who acted them. In short, there is no indecorum in any of our modern plays which, if I would excuse, I could not shadow with some authority from the Ancients.

"And one farther note of them let me leave you: tragedies and comedies were not writ then as they are now, promiscuously, by the same person, but he who found his genius bending to the one, never attempted the other way. This so plain, that I need not instance to you that Aristophanes, Plautus, Terence, never any of them writ a tragedy; Aeschylus, Euripides, Sophocles, and Seneca never meddled with comedy: the sock and buskin were not worn by the same poet. Having then so much care to excel in one kind, very little is to be pardoned them if they miscarried in it, and this would lead me to the consideration of their wit, had not Crites given me sufficient warning not to be too bold in my judgment of it because, the languages being dead and many of the customs and little accidents on which it depended lost to us, we are not competent judges of it. But though I grant that here and there we may miss the application of a proverb or a custom, yet a thing well said will be wit in all languages, and, though it may lose something in the translation, yet to him who reads it in the original, 'tis still the same: he has an idea of its excellency, though it cannot pass from his mind into any other expression or words than those in which he finds it. . . .

"But, to return from whence I have digressed, to the consideration of the Ancients' writing and their wit, of which by this time you will grant us in some measure to be fit judges. Though I see many excellent thoughts in Seneca, yet he of them who had a genius most proper for the stage was Ovid; he had a way of writing so fit to stir up a pleasing admiration and concernment, which are the objects of a tragedy, and to show the various movements of a soul combating betwixt two different passions that, had he lived in our age, or in his own could have writ with our advantages, no man but must have yielded to him; and therefore I am confident that the *Medea* is

none of his, for, though I esteem it for the gravity and sententiousness
of it, which he himself concludes to be suitable to a tragedy . . . ,
yet it moves not my soul enough to judge that he, who in the epic
way wrote things so near the drama as the story of Myrrha, of
Caunus and Biblis, and the rest, should stir up no more concernment where he most endeavored it. The masterpiece of Seneca I hold
to be that scene in the *Troades* where Ulysses is seeking for Astyanax
to kill him; there you see the tenderness of a mother so represented
in Andromache that it raises compassion to a high degree in the
reader and bears the nearest resemblance of anything in their tragedies to the excellent scenes of passion in Shakespeare or in Fletcher.
For love-scenes, you will find few among them; their tragic poets dealt
not with that soft passion, but with lust, cruelty, revenge, ambition,
and those bloody actions they produced, which were more capable
of raising horror than compassion in an audience, leaving love un-
touched, whose gentleness would have tempered them, which is the
most frequent of all the passions, and which, being the private concernment of every person, is soothed by viewing its own image in
a public entertainment.

"Among their comedies, we find a scene or two of tenderness, and
that where you would least expect it, in Plautus, but, to speak generally, their lovers say little when they see each other but *anima mea,
vita mea* . . . , as the women in Juvenal's time used to cry out in the
fury of their kindness; then indeed to speak sense were an offense.
Any sudden gust of passion (as an ecstasy of love in an unexpected
meeting) cannot better be expressed than in a word and a sigh,
breaking one another. Nature is dumb on such occasions and to
make her speak would be to represent her unlike herself. But there
are a thousand other concernments of lovers, as jealousies, complaints,
contrivances, and the like, where not to open their minds at large to
each other were to be wanting to their own love and to the expectation of the audience, who watched the movements of their minds as
much as the changes of their fortunes. For the imaging of the first
is properly the work of a poet; the latter he borrows of the
historian."

Eugenius was proceeding in that part of his discourse, when Crites
interrupted him. "I see," said he, "Eugenius and I are never like to

have this question decided betwixt us, for he maintains the Moderns have acquired a new perfection in writing; I can only grant they have altered the mode of it. . . ."

This moderation of Crites, as it was pleasing to all the company, so it put an end to that dispute, which Eugenius, who seemed to have the better of the argument, would urge no farther; but Lisideius, after he had acknowledged himself of Eugenius's opinion concerning the Ancients, yet told him he had forborne, till his discourse were ended, to ask him why he preferred the English plays above those of other nations and whether we ought not to submit our stage to the exactness of our next neighbors.

"Though," said Eugenius, "I am at all times ready to defend the honor of my country against the French and to maintain, we are as well able to vanquish them with our pens as our ancestors have been with their swords; yet, if you please," added he, looking upon Neander, "I will commit this cause to my friend's management; his opinion of our plays is the same with mine, and, besides, there is no reason that Crites and I, who have now left the stage, should re-enter so suddenly upon it, which is against the laws of comedy."

"If the question had been stated," replied Lisideius, "who had writ best, the French or English, forty years ago, I should have been of your opinion and adjudged the honor to our own nation, but since that time" (said he, turning towards Neander) "we have been so long together bad Englishmen that we had not leisure to be good poets. Beaumont, Fletcher, and Jonson (who were only capable of bringing us to that degree of perfection which we have) were just then leaving the world, as if (in an age of so much horror) wit, and those milder studies of humanity, had no farther business among us. But the Muses, who ever follow peace, went to plant in another country: it was then that the great Cardinal of Richelieu began to take them into his protection and that, by his encouragement, Corneille and some other Frenchmen reformed their theater, which before was as much below ours as it now surpasses it and the rest of Europe. But because Crites in his discourse for the Ancients has prevented me, by touching upon many rules of the stage which the Moderns have borrowed from them, I shall only, in short, demand of you whether you are not convinced that of all nations the French have best observed them? In the Unity of Time you find them so scrupulous that it yet remains a dispute among their poets whether the artificial day of twelve hours, more or less, be not meant by Aristotle, rather than the natural one of twenty-four, and, consequently, whether all plays ought not to be reduced into that compass. . . . The Unity of Action in all plays is yet more conspicuous, for they do not burden them with underplots, as the English do; which is the reason why many scenes of our tragicomedies carry on a design that is nothing of kin to the main plot and that we see two distinct webs in a play, like those in ill-wrought stuffs, and two actions, that is, two plays, carried on together, to the confounding of the audience, who, before they are warm in their concernments for one part, are diverted to another and by that means espouse the interest of neither. From hence likewise it arises that the one half of our actors are not known to the other. They keep their distances, as if they were Montagues and Capulets, and seldom begin an acquaintance till the last scene of the fifth act, when they are all to meet upon the stage. There is no theater in the world has any thing so absurd as the English tragicomedy; 'tis a drama of our own invention, and the fashion of it is enough to proclaim it so: here a course of mirth, there another of sadness and passion, a third of honor, and a fourth a duel. Thus, in two hours and a half, we run through all the fits of Bedlam. The French affords you as much variety on the same day, but they do it not so unseasonably, or *mal à propos*, as we; our poets present you the play and the farce together, and our stages still retain somewhat of the original civility of the *Red Bull: Atque ursum et pugiles media inter carmina poscunt* ['In the middle of plays call for a bear and pugilists']. The end of tragedies or serious plays, says Aristotle, is to beget admiration, compassion, or concernment, but are not mirth and compassion things incompatible? And is it not evident that the poet must of necessity destroy the former by intermingling of the latter? That is, he must ruin the sole end and object of his tragedy to introduce somewhat that is forced in and is not of the body of it. Would you not think that physician mad who, having prescribed a purge, should immediately order you to take restringents upon it?

"But to leave our plays and return to theirs. I have noted one great advantage they have had in the plotting of their tragedies; that is, they are always grounded upon some known history . . . ; in that they have so imitated the Ancients that they have surpassed them. For the Ancients, as was observed before, took for the foundation of their plays some poetical fiction, such as under that consideration could move but little concernment in the audience because they already knew the event of it. But the French goes farther: . . . he so interweaves truth with probable fiction that he puts a pleasing fallacy upon us, mends the intrigues of fate, and dispenses with the severity of history, to reward that virtue which has been rendered to us there unfortunate. . . .

"Another thing in which the French differ from us and from the Spaniards, is that they do not embarrass or cumber themselves with too much plot; they only represent so much of a story as will constitute one whole and great action sufficient for a play. We, who undertake more, do but multiply adventures which, not being produced from one another, as effects from causes, but barely following, constitute many actions in the drama, and consequently make it many plays. . . .

"But I return again to the French writers, who, as I have said, do not burden themselves too much with plot, which has been reproached to them by an *ingenious person* of our nation as a fault, for, he says, they commonly make but one person considerable in a play; they dwell on him and his concernments, while the rest of the persons are only subservient to set him off. If he intends this by it, that there is one person in the play who is of greater dignity than the rest, he must tax, not only theirs, but those of the Ancients, and which he would be loath to do, the best of ours, for it is impossible but that one person must be more conspicuous in it than any other, and consequently the greatest share in the action must devolve on him. We see it so in the management of all affairs; even in the most equal aristocracy the balance cannot be so justly poised but someone will be superior to the rest either in parts, fortune, interest, or the consideration of some glorious exploit, which will reduce the greatest part of business into his hands.

"But, if he would have us to imagine that in exalting one character the rest of them are neglected and that all of them have not some share or other in the action of the play, I desire him to produce any of Corneille's tragedies, wherein every person, like so many servants in a well-governed family, has not some employment, and who is not necessary to the carrying on of the plot, or at least to your understanding it.

"There are indeed some protatic persons in the Ancients, whom they make use of in their plays, either to hear or give the relation, but the French avoid this with great address, making their narrations only to or by such who are some way interested in the main design. And now I am speaking of relations, I cannot take a fitter opportunity to add this in favor of the French, that they often use them with better judgment and more *à propos* than the English do. Not that I commend narrations in general—but there are two sorts of them. One, of those things which are antecedent to the play and are related to make the conduct of it more clear to us. But 'tis a fault to choose such subjects for the stage as will force us on that rock because we see they are seldom listened to by the audience, and that is many times the ruin of the play, for, being once let pass without attention, the audience can never recover themselves to understand the plot; and indeed it is somewhat unreasonable that they should be put to so much trouble, as that, to comprehend what passes in their sight, they must have recourse to what was done, perhaps, ten or twenty years ago.

"But there is another sort of relations, that is, of things happening in the action of the play and supposed to be done behind the scenes, and this is many times both convenient and beautiful, for by it the French avoid the tumult which we are subject to in England by representing duels, battles, and the like, which renders our stage too like the theaters where they fight prizes. For what is more ridiculous than to represent an army with a drum and five men behind it, all which the hero of the other side is to drive in before him, or to see a duel fought and one slain with two or three thrusts of the foils, which we know are so blunted that we might give a man an hour to kill another in good earnest with them.

"I have observed that in all our tragedies the audience cannot forbear laughing when the actors are to die; it is the most comic part of the whole play. All *passions* may be lively represented on the stage if to the well-writing of them the actor supplies a good commanded voice, and limbs that move easily, and without stiffness; but there are many *actions* which can never be imitated to a just height: dying especially is a thing which none but a Roman gladiator could naturally perform on the stage, when he did not imitate or represent, but naturally do it; and therefore it is better to omit the representation of it. . . . That is, those actions which by reason of their cruelty will cause aversion in us or by reason of their impossibility, unbelief, ought either wholly to be avoided by a poet, or only delivered by narration. . . .

"But I find I have been too long in this discourse, since the French have many other excellencies not common to us, as that you never see any of their plays end with a conversion or simple change of will, which is the ordinary way which our poets use to end theirs. It shows little art in the conclusion of a dramatic poem, when they who have hindered the felicity during the four acts, desist from it in the fifth, without some powerful cause to take them off; and, though I deny not but such reasons may be found, yet it is a path that is cautiously to be trod, and the poet is to be sure he convinces the audience that the motive is strong enough. As for example the conversion of the Usurer in *The Scornful Lady* seems to me a little forced, for, being a usurer, which implies a lover of money to the highest degree of covetousness (and such the poet has represented him), the account he gives for the sudden change is that he has been duped by the wild young fellow, which in reason might render him more wary another time and make him punish himself with harder fare and coarser clothes, to get it up again; but that he should look on it as a judgment, and so repent, we may expect to hear of in a sermon but I should never endure it in a play.

"I pass by this; neither will I insist on the care they take that no person after his first entrance shall ever appear but the business which brings him upon the stage shall be evident, which, if observed, must needs render all the events in the play more natural, for there you see the probability of every accident in the cause that produced it, and that which appears chance in the play will seem so reasonable to you that you will there find it almost necessary, so that in the exits of the actors you have a clear account of their purpose and design in the next entrance (though, if the scene be well wrought, the event will commonly deceive you), for there is nothing so absurd, says Corneille, as for an actor to leave the stage only because he has no more to say.

"I should now speak of the beauty of their rhyme and the just reason I have to prefer that way of writing in tragedies before ours in blank verse, but, because it is partly received by us and therefore not altogether peculiar to them, I will say no more of it in relation to their plays. For our own, I doubt not but it will exceedingly beautify them, and I can see but one reason why it should not generally obtain; that is, because our poets write so ill in it. . . ."

Lisideius concluded in this manner, and Neander, after a little pause, thus answered him:

"I shall grant Lisideius without much dispute a great part of what he has urged against us, for I acknowledge that the French contrive their plots more regularly and observe the laws of comedy and decorum of the stage (to speak generally) with more exactness than the English. Farther, I deny not but he has taxed us justly in some irregularities of ours, which he has mentioned; yet, after all, I am of opinion that neither our faults nor their virtues are considerable enough to place them above us.

"For the lively imitation of nature being in the definition of a play, those which best fulfill that law ought to be esteemed superior to the others. 'Tis true, those beauties of the French poesy are such as will raise perfection higher where it is, but are not sufficient to give it where it is not. They are indeed the beauties of a statue, but not of a man, because not animated with the soul of poesy, which is imitation of humor and passions, and this Lisideius himself, or any other, however biased to their party, cannot but acknowledge if he will either compare the humors of our comedies or the characters of our serious plays with theirs. He that will look upon theirs which have been written till these last ten years or thereabouts will find it a hard matter to pick out two or three passable humors amongst them. Corneille himself, their arch-poet, what has he produced except *The Liar,* and you know how it was cried up in France, but when it came upon the English stage, though well translated and that part of Dorant acted to so much advantage by Mr. Hart as I am confident it never received in its own country, the most favorable to it would not put it in competition with many of Fletcher's or Ben Jonson's. In the rest of Corneille's comedies you have little humor; he tells you himself his way is first to show two lovers in good intelligence with each other, in the working up of the play to embroil them by some mistake, and in the latter end to clear it and reconcile them.

"But of late years Molière, the younger Corneille, Quinault, and some others have been imitating afar off the quick turns and graces of the English stage. They have mixed their serious plays with mirth, like our tragicomedies, since the death of Cardinal Richelieu, which Lisideius and many others not observing have commended that in them for a virtue which they themselves no longer practice. Most of their new plays are, like some of ours, derived from the Spanish novels. There is scarce one of them without a veil and a trusty Diego who drolls much after the rate of the *Adventures*. But their humors, if I may grace them with that name, are so thin-sown that never above one of them comes up in any play. I dare take upon me to find more variety of them in some one play of Ben Jonson's than in all theirs together, as he who has seen *The Alchemist, The Silent Woman,* or *Bartholomew Fair* cannot but acknowledge with me.

"I grant the French have performed what was possible on the groundwork of the Spanish plays; what was pleasant before, they have made regular. But there is not above one good play to be writ on all those plots; they are too much alike to please often, which we need not the experience of our own stage to justify. As for their new way of mingling mirth with serious plot, I do not, with Lisideius, condemn the thing though I cannot approve their manner of doing it. He tells us we cannot so speedily recollect ourselves after a scene of great passion and concernment as to pass to another of mirth and humor and to enjoy it with any relish, but why should he imagine the soul of man more heavy than his senses? Does not the eye pass from an unpleasant object to a pleasant in a much shorter time than is required to this? And does not the unpleasantness of the first commend the beauty of the latter? The old rule of logic might have convinced him that contraries, when placed near, set off each other. A continued gravity keeps the spirit too much bent; we must refresh it sometimes, as we bait in a journey, that we may go on with great ease. A scene of mirth mixed with tragedy has the same effect upon us which our music has betwixt the acts, and that we find a relief to us from the best plots and language of the stage if the discourses have been long. I must therefore have stronger arguments ere I am convinced that compassion and mirth in the same subject destroy each other and in the meantime cannot but conclude, to the honor of our nation, that we have invented, increased, and perfected a more pleasant way of writing for the stage than was ever known to the ancients or moderns of any nation, which is tragicomedy.

"And this leads me to wonder why Lisideius and many others should cry up the barrenness of the French plots above the variety and copiousness of the English. Their plots are single; they carry on one design, which is pushed forward by all the actors, every scene in the play contributing and moving towards it. Our plays, besides the main design, have underplots or by-concernments, of less considerable persons and intrigues, which are carried on with the motion of the main plot, just as they say the orb of the fixed stars and those of the planets, though they have motions of their own, are whirled about by the motion of the *Primum Mobile,* in which they are contained. That similitude expresses much of the English stage, for if contrary motions may be found in nature to agree, if a planet can go east and west at the same time—one way by virtue of his own motion, the other by the force of the First Mover—it will not be difficult to imagine how the underplot, which is only different, not contrary to the great design, may naturally be conducted along with it.

"Eugenius has already shown us, from the confession of the French poets, that the Unity of Action is sufficiently preserved if all the imperfect actions of the play are conducing to the main design, but, when those petty intrigues of a play are so ill ordered that they have no coherence with the other, I must grant that Lisideius has reason to tax that want of due connection, for co-ordination in a play is as dangerous and unnatural as in a state. In the meantime, he must acknowledge, our variety, if well ordered, will afford a greater pleasure to the audience.

"As for his other argument, that by pursuing one single theme they gain an advantage to express and work up the passions, I wish any example he could bring from them would make it good, for I confess their verses are to me the coldest I have ever read. Neither, indeed, is it possible for them, in the way they take, so to express passion as that the effects of it should appear in the concernment of an audience, their speeches being so many declamations, which tire us with the length, so that instead of persuading us to grieve for their imaginary heroes we are concerned for our own trouble, as we are in the tedious visits of bad company; we are in pain till they are gone. When the French stage came to be reformed by Cardinal Richelieu, those long harangues were introduced to comply with the gravity of a churchman. Look upon the *Cinna* and the *Pompey;* they are not so properly to be called plays as long discourses of reason of state; and *Polieucte* in matters of religion is as solemn as the long stops upon our organs. Since that time it is grown into a custom, and their actors speak by the hour-glass, as our parsons do; nay, they account it the grace of their parts and think themselves disparaged by the poet if they may not twice or thrice in a play entertain the audience with a speech of a hundred or two hundred lines. I deny not but this may suit well enough with the French, for as we, who are a more sullen people, come to be diverted at our plays, so they, who are of an airy and gay temper, come thither to make themselves more serious, and this I conceive to be one reason why comedy is more pleasing to us and tragedies to them. But, to speak generally, it cannot be denied that short speeches and replies are more apt to move the passions and beget concernment in us, than the other, for it is unnatural for any one in a gust of passion to speak long together, or for another in the same condition to suffer him, without interruption. Grief and passion are like floods raised in little brooks by a sudden rain: they are quickly up, and, if the concernment be poured unexpectedly in upon us, it overflows us, but a long sober shower gives them leisure to run out as they came in, without troubling the ordinary current. As for comedy, repartee is one of its chiefest graces; the greatest pleasure of the audience is a chase of wit kept up on both sides and swiftly managed. And this our forefathers, if not we, have had in Fletcher's plays to a much higher degree of perfection than the French poets can arrive at.

"There is another part of Lisideius's discourse, in which he has rather excused our neighbors than commended them, that is, for aiming only to make one person considerable in their plays. 'Tis very true what he has urged, that one character in all plays, even without the poet's care, will have advantage of all the others and that the design of the whole drama will chiefly depend on it. But this hinders not that there may be more shining characters in the play: many persons of a second magnitude, nay, some so very near, so almost equal to the first, that greatness may be opposed to greatness, and all the persons be made considerable, not only by their quality, but their action. 'Tis evident that the more the persons are, the greater will be the variety of the plot. If then the parts are managed so regularly that the beauty of the whole be kept entire and that the variety become not a perplexed and confused mass of accidents, you will find it infinitely pleasing to be led in a labyrinth of design where you see some of your way before you, yet discern not the end till you arrive at it. And that all this is practicable, I can produce for examples many of our English plays, as *The Maid's Tragedy, The Alchemist, The Silent Woman.* I was going to have named *The Fox,* but that the unity of design seems not exactly observed in it, for there appear two actions in the play: the first naturally ending with the fourth act, the second forced from it in the fifth, which yet is the less to be condemned in him because the disguise of Volpone, though it suited not with his character as a crafty or covetous person, agreed well enough with that of a voluptuary, and by it the poet gained the end he aimed at, the punishment of vice and the reward of virtue, which that disguise produced. So that to judge equally of it, it was an excellent fifth act, but not so naturally proceeding from the former.

"But to leave this and pass to the latter part of Lisideius's discourse, which concerns relations: I must acknowledge with him that the French have reason when they hide that part of the action which would occasion too much tumult on the stage and choose rather to have it made known by narration to the audience. Farther, I think it very convenient, for the reasons he has given, that all incredible actions were removed, but, whether custom has so insinuated itself into our countrymen or nature has so formed them to fierceness, I know not, but they will scarcely suffer combat and other objects of horror to be taken from them. And, indeed, the indecency of tumults is all which can be objected against fighting, for why may not our imagination as well suffer itself to be deluded with the probability of it as with any other thing in the play? For my part, I can with as great ease persuade myself that the blows which are struck are given in good earnest as I can that they who strike them are kings or princes, or those persons which they represent. . . . To conclude on this subject of relations: if we are to be blamed for showing too much of the action, the French are as faulty for discovering too little of it. A mean betwixt both should be observed by every judicious writer, so as the audience may neither be left unsatisfied by not seeing what is beautiful or shocked by beholding what is either incredible or undecent.

"I hope I have already proved in this discourse that, though we are not altogether so punctual as the French in observing the laws of comedy, yet our errors are so few, and little, and those things wherein we excel them so considerable, that we ought of right to be preferred before them. But what will Lisideius say if they themselves acknowledge they are too strictly tied up by those laws for breaking which he has blamed the English? I will allege Corneille's words, as I find them in the end of his Discourse of the Three Unities: *Il est facile aux speculatifs d'estre severes, etc.* ' 'Tis easy for speculative persons to judge severely, but if they would produce to public view ten or twelve pieces of this nature, they would perhaps give more latitude to the rules than I have done when, by experience, they had known how much we are bound up and constrained by them and how many beauties of the stage they banished from it.' To illustrate a little what he has said: by their servile observations of the Unities of Time and Place and integrity of scenes, they have brought on themselves that dearth of plot and narrowness of imagination which may be observed in all their plays. How many beautiful accidents might naturally happen in two or three days which cannot arrive with any probability in the compass of twenty-four hours? There is time to be allowed also for maturity of design, which, amongst great and prudent persons, such as are often represented in tragedy, cannot with any likelihood of truth be brought to pass at so short a warning. Farther, by tying themselves strictly to the Unity of Place and unbroken scenes, they are forced many times to omit some beauties which cannot be shown where the act began but might, if the scene were interrupted and the stage cleared for the persons to enter in another place, and therefore the French poets are often forced upon absurdities, for, if the act begins in a chamber, all the persons in the play must have some business or other to come thither, or else they are not to be shown that act, and sometimes their characters are very unfitting to appear there. As, suppose it were the king's bedchamber, yet the meanest man in the tragedy must come and dispatch his business there, rather than in the lobby or courtyard (which is fitter for him), for fear the stage should be cleared and the scenes broken. Many times they fall by it in a greater inconvenience. . . . Now what, I beseech you, is more easy than to write a regular French play or more difficult than write an irregular English one, like those of Fletcher or of Shakespeare?

". . . For, if you consider the plots, our own are fuller of variety; if the writing, ours are more quick and fuller of spirit; and therefore 'tis a strange mistake in those who decry the way of writing plays in verse, as if the English therein imitated the French. We have borrowed nothing from them: our plots are weaved in English looms; we endeavor therein to follow the variety and greatness of characters which are derived to us from Shakespeare and Fletcher; the copiousness and well-knitting of the intrigues we have from Jonson; and for the verse itself we have English precedents of elder date than any of Corneille's plays. . . .

"But to return from whence I have digressed: I dare boldly affirm these two things of the English drama—first, that we have many plays of ours as regular as any of theirs and which, besides, have more variety of plot and characters, and, secondly, that in most of the irregular plays of Shakespeare or Fletcher (for Ben Jonson's are for the most part regular) there is a more masculine fancy and greater spirit in the writing than there is in any of the French. I could produce, even in Shakespeare's and Fletcher's works, some plays which are almost exactly formed, as *The Merry Wives of Windsor* and *The Scornful Lady,* but because (generally speaking) Shakespeare, who writ first, did not perfectly observe the laws of comedy, and Fletcher, who came nearer to perfection, yet through carelessness made many faults, I will take the pattern of a perfect play from Ben Jonson, who was a careful and learned observer of the dramatic laws, and from all his comedies I shall select *The Silent Woman,* of which I will make a short examen, according to those rules which the French observe."

As Neander was beginning to examine *The Silent Woman,* Eugenius, looking earnestly upon him: "I beseech you, Neander," said he, "gratify the company, and me in particular, so far as, before you speak of the play, to give us a character of the author; and tell us frankly your opinion, whether you do not think all writers, both French and English, ought to give place to him."

"I fear," replied Neander, "that in obeying your commands I shall draw a little envy on myself. Besides, in performing them it will be first necessary to speak somewhat of Shakespeare and Fletcher, his rivals in poesy, and one of them, in my opinion, at least his equal, perhaps his superior.

"To begin, then, with Shakespeare. He was the man who, of all modern and perhaps ancient poets, had the largest and most comprehensive soul. All the images of nature were still present to him, and he drew them, not laboriously, but luckily; when he describes anything, you more than see it, you feel it too. Those who accuse him to have wanted learning give him the greater commendation: he was naturally learned; he needed not the spectacles of books to read nature; he looked inwards and found her there. I cannot say he is everywhere alike; were he so, I should do him injury to compare him with the greatest of mankind. He is many times flat, insipid, his comic wit degenerating into clenches, his serious swelling into bombast. But he is always great when some great occasion is presented to him; no man can say he ever had a fit subject for his wit and did not then raise himself as high above the rest of poets, *Quantum lenta solent inter viburna cupressi* ['As cypresses commonly do among bending shrubs']. The consideration of this made Mr. Hales of Eaton say that there was no subject of which any poet ever writ, but he would produce it much better treated of in Shakespeare; and, however others are now generally preferred before him, yet the age wherein he lived, which had contemporaries with him Fletcher and Jonson, never equalled them to him in their esteem; and in the last King's court, when Ben's reputation was at highest, Sir John Suckling, and with him the greater part of the courtiers, set our Shakespeare far above him.

"Beaumont and Fletcher, of whom I am next to speak, had, with the advantage of Shakespeare's wit, which was their precedent, great natural gifts, improved by study: Beaumont especially being so accurate a judge of plays that Ben Jonson, while he lived, submitted all his writings to his censure and, 'tis thought, used his judgment in correcting, if not contriving, all his plots. What value he had for him appears by the verses he writ to him, and therefore I need speak no farther of it. The first play that brought Fletcher and him in esteem was their *Philaster*, for, before that, they had written two or three very unsuccessfully, as the like is reported of Ben Jonson before he writ *Every Man in his Humour*. Their plots were generally more regular than Shakespeare's, especially those which were made before Beaumont's death, and they understood and imitated the conversation of gentlemen much better, whose wild debaucheries and quickness of wit in repartees no poet can ever paint as they have done. Humor, which Ben Jonson derived from particular persons, they made it not their business to describe; they represented all the passions very lively, but, above all, love. I am apt to believe the English language in them arrived to its highest perfection; what words have since been taken in are rather superfluous than ornamental. Their plays are now the most pleasant and frequent entertainments of the stage, two of theirs being acted through the year for one of Shakespeare's or Jonson's; the reason is because there is a certain gaiety in their comedies and pathos in their more serious plays which suits generally with all men's humors. Shakespeare's language is likewise a little obsolete, and Ben Jonson's wit comes short of theirs.

"As for Jonson, to whose character I am now arrived, if we look upon him while he was himself (for his last plays were but his dotages), I think him the most learned and judicious writer which any theater ever had. He was a most severe judge of himself as well as others. One cannot say he wanted wit but rather that he was frugal of it. In his works you find little to retrench or alter. Wit and language and humor also in some measure, we had before him, but something of art was wanting to the drama till he came. He managed his strength to more advantage than any who preceded him. You seldom find him making love in any of his scenes or endeavoring to move the passions; his genius was too sullen and saturine to do it gracefully, especially when he knew he came after those who had performed both to such a height. Humor was his proper sphere, and in that he delighted most to represent mechanic people. He was deeply conversant in the Ancients, both Greek and Latin, and he borrowed boldly from them: there is scarce a poet or historian among the Roman authors of those times whom he has not translated in *Sejanus* and *Catiline*. But he has done his robberies so openly that one may see he fears not to be taxed by any law. He invades authors like a monarch, and what would be theft in other poets is only victory in him. With the spoils of these writers he so represents old Rome to us, in its rites, ceremonies, and customs, that if one of their poets had written either of his tragedies, we had seen less of it than in him. If there was any fault in his language, 'twas that he weaved it too closely and laboriously in his serious plays. Perhaps too, he did a little too much Romanize our tongue, leaving the words which he translated almost as much Latin as he found them—wherein, though he learnedly followed the idiom of their language, he did not enough comply with the idiom of ours. If I would compare him with Shakespeare, I must acknowledge him the more correct poet but Shakespeare the greater wit. Shakespeare was the Homer, or father of our dramatic poets; Jonson was the Virgil, the pattern of elaborate writing; I admire him, but I love Shakespeare. To conclude of him: as he has given us the most correct plays, so in the precepts which he has laid down in his *Discoveries* we have as many and profitable rules for perfecting the stage as any wherewith the French can furnish us.

"Having thus spoken of the author, I proceed to the examination of his comedy, *The Silent Woman.*

Examen of The Silent Woman.

"To begin first with the length of the action: it is so far from exceeding the compass of a natural day that it takes not up an artificial one. 'Tis all included in the limits of three hours and a half, which is no more than is required for the presentment on the stage. A beauty perhaps not much observed; if it had, we should not have looked on the Spanish translation of *Five Hours* with so much wonder. The scene of it is laid in London; the latitude of place is almost as little as you can imagine, for it lies all within the compass of two houses and, after the first act, in one. The continuity of scenes is observed more than in any of our plays except his own *Fox* and *Alchemist*. They are not broken above twice or thrice at most in the whole comedy, and in the two best of Corneille's plays, the *Cid* and *Cinna*, they are interrupted once apiece. The action of the play is entirely one, the end or aim of which is the settling Morose's estate on Dauphine. The intrigue of it is the greatest and most noble of any pure unmixed comedy in any language; you see in it many persons of various characters and humors, and all delightful: as, first, Morose, or an old man, to whom all noise but his own talking is offensive. Some who would be thought critics say this humor of his is forced; but to remove that objection we may consider him first to be naturally of a delicate hearing, as many are to whom all sharp sounds are unpleasant, and secondly we may attribute much of it to the peevishness of his age, or the wayward authority of an old man in his own house, where he may make himself obeyed; and this the poet seems to allude to in his name Morose. Besides this, I am assured from divers persons that Ben Jonson was actually acquainted with such a man, one altogether as ridiculous as he is here represented. Others say it is not enough to find one man of such a humor; it must be common to more, and the more common the more natural. To prove this, they instance in the best of comical characters, Falstaff. There are many men resembling him: old, fat, merry, cowardly, drunken, amorous, vain, and lying. But, to convince these people, I need but tell them that humor is the ridiculous extravagance of conversation, wherein one man differs from all others. If then it be common, or communicated to many, how differs it from other men's, or what indeed causes it to be ridiculous so much as the singularity of it? As for Falstaff, he is not properly one humor but a miscellany of humors or images drawn from so many several men. That wherein he is singular is his wit, or those things he says *præter expectatum*, unexpected by the audience; his quick evasions, when you imagine him surprised, which, as they are extremely diverting of themselves, so receive a great addition from his person, for the very sight of such an unwieldy old debauched fellow is a comedy alone. And here, having a place so proper for it, I cannot but enlarge somewhat upon this subject of humor into which I am fallen. The ancients had little of it in their comedies, for the *to geloion* of the Old Comedy, of

which Aristophanes was chief, was not so much to imitate a man as
to make the people laugh at some odd conceit which had commonly somewhat of unnatural or obscene in it. Thus, when you see
Socrates brought upon the stage, you are not to imagine him made
ridiculous by the imitation of his actions, but rather by making him
perform something very unlike himself, something so childish and
absurd, as by comparing it with the gravity of the true Socrates makes
a ridiculous object for the spectators. In their New Comedy which
succeeded, the poets sought indeed to express the *ethos,* as in their
tragedies the *pathos* of mankind. But this *ethos* contained only the
general characters of men and manners (as old men, lovers, serving-
men, courtesans, parasites, and such other persons as we see in their
comedies); all which they made alike: that is, one old man or father,
one lover, one courtesan, so like another, as if the first of them had
begot the rest of every sort: *Ex homine hunc natum dicas* ['You
would say he was born from that man']. The same custom they observed likewise in their tragedies. As for the French, though they
have the word *humeur* among them, yet they have small use of it
in their comedies or farces, they being but ill imitations of the
ridiculum, or that which stirred up laughter in the Old Comedy. But
among the English 'tis otherwise: where by humor is meant some
extravagant habit, passion, or affection, particular (as I said before)
to some one person, by the oddness of which he is immediately distinguished from the rest of men, which, being lively and naturally
represented, most frequently begets that malicious pleasure in the
audience which is testified by laughter; as all things which are de-
viations from common customs are ever the aptest to produce it
though by the way this laughter is only accidental, as the person
represented is fantastic or bizarre, but pleasure is essential to it, as the
imitation of what is natural. The description of these humors, drawn
from the knowledge and observation of particular persons, was the
peculiar genius and talent of Ben Jonson, to whose play I now
return.

"Besides Morose, there are at least nine or ten different characters
and humors in *The Silent Woman*—all which persons have several
concernments of their own, yet are all used by the poet to the con-
ducting of the main design to perfection. I shall not waste time in

commending the writing of this play, but I will give you my opinion that there is more wit and acuteness of fancy in it than in any of Ben Jonson's. Besides that he has here described the conversation of gentlemen in the persons of True-Wit and his friends with more gaiety, air, and freedom than in the rest of his comedies. For the contrivance of the plot, 'tis extreme, elaborate, and yet withal easy, for the *lysis*, or untying of it, 'tis so admirable that when it is done no one of the audience would think the poet could have missed it, and yet it was concealed so much before the last scene that any other way would sooner have entered into your thoughts. But I dare not take upon me to commend the fabric of it because it is altogether so full of art that I must unravel every scene in it to commend it as I ought. And this excellent contrivance is still the more to be admired because 'tis comedy, where the persons are only of common rank, and their business private, not elevated by passions or high concernments as in serious plays. Here everyone is a proper judge of all he sees, nothing is represented but that with which he daily converses, so that by consequence all faults lie open to discovery, and few are pardonable. 'Tis this which Horace has judiciously observed: *Creditur, ex medio quia res arcessit, habere sudoris minimum; sed habet Comedia tanto plus oneris, quanto veniæ minus* ['Comedy is thought to require the least work because it draws its subjects from common life; but the less indulgence it has, the more work it requires' (*Epistles*, II, i)]. But our poet who was not ignorant of these difficulties had prevailed himself of all advantages, as he who designs a large leap takes his rise from the highest ground. One of these advantages is that which Corneille has laid down as the greatest which can arrive to any poem and which he himself could never compass above thrice in all his plays: viz., the making choice of some signal and long-expected day whereon the action of the play is to depend. This day was that designed by Dauphine for the settling of his uncle's estate upon him, which, to compass, he contrives to marry him. That the marriage had been plotted by him long beforehand is made evident by what he tells True-Wit in the second act, that in one moment he had destroyed what he had been raising many months.

"There is another artifice of the poet which I cannot here omit because by the frequent practice of it in his comedies he has left it to

us almost as a rule; that is, when he has any character or humor
wherein he would show a *coup de Maistre,* or his highest skill, he
recommends it to your observation by a pleasant description of it
before the person first appears. Thus, in *Bartholomew Fair* he gives
you the pictures of Numps and Cokes, and in this those of Daw,
Lafoole, Morose, and the Collegiate Ladies, all which you hear described before you see them. So that, before they come upon the
stage, you have a longing expectation of them which prepares you
to receive them favorably, and, when they are there, even from
their first appearance you are so far acquainted with them that
nothing of their humor is lost to you.

"I will observe yet one thing further of this admirable plot; the
business of it rises in every act. The second is greater than the first,
the third than the second, and so forward to the fifth. There too you
see, till the very last scene, new difficulties arising to obstruct the action of the play; and, when the audience is brought into despair
that the business can naturally be effected, then, and not before,
the discovery is made. But that the poet might entertain you with
more variety all this while, he reserves some new characters to show
you, which he opens not till the second and third act. In the second
Morose, Daw, the Barber, and Otter; in the third the Collegiate
Ladies—all which he moves afterwards in by-walks, or underplots,
as diversions to the main design, lest it should grow tedious, though
they are still naturally joined with it and somewhere or other subservient to it. Thus, like a skillful chess player, by little and little he
draws out his men and makes his pawns of use to his greater persons.

"If this comedy and some others of his were translated into French
prose (which would now be no wonder to them, since Molière has
lately given them plays out of verse, which have not displeased them),
I believe the controversy would soon be decided betwixt the two
nations, even making them the judges. But we need not call our heroes
to our aid; be it spoken to the honor of the English, our nation can
never want in any age such who are able to dispute the empire of
wit with any people in the universe. And though the fury of a civil
war and power for twenty years together abandoned to a barbarous
race of men, enemies of all good learning, had buried the Muses
under the ruins of monarchy, yet, with the restoration of our hap-

piness, we see revived poesy lifting up its head and already shaking off the rubbish which lay so heavy on it. We have seen since his Majesty's return many dramatic poems which yield not to those of any foreign nation and which deserve all laurels but the English. I will set aside flattery and envy; it cannot be denied but we have had some little blemish either in the plot or writing of all those plays which have been made within these seven years (and perhaps there is no nation in the world so quick to discern them or so difficult to pardon them as ours). Yet if we can persuade ourselves to use the candor of that poet who, though the most severe of critics, has left us this caution by which to moderate our censures—*ubi plura nitent in carmine, non ego paucis offendar maculis* ['Where many beauties shine out in a poem, I am not offended at small faults']—if, in consideration of their many and great beauties, we can wink at some slight and little imperfections, if we, I say, can be thus equal to ourselves, I ask no favor from the French. And if I do not venture upon any particular judgment of our late plays, 'tis out of the consideration which an ancient writer gives me . . . : betwixt the extremes of admiration and malice, 'tis hard to judge uprightly of the living. Only I think it may be permitted me to say that, as it is no lessening to us to yield to some plays, and those not many, of our own nation in the last age, so can it be no addition to pronounce of our present poets that they have far surpassed all the Ancients and the modern writers of other countries."

This, my Lord, was the substance of what was then spoke on that occasion; and Lisideius, I think, was going to reply, when he was prevented thus by Crites: "I am confident," said he, "that the most material things that can be said have been already urged on either side; if they have not, I must beg of Lisideius that he will defer his answer till another time, for I confess I have a joint quarrel to you both because you have concluded without any reason given for it that rhyme is proper for the stage. I will not dispute how ancient it hath been among us to write this way; perhaps our ancestors knew no better till Shakespeare's time. I will grant it was not altogether left by him and that Fletcher and Ben Jonson used it frequently in their pastorals and sometimes in other plays. Farther, I will not argue whether we received it originally from our own countrymen or from

the French, for that is an inquiry of as little benefit as theirs who, in
the midst of the great plague, were not so solicitious to provide against
it as to know whether we had it from the malignity of our own air
or by transportation from Holland. I have therefore only to affirm
that it is not allowable in serious plays; for comedies, I find you
already concluding with me. To prove this, I might satisfy myself
to tell you how much in vain it is for you to strive against the stream
of the people's inclination, the greatest part of which are prepossessed so much with those excellent plays of Shakespeare, Fletcher,
and Ben Jonson, which have been written out of rhyme, that except
you could bring them such as were written better in it, and those too
by persons of equal reputation with them, it will be impossible for
you to gain your cause with them, who will still be judges. This it
is to which, in fine, all your reasons must submit. The unanimous consent of an audience is so powerful that even Julius Cæsar (as Macrobius reports of him), when he was perpetual dictator, was not able
to balance it on the other side. But when Laberius, a Roman knight,
at his request contended in the mime with another poet, he was
forced to cry out, *Etiam favente me victus es, Laberi* ['Even with me
favoring you, you are defeated, Laberius']. But I will not on this
occasion take the advantage of the greater number but only urge
such reasons against rhyme as I find in the writings of those who have
argued for the other way. First, then, I am of opinion that rhyme is
unnatural in a play because dialogue there is presented as the effect
of sudden thought; for a play is the imitation of nature, and, since
no man without premeditation speaks in rhyme, neither ought he to
do it on the stage. This hinders not but the fancy may be there
elevated to a higher pitch of thought than it is in ordinary discourse,
for there is a probability that men of excellent and quick parts may
speak noble things *ex tempore*, but those thoughts are never fettered
with the numbers or sound of verse without study, and therefore it
cannot be but unnatural to present the most free way of speaking in
that which is the most constrained. For this reason, says Aristotle,
'tis best to write tragedy in that kind of verse which is the least
such, or which is nearest prose; and this amongst the Ancients was
the iambic and with us is blank verse, or the measure of verse kept
exactly without rhyme. These numbers therefore are fittest for a

natural imitation of the English language

play, the others for a paper of verses or a poem, blank verse being as much below them as rhyme is improper for the drama. . . .

"Thus, you see, your rhyme is uncapable of expressing the greatest thoughts naturally, and the lowest it cannot with any grace, for what is more unbefitting the majesty of verse than to call a servant or bid a door be shut in rhyme? And yet this miserable necessity you are forced upon. But verse, you say, circumscribes a quick and luxuriant fancy which would extend itself too far on every subject, did not the labor which is required to well-turned and polished rhyme set bounds to it. Yet this argument, if granted, would only prove that we may write better in verse, but not more naturally. Neither is it able to evince that, for he who wants judgment to confine his fancy in blank verse may want it as much in rhyme, and he who has it will avoid errors in both kinds. Latin verse was as great a confinement to the imagination of those poets as rhyme to ours, and yet you find Ovid saying too much on every subject. *Nescivit* (says Seneca) *quod bene cessit relinquere* ['He did not know how to end it when it was proper to']: of which he gives you one famous instance in his description of the deluge: *Omnia pontus erat, deerant quoque litora ponto* ('Now all was sea, nor had that sea a shore'). Thus Ovid's fancy was not limited by verse, and Virgil needed not verse to have bounded his.

"In our own language we see Ben Jonson confining himself to what ought to be said, even in the liberty of blank verse, and yet Corneille, the most judicious of the French poets, is still varying the same sense a hundred ways and dwelling eternally on the same subject, though confined by rhyme. Some other exceptions I have to verse, but being these I have named are for the most part already public, I conceive it reasonable they should first be answered."

"It concerns me less than any," said Neander (seeing he had ended), "to reply to this discourse because, when I should have proved that verse may be natural in plays, yet I should aways be ready to confess that those which I have written in this kind come short of that perfection which is required. Yet, since you are pleased I should undertake this province, I will do it, though with all imaginable respect and deference, both to that person from whom you have borrowed your strongest arguments and to whose judgment, when I have said all, I finally submit. But before I proceed to answer your objections I must first remember you that I exclude all comedy from my defense and next that I deny not but blank verse may be also used and content myself only to assert that in serious plays, where the subject and characters are great and the plot unmixed with mirth which might allay or divert these concernments which are produced, rhyme is there as natural and more effectual than blank verse.

"And now having laid down this as a foundation, to begin with Crites I must crave leave to tell him that some of his arguments against rhyme reach no farther than from the faults or defects of ill rhyme to conclude against the use of it in general. May not I conclude against blank verse by the same reason? If the words of some poets who write in it are either ill chosen or ill placed, which makes not only rhyme, but all kind of verse in any language unnatural, shall I, for their vicious affectation, condemn those excellent lines of Fletcher which are written in that kind? Is there anything in rhyme more constrained than this line in blank verse, *I heaven invoke, and strong resistance make,* where you see both the clauses are placed unnaturally, that is, contrary to the common way of speaking, and that without the excuse of a rhyme to cause it? Yet you would think me very ridiculous if I should accuse the stubbornness of blank verse for this and not rather the stiffness of the poet. Therefore, Crites, you must either prove that words, though well chosen and duly placed, yet render not rhyme natural in itself, or that, however natural and easy the rhyme may be, yet it is not proper for a play. If you insist on the former part, I would ask you what other conditions are required to make rhyme natural in itself, besides an election of apt words and a right disposing of them? For the due choice of your words expresses your sense naturally, and the due placing them adapts the rhyme to it. If you object that one verse may be made for the sake of another, though both the words and rhyme be apt, I answer it cannot possibly so fall out, for either there is a dependence of sense betwixt the first line and the second or there is none. If there be that connection, then in the natural position of the words the latter line must of necessity flow from the former; if there be no dependence, yet still the due ordering of words makes the last line as natural in itself as the other, so that the necessity of a rhyme never forces any but bad or lazy writers to say what they would not otherwise. 'Tis true, there is both care and art required to write in verse. A good poet never concludes upon the first line till he has sought out such a rhyme as may fit the sense, already prepared to heighten the second. Many times the close of the sense falls into the middle of the next verse, or farther off, and he may often prevail himself of the same advantages in English which Virgil had in Latin: he may break off in the hemistich and begin another line. Indeed, the not observing these two last things makes plays which are writ in verse so tedious, for though most commonly the sense is to be confined to the couplet, yet nothing that does *perpetuo tenore fluere*, run in the same channel, can please always. 'Tis like the murmuring of a stream, which not varying in the fall, causes at first attention, at last drowsiness. Variety of cadences is the best rule—the greatest help to the actors and refreshment to the audience.

"If then verse may be made natural in itself, how becomes it improper to a play? You say the stage is the representation of nature and no man in ordinary conversation speaks in rhyme. But you foresaw when you said this that it might be answered: neither does any man speak in blank verse or in measure without rhyme. Therefore you concluded that which is nearest nature is still to be preferred. But you took no notice that rhyme might be made as natural as blank verse by the well placing of the words, *etc.* All the difference between them, when they are both correct, is the sound in one, which the other wants, and, if so, the sweetness of it and all the advantage resulting from it which are handled in the preface to *The Rival Ladies* will yet stand good. As for that place of Aristotle where he says plays should be writ in that kind of verse which is nearest prose, it makes little for you, blank verse being properly but measured prose. Now measure alone, in any modern language, does not constitute verse; those of the Ancients in Greek and Latin consisted in quantity of words and a determinate number of feet. But when, by the inundation of the Goths and Vandals into Italy, new languages were brought in and barbarously mingled with the Latin, of which the Italian, Spanish, French, and ours (made out of them and the Teutonic) are dialects, a new way of poesy was practiced—new, I say, in those countries, for in all probability it was that of the conquerors in their own nations. This new way consisted in measure or number of feet and rhyme, the sweetness of rhyme and observation of accent supplying the place of quantity in words, which could neither exactly be observed by those barbarians, who knew not the rules of it; neither was it suitable to their tongues, as it had been to the Greek and Latin. No man is tied in modern poesy to observe any farther rule in the feet of his verse but that they be dissyllables; whether spondee, trochee, or iambic, it matters not; only he is obliged to rhyme. Neither do the Spanish, French, Italians, or Germans acknowledge at all, or very rarely, any such kind of poesy as blank verse amongst them. Therefore, at most 'tis but a poetic prose, a *sermo pedestris,* and as such most fit for comedies, where I acknowledge rhyme to be improper. Farther, as to that quotation of Aristotle, our couplet verses may be rendered as near prose as blank verse itself by using those advantages I lately named, as breaks in a hemistich, or running the sense into another line, thereby making art and order appear as loose and free as nature; or, not tying ourselves to couplets strictly, we may use the benefit of the Pindaric way practiced in *The Siege of Rhodes,* where the numbers vary and the rhyme is disposed carelessly and far from often chiming. Neither is that other advantage of the Ancients to be despised, of changing the kind of verse when they please, with the change of the scene or some new entrance, for they confine not themselves always to iambics but extend their liberty to all lyric numbers and sometimes even to hexameter. But I need not go so far to prove that rhyme, as it succeeds to all other offices of Greek and Latin verse, so especially to this of plays, since the custom of all nations at this day confirms it; all the French, Italian, and Spanish tragedies are generally writ in it; and sure the universal consent of the most civilized parts of the world ought in this, as it doth in other customs, to include the rest.

"But perhaps you may tell me I have proposed such a way to make rhyme natural, and consequently proper to plays, as is unpracticable and that I shall scarce find six or eight lines together in any play where the words are so placed and chosen as is required to make it natural. I answer, no poet need constrain himself at all times to it. It is enough he makes it his general rule, for I deny not but sometimes there may be a greatness in placing the words otherwise, and sometimes they may sound better, sometimes also the variety itself is excuse enough. But if, for the most part, the words be placed as they are in the negligence of prose, it is sufficient to denominate the way practicable, for we esteem that to be such which in the trial oftener succeeds than misses. And thus far you may find the practice made good in many plays; where you do not, remember still that if you cannot find six natural rhymes together it will be as hard for you to produce as many lines in blank verse, even among the greatest of our poets, against which I cannot make some reasonable exception.

"And this, Sir, calls to my remembrance the beginning of your discourse, where you told us we should never find the audience favorable to this kind of writing till we could produce as good plays in rhyme as Ben Jonson, Fletcher, and Shakespeare had writ out of it. But it is to raise envy to the living, to compare them with the dead. They are honored and almost adored by us, as they deserve; neither do I know any so presumptuous of themselves as to contend with them. Yet give me leave to say thus much, without injury to their ashes, that not only we shall never equal them, but they could never equal themselves were they to rise and write again. We acknowledge them our fathers in wit, but they have ruined their estates themselves before they came to their children's hands. There is scarce a humor, a character, or any kind of plot, which they have not blown upon. All comes sullied or wasted to us, and were they to entertain this age, they could not make so plenteous treatments out of such decayed fortunes. This therefore will be a good argument to us either not to write at all or to attempt some other way. There is no bays to be expected in their walks. . . .

"This way of writing in verse they have only left free to us; our age is arrived to a perfection in it which they never knew and which (if we may guess by what of theirs we have seen in verse, as *The Faithful Shepherdess* and *Sad Shepherd*) 'tis probable they never could have reached. For the genius of every age is different, and, though ours excel in this, I deny not but that to imitate nature in that perfection which they did in prose is a greater commendation than to write in verse exactly. As for what you have added, that the people are not generally inclined to like this way, if it were true, it would be no wonder, that betwixt the shaking off an old habit and the introducing of a new there should be difficulty. Do we not see them stick to Hopkins' and Sternhold's psalms and forsake those of David, I mean Sandys's translation of them? If by the people you understand the multitude, the hoi polloi, 'tis no matter what they think; they are sometimes in the right, sometimes in the wrong: their judgment is a mere lottery. . . . But if you mean the mixed audience of the populace and the noblesse, I dare confidently affirm that a great part of the latter sort are already favorable to verse and that no serious plays written since the King's return have been more kindly received by them than *The Siege of Rhodes,* the *Mustapha, The Indian Queen,* and *Indian Emperor.*

"But I come now to the inference of your first argument. You said the dialogue of plays is presented as the effect of sudden thought, but no man speaks suddenly, or *ex tempore,* in rhyme, and you inferred from thence that rhyme, which you acknowledge to be proper to epic poesy, cannot equally be proper to dramatic unless we could suppose all men born so much more than poets that verses should be made in them, not by them.

"It has been formerly urged by you and confessed by me that, since no man spoke any kind of verse *ex tempore,* that which was nearest nature was to be preferred. I answer you therefore by distinguishing betwixt what is nearest to the nature of comedy, which is the imitation of common persons and ordinary speaking, and what is nearest the nature of a serious play. This last is indeed the representation of nature, but 'tis nature wrought up to a higher pitch. The plot, the characters, the wit, the passions, the descriptions are all exalted above the level of common converse, as high as the imagination of the poet can carry them, with proportion to verisimility. Tragedy, we know, is wont to image to us the minds and fortunes of noble persons and to portray these exactly; heroic rhyme is nearest nature, as being the noblest kind of modern verse. . . . Blank verse is acknowledged to be too low for a poem, nay, more, for a paper of verses, but if too low for an ordinary sonnet, how much more for tragedy, which is by Aristotle, in the dispute betwixt the epic poesy and the dramatic, for many reasons he there alleges, ranked above it?

"But setting this defense aside, your argument is almost as strong against the use of rhyme in poems as in plays, for the epic way is everywhere interlaced with dialogue, or discursive scenes, and therefore you must either grant rhyme to be improper there, which is contrary to your assertion, or admit it into plays by the same title which you have given it to poems. For though tragedy be justly preferred above the other, yet there is a great affinity between them, as may easily be discovered in that definition of a play which Lisideius gave us. The *genus* of them is the same, a just and lively image of human nature, in its actions, passions, and traverses of fortune; so is the end, namely, for the delight and benefit of mankind. The characters and persons are still the same, viz., the greatest of both sorts; only the manner of acquainting us with those actions, passions, and fortunes is different. Tragedy performs in *viva voce*, or by action, in dialogue, wherein it excels the epic poem, which does it chiefly by narration and therefore is not so lively an image of human nature. However, the agreement betwixt them is such that if rhyme be proper for one it must be for the other. Verse, 'tis true, is not the effect of sudden thought, but this hinders not that sudden thought may be represented in verse since those thoughts are such as must be higher than nature can raise them without premeditation, especially to a continuance of them, even out of verse, and consequently you cannot imagine them to have been sudden either in the poet or in the actors. A play, as I have said, to be like nature, is to be set above it, as statues which are placed on high are made greater than the life that they may descend to the sight in their just proportion.

"Perhaps I have insisted too long on this objection, but the clearing of it will make my stay shorter on the rest. You tell us, Crites, that rhyme appears most unnatural in repartees, or short replies, when he who answers, it being presumed he knew not what the other would say, yet makes up that part of the verse which was left incomplete and supplies both the sound and measure of it. This, you say, looks rather like the confederacy of two than the answer of one.

"This, I confess, is an objection which is in everyone's mouth who loves not rhyme, but suppose, I beseech you, the repartee were made only in blank verse; might not part of the same argument be turned against you? For the measure is as often supplied there as it is in rhyme; the latter half of the hemistich as commonly made up, or a second line subjoined as a reply to the former, which any one leaf in Jonson's plays will sufficiently clear to you. You will often find in the Greek tragedians, and in Seneca, that when a scene grows up into the warmth of repartees, which is the close fighting of it, the latter part of the trimeter is supplied by him who answers, and yet it was never observed as a fault in them by any of the ancient or modern critics. The case is the same in our verse as it was in theirs, rhyme to us being in lieu of quantity to them. But if no latitude is to be allowed a poet, you take from him not only his license of *quidlibet audendi* ['taking what liberty he wishes'], but you tie him up in a straiter compass than you would a philosopher. This is indeed *Musas colere severiores* ['to cultivate the more serious Muses']. You would have him follow nature, but he must follow her on foot: you have dismounted him from his Pegasus. But, you tell us, this supplying the last half of a verse, or adjoining a whole second to the former, looks more like the design of two than the answer of one. Supposing we acknowledge it: how comes this confederacy to be more displeasing to you than in a dance which is well contrived? You see there the united design of many persons to make up one figure: after they have separated themselves in many petty divisions, they rejoin one by one into a gross. The confederacy is plain amongst them, for chance could never produce any thing so beautiful, and yet there is nothing in it that shocks your sight. I acknowledge the hand of art appears in repartee, as of necessity it must in all kinds of verse. But there is also the quick and poignant brevity of it (which is a high imitation of nature in those sudden gusts of passion) to mingle with it, and this, joined with the cadency and sweetness of the rhyme, leaves nothing in the soul of the hearer to desire. 'Tis an art which appears, but it appears only like the shadowings of painture which, being to cause the rounding of it, cannot be absent, but, while that is considered, they are lost. So, while we attend to the other beauties of the matter, the care and labor of the rhyme is carried from us, or at least drowned in its own sweetness, as bees are sometimes buried in their honey. When a poet has found the repartee, the last perfection he can add to it is to put it into verse. However good the thought may be, however apt the words in which 'tis couched, yet he finds himself at a little unrest while rhyme is wanting; he cannot leave it till that comes naturally and then is at ease and sits down contented.

"From replies, which are the most elevated thoughts of verse, you pass to the most mean ones, those which are common with the lowest of household conversation. In these, you say, the majesty of verse suffers. You instance in the calling of a servant, or commanding a door to be shut, in rhyme. This, Crites, is a good observation of yours, but no argument, for it proves no more but that such thoughts should be waived, as often as may be, by the address of the poet. But suppose they are necessary in the places where he uses them, yet there is no need to put them into rhyme. He may place them in the beginning of a verse and break it off as unfit, when so debased, for any other use, or, granting the worst, that they require more room than the hemistich will allow, yet still there is a choice to be made of the best words and least vulgar (provided they be apt) to express such thoughts. Many have blamed rhyme in general for this fault, when the poet with a little care might have redressed it. But they do it with no more justice than if English poesy should be made ridiculous for the sake of the Water Poet's rhymes. Our language is noble, full, and significant, and I know not why he who is master of it may not clothe ordinary things in it as decently as the Latin if he use the same diligence in his choice of words. *Delectus verborum origo est eloquentiae* ['Proper choice of words is the source of eloquence']. It was the saying of Julius Cæsar, one so curious in his that none of them can be changed but for a worse. One would think *unlock the door* was a thing as vulgar as could be spoken, and yet Seneca could make it sound high and lofty in his Latin: *Reserate clusos regii postes laris* ('Set wide the palace gates').

"But I turn from this exception both because it happens not above twice or thrice in any play that those vulgar thoughts are used, and then too, were there no other apology to be made, yet the necessity of them, which is alike in all kind of writing, may excuse them. Besides that the great eagerness and precipitation with which they are spoken makes us rather mind the substance than the dress: that for which they are spoken rather than what is spoke. For they are always the effect of some hasty concernment, and something of consequence depends on them.

"Thus, Crites, I have endeavored to answer your objections; it remains only that I should vindicate an argument for verse which you have gone about to overthrow. It had formerly been said that the easiness of blank verse renders the poet too luxuriant, but that the labor of rhyme bounds and circumscribes an overfruitful fancy, the sense there being commonly confined to the couplet and the words so ordered that the rhyme naturally follows them, not they the rhyme. To this you answered, that it was no argument to the question in hand, for the dispute was not which way a man may write best, but which is most proper for the subject on which he writes.

"First, give me leave, Sir, to remember you that the argument against which you raised this objection was only secondary: it was built on this hypothesis, that to write in verse was proper for serious plays. Which supposition being granted (as it was briefly made out in that discourse, by showing how verse might be made natural), it asserted that this way of writing was a help to the poet's judgment by putting bounds to a wild overflowing fancy. I think, therefore, it will not be hard for me to make good what it was to prove. But you add that, were this let pass, yet he who wants judgment in the liberty of his fancy may as well show the defect of it when he is confined to verse, for he who has judgment will avoid errors, and he who has it not will commit them in all kinds of writing.

"This argument, as you have taken it from a most acute person, so I confess it carries much weight in it, but by using the word *judgment* here indefinitely, you seem to have put a fallacy upon us. I grant he who has judgment that is so profound, so strong, so infallible a judgment that he needs no helps to keep it always poised and upright, will commit no faults either in rhyme or out of it. And, on the other extreme, he who has a judgment so weak and crazed that no helps can correct or amend it shall write scurvily out of rhyme and worse in it. But the first of these judgments is nowhere to be found, and the latter is not fit to write at all. To speak therefore of judgment as it is in the best poets, they who have the greatest proportion of it want other helps than from it, within. As, for example, you would be loath to say that he who was endued with a sound judgment had no need of history, geography, or moral philosophy to write correctly. Judgment is indeed the master-workman in a play, but he requires many subordinate hands, many tools to his assistance. And

no imagination must adhere to rules

verse I affirm to be one of these; 'tis a rule and line by which he
keeps his building compact and even, which otherwise lawless imagination would raise either irregularly or loosely. At least, if the poet
commits errors with this help, he would make greater and more
without it; 'tis, in short, a slow and painful, but the surest kind of
working. Ovid, whom you accuse for luxuriancy in verse, had perhaps been farther guilty of it had he writ in prose. And for your
instance of Ben Jonson, who, you say, writ exactly without the help
of rhyme, you are to remember 'tis only an aid to a luxuriant fancy,
which his was not: as he did not want imagination, so none ever said
he had much to spare. Neither was verse then refined so much to be
a help to that age, as it is to ours. Thus then the second thoughts
being usually the best, as receiving the maturest digestion from judgment, and the last and most mature product of those thoughts being
artful and labored verse, it may well be inferred that verse is a
great help to a luxuriant fancy, and this is what that argument which
you oppose was to evince."

Neander was pursuing this discourse so eagerly that Eugenius had
called to him twice or thrice ere he took notice that the barge stood
still and that they were at the foot of Somerset Stairs, where they had
appointed it to land. The company were all sorry to separate so soon,
though a great part of the evening was already spent, and stood
awhile looking back on the water, which the moonbeams played upon
and made it appear like floating quicksilver. At last they went up
through a crowd of French people who were merrily dancing in the
open air and nothing concerned for the noise of guns which had
alarmed the town that afternoon. Walking thence together to the
Piazze, they parted there, Eugenius and Lisideius to some pleasant
appointment they had made, and Crites and Neander to their several
lodgings.

argument about the Nature of poetry. arg. about nature and speaking in Rhyme is Rhyme natural

Alexander Pope

(1688–1744)

The brilliant and precocious Alexander Pope wrote *An Essay on Criticism* (1711) before reaching his twenty-first birthday. Inspired by Horace's *Art of Poetry* and by Boileau's *Art Poétique* (1674), which it surpasses in smoothness and conciseness, the *Essay* is a compendium of traditional neoclassical principles. Pope's famous definition of wit as "what oft was thought but ne'er so well expressed," was to be criticized by Dr. Johnson for its failure to give sufficient credit to originality or "strength of thought." Johnson had no way of knowing that the earlier manuscript version had read "ne'er before expressed." But Pope's printed version is certainly more applicable to his own poem, which is made up of borrowings from more than fifty earlier writers, including Horace, Quintilian, Vida, Cowley, Roscommon, Boileau, and especially John Dryden—borrowings given point and pithiness in Pope's epigrammatic style. Following the conventions of his age, he emphasizes decorum, imitation of models, concern for general ideas and the whole rather than parts, disinterested judgment, and veneration of the past. But his satirical treatment of time-bound, fashion-ridden criticism and of partial and biased judgments is applicable to any age. Pope also recognizes that any poet need not observe all the rules and that the great poet may sometimes "gloriously offend," although in counseling moderation he falls far short of the modern idea of the necessity of renovating conventions. His praise of the "ardor" of Longinus, then at the height of his reputation, may

be understood as one eighteenth century sign of the impending reaction against the rule of reason and wit. The appeal of Pope's work
to modern readers is not so much in its rational discursiveness as in
its satirical wit. One of Pope's central assumptions is his idea that
the critic is social arbiter and enemy of the vices of his society.
The best and most fully annotated text of the *Essay* is E. Audra
and Aubrey Williams, eds., *Pastoral Poetry and an Essay on Criticism* (1961), in the Twickenham Edition of the works. R. M. Schmitz,
ed., *Pope's Essay on Criticism, 1709* (1962) is a carefully edited
text of the earlier manuscript version.

AN ESSAY ON CRITICISM

(1711)

Part I

'Tis hard to say, if greater want of skill
Appear in writing or in judging ill;
But, of the two, less dangerous is the offense
To tire our patience, than mislead our sense.
Some few in that, but numbers err in this,
Ten censure wrong for one who writes amiss;
A fool might once himself alone expose,
Now one in verse makes many more in prose.
    'Tis with our judgments as our watches, none
Go just alike, yet each believes his own.   10
In poets as true genius is but rare,
True taste as seldom is the critic's share;
Both must alike from heaven derive their light,
These born to judge, as well as those to write.
Let such teach others who themselves excel,
And censure freely who have written well.
Authors are partial to their wit, 'tis true,

The text is based on that of the first edition of 1711.

But are not critics to their judgment too?
   Yet if we look more closely, we shall find
Most have the seeds of judgment in their mind.   20
Nature affords at least a glimmering light;
The lines, though touched but faintly, are drawn right.
But as the slightest sketch, if justly traced,
Is by ill-coloring but the more disgraced,
So by false learning is good sense defaced:
Some are bewildered in the maze of schools,
And some made coxcombs nature meant but fools.
In search of wit these lose their common sense,
And then turn critics in their own defense:
Each burns alike, who can, or cannot write,   30
Or with a rival's, or a eunuch's spite.
All fools have still an itching to deride,
And fain would be upon the laughing side.
If Mævius scribble in Apollo's spite,
There are who judge still worse than he can write.
   Some have at first for wits, then poets passed,
Turned critics next, and proved plain fools at last.
Some neither can for wits nor critics pass,
As heavy mules are neither horse nor ass.
Those half-learned witlings, numerous in our isle,   40
As half-formed insects on the banks of Nile;
Unfinished things, one knows not what to call,
Their generation's so equivocal;
To tell 'em, would a hundred tongues require,
Or one vain wit's, that might a hundred tire.
   But you who seek to give and merit fame,
And justly bear a critic's noble name,
Be sure yourself and your own reach to know,
How far your genius, taste, and learning go;
Launch not beyond your depth, but be discreet,   50
And mark that point where sense and dullness meet.
   Nature to all things fixed the limits fit,
And wisely curbed proud man's pretending wit.
As on the land while here the ocean gains,

In other parts it leaves wide sandy plains;
Thus in the soul while memory prevails,
The solid power of understanding fails;
Where beams of warm imagination play,
The memory's soft figures melt away.
One science only will one genius fit;   60
So vast is art, so narrow human wit:
Not only bounded to peculiar arts,
But oft in those confined to single parts.
Like kings we lose the conquests gained before,
By vain ambition still to make them more;
Each might his several province well command,
Would all but stoop to what they understand.
    First follow nature, and your judgment frame
By her just standard, which is still the same;
Unerring Nature, still divinely bright,   70
One clear, unchanged, and universal light,
Life, force, and beauty, must to all impart,
At once the source, and end, and test of art.
Art from that fund each just supply provides,
Works without show, and without pomp presides;
In some fair body thus the informing soul
With spirits feeds, with vigor fills the whole,
Each motion guides, and every nerve sustains,
Itself unseen, but in the effects, remains.
Some, to whom Heaven in wit has been profuse,   80
Want as much more, to turn it to its use;
For wit and judgment often are at strife,
Though meant each other's aid, like man and wife.
'Tis more to guide, than spur the Muse's steed;
Restrain his fury, than provoke his speed;
The wingèd courser, like a generous horse,
Shows most true mettle when you check his course.
    Those rules of old discovered, not devised,
Are nature still, but nature methodized;
Nature, like liberty, is but restrained   90
By the same laws which first herself ordained.

  Hear how learned Greece her useful rules indites,
When to repress, and when indulge our flights:
High on Parnassus' top her sons she showed,
And pointed out those arduous paths they trod;
Held from afar, aloft, the immortal prize,
And urged the rest by equal steps to rise.
Just precepts thus from great examples given,
She drew from them what they derived from Heaven.
The generous critic fanned the poet's fire,　　　　100
And taught the world with reason to admire.
Then criticism the Muses' handmaid proved,
To dress her charms, and make her more beloved:
But following wits from that intention strayed;
Who could not win the mistress, wooed the maid;
Against the poets their own arms they turned,
Sure to hate most the men from whom they learned.
So modern 'pothecaries, taught the art
By doctor's bills to play the doctor's part,
Bold in the practice of mistaken rules,　　　　110
Prescribe, apply, and call their masters fools.
Some on the leaves of ancient authors prey,
Nor time nor moths e'er spoiled so much as they.
Some drily plain, without invention's aid,
Write dull receipts how poems may be made.
These leave the sense, their learning to display,
And those explain the meaning quite away.
  You then whose judgment the right course would steer,
Know well each Ancient's proper character;
His fable, subject, scope in every page;　　　　120
Religion, country, genius of his age:
Without all these at once before your eyes,
Cavil you may, but never criticize.
Be Homer's works your study and delight,
Read them by day, and meditate by night;
Thence form your judgment, thence your maxims bring,
And trace the Muses upward to their spring.
Still with itself compared, his text peruse;

And let your comment be the Mantuan Muse.
    When first young Maro[1] in his boundless mind   130
A work to outlast immortal Rome designed,
Perhaps he seemed above the critic's law,
And but from nature's fountains scorned to draw:
But when to examine every part he came,
Nature and Homer were, he found, the same.
Convinced, amazed, he checks the bold design,
And rules as strict his labored work confine,
As if the Stagirite[2] o'erlooked each line.
Learn hence for ancient rules a just esteem;
To copy nature is to copy them.   140
    Some beauties yet no precepts can declare,
For there's a happiness as well as care.
Music resembles poetry; in each
Are nameless graces which no methods teach,
And which a master-hand alone can reach.
If, where the rules not far enough extend
(Since rules were made but to promote their end),
Some lucky license answers to the full
The intent proposed, that license is a rule.
Thus Pegasus, a nearer way to take,   150
May boldly deviate from the common track.
Great wits sometimes may gloriously offend,
And rise to faults true critics dare not mend;
From vulgar bounds with brave disorder part,
And snatch a grace beyond the reach of art,
Which without passing through the judgment, gains
The heart, and all its end at once attains.
In prospects thus, some objects please our eyes,
Which out of nature's common order rise,
The shapeless rock, or hanging precipice.   160
But though the Ancients thus their rules invade
(As kings dispense with laws themselves have made)
Moderns, beware! or if you must offend

    [1] Virgil.
    [2] Aristotle, a native of Stagiria in Macedonia.

Against the precept, ne'er transgress its end;
Let it be seldom, and compelled by need;
And have, at least, their precedent to plead.
The critic else proceeds without remorse,
Seizes your fame, and puts his laws in force.
   I know there are, to whose presumptuous thoughts
Those freer beauties, even in them, seem faults.   170
Some figures monstrous and misshaped appear,
Considered singly, or beheld too near,
Which, but proportioned to their light, or place,
Due distance reconciles to form and grace.
A prudent chief not always must display
His powers in equal ranks, and fair array,
But with the occasion and the place comply,
Conceal his force, nay seem sometimes to fly.
Those oft are stratagems which errors seem,
Nor is it Homer nods, but we that dream.   180
   Still green with bays each ancient altar stands,
Above the reach of sacrilegious hands;
Secure from flames, from envy's fiercer rage,
Destructive war, and all-involving age.
See, from each clime, the learned their incense bring!
Hear, in all tongues consenting pæans ring!
In praise so just let every voice be joined,
And fill the general chorus of mankind.
Hail, bards triumphant! born in happier days;
Immortal heirs of universal praise!   190
Whose honors with increase of ages grow,
As streams roll down, enlarging as they flow;
Nations unborn your mighty names shall sound,
And worlds applaud that must not yet be found!
Oh may some spark of your celestial fire,
The last, the meanest of your sons inspire,
(That on weak wings, from far, pursues your flights;
Glows while he reads, but trembles as he writes)
To teach vain wits a science little known,
To admire superior sense, and doubt their own!   200

Part II

Of all the causes which conspire to blind
Man's erring judgment and misguide the mind,
What the weak head with strongest bias rules
Is pride, the never-failing vice of fools.
Whatever nature has in worth denied,
She gives in large recruits of needful pride;
For as in bodies, thus in souls, we find
What wants in blood and spirits, swelled with wind:
Pride, where wit fails, steps in to our defense,
And fills up all the mighty void of sense.   210
If once right reason drives that cloud away,
Truth breaks upon us with resistless day.
Trust not yourself; but your defects to know,
Make use of every friend—and every foe.

A little learning is a dangerous thing;
Drink deep, or taste not the Pierian spring:
There shallow draughts intoxicate the brain,
And drinking largely sobers us again.
Fired at first sight with what the Muse imparts,
In fearless youth we tempt the heights of arts,   220
While from the bounded level of our mind
Short views we take, nor see the lengths behind;
But more advanced, behold with strange surprise
New distant scenes of endless science rise!
So pleased at first the towering Alps we try,
Mount o'er the vales, and seem to tread the sky,
The eternal snows appear already past,
And the first clouds and mountains seem the last;
But, those attained, we tremble to survey
The growing labors of the lengthened way;   230
The increasing prospect tires our wandering eyes,

Hills peep o'er hills, and Alps on Alps arise!
  A perfect judge will read each work of wit
With the same spirit that its author writ;
Survey the whole, nor seek slight faults to find
Where nature moves, and rapture warms the mind;
Nor lose, for that malignant dull delight,
The generous pleasure to be charmed with wit.
But in such lays as neither ebb, nor flow,
Correctly cold, and regularly low,   240
That shunning faults, one quiet tenor keep;
We cannot blame indeed——but we may sleep.
In wit, as nature, what affects our hearts
Is not the exactness of peculiar parts;
'Tis not a lip, or eye, we beauty call,
But the joint force and full result of all.
Thus when we view some well-proportioned dome,
(The world's just wonder, and even thine, O Rome!)
No single parts unequally surprise,
All comes united to the admiring eyes;   250
No monstrous height, or breadth, or length appear;
The whole at once is bold, and regular.
  Whoever thinks a faultless piece to see,
Thinks what ne'er was, nor is, nor e'er shall be.
In every work regard the writer's end,
Since none can compass more than they intend;
And if the means be just, the conduct true,
Applause, in spite of trivial faults, is due.
As men of breeding, sometimes men of wit,
To avoid great errors, must the less commit,   260
Neglect the rules each verbal critic lays,
For not to know some trifles is a praise.
Most critics, fond of some subservient art,
Still make the whole depend upon a part:
They talk of principles, but notions prize,
And all to one loved folly sacrifice.
  Once on a time, La Mancha's Knight, they say,
A certain bard encountering on the way,

Discoursed in terms as just, with looks as sage,
As e'er could Dennis[3] of the Grecian stage;   270
Concluding all were desperate sots and fools,
Who durst depart from Aristotle's rules.
Our author, happy in a judge so nice,
Produced his play, and begged the Knight's advice;
Made him observe the subject, and the plot,
The manners, passions, unities; what not?
All which, exact to rule, were brought about,
Were but a combat in the lists left out.
"What! leave the combat out?" exclaims the Knight;
"Yes, or we must renounce the Stagirite."   280
"Not so by Heaven" (he answers in a rage),
"Knights, squires, and steeds, must enter on the stage."
"So vast a throng the stage can ne'er contain."
"Then build a new, or act it in a plain."

     Thus critics, of less judgment than caprice,
Curious, not knowing, not exact but nice,
Form short ideas and offend in arts
(As most in manners) by a love to parts.

     Some to conceit[4] alone their taste confine,
And glittering thoughts struck out at every line;   290
Pleased with a work where nothing's just or fit;
One glaring chaos and wild heap of wit.
Poets like painters, thus, unskilled to trace
The naked nature and the living grace,
With gold and jewels cover every part,
And hide with ornaments their want of art.
True wit is nature to advantage dressed,
What oft was thought, but ne'er so well expressed;
Something, whose truth convinced at sight we find,
That gives us back the image of our mind.   300
As shades more sweetly recommend the light,

     [3] John Dennis, a critic and enemy of Pope's; also referred to as Appius,
in line 585.
     [4] In the sense of ingenious figurative and metaphoric language, as in the
metaphysical conceit.

So modest plainness sets off sprightly wit.
For works may have more wit than does 'em good,
As bodies perish through excess of blood.
    Others for language all their care express,
And value books, as women men, for dress:
Their praise is still—the style is excellent;
The sense, they humbly take upon content.
Words are like leaves; and where they most abound,
Much fruit of sense beneath is rarely found.   310
False eloquence, like the prismatic glass,
Its gaudy colors spreads on every place;
The face of nature we no more survey,
All glares alike, without distinction gay;
But true expression, like the unchanging sun,
Clears and improves whate'er it shines upon,
It gilds all objects, but it alters none.
Expression is the dress of thought, and still
Appears more decent, as more suitable;
A vile conceit in pompous words expressed,   320
Is like a clown in regal purple dressed:
For different styles with different subjects sort,
As several garbs with country, town, and court.
Some by old words to fame have made pretense,
Ancients in phrase, mere moderns in their sense;
Such labored nothings, in so strange a style,
Amaze the unlearned, and make the learnèd smile.
Unlucky, as Fungoso in the play,
These sparks with awkward vanity display
What the fine gentleman wore yesterday;   330
And but so mimic ancient wits at best,
As apes our grandsires, in their doublets dressed.
In words, as fashions, the same rule will hold;
Alike fantastic, if too new, or old:
Be not the first by whom the new are tried,
Nor yet the last to lay the old aside.
    But most by numbers judge a poet's song;
And smooth or rough, with them is right or wrong:

In the bright Muse though thousand charms conspire,
Her voice is all these tuneful fools admire;   340
Who haunt Parnassus but to please their ear,
Not mend their minds; as some to church repair,
Not for the doctrine, but the music there.
These equal syllables alone require,
Though oft the ear the open vowels tire;
While expletives their feeble aid do join;
And ten low words oft creep in one dull line:
While they ring round the same unvaried chimes,
With sure returns of still expected rhymes;
Where'er you find "the cooling western breeze,"   350
In the next line, it "whispers through the trees":
If crystal streams "with pleasing murmurs creep,"
The reader's threatened (not in vain) with "sleep."
Then, at the last and only couplet fraught
With some unmeaning thing they call a thought,
A needless Alexandrine ends the song
That, like a wounded snake, drags its slow length along.
Leave such to tune their own dull rhymes, and know
What's roundly smooth or languishingly slow;
And praise the easy vigor of a line,   360
Where Denham's strength and Waller's sweetness join.
True ease in writing comes from art, not chance,
As those move easiest who have learned to dance.
'Tis not enough no harshness gives offense,
The sound must seem an echo to the sense:
Soft is the strain when Zephyr gently blows,
And the smooth stream in smoother numbers flows;
But when loud surges lash the sounding shore,
The hoarse, rough verse should like the torrent roar.
When Ajax strives some rock's vast weight to throw,   370
The line too labors, and the words move slow;
Not so, when swift Camilla scours the plain,
Flies o'er the unbending corn, and skims along the main.
Hear how Timotheus'[5] varied lays surprise,

[5] A reference to Dryden's ode "Alexander's Feast: or, The Power of Music."

And bid alternate passions fall and rise!
While, at each change, the son of Libyan Jove
Now burns with glory, and then melts with love;
Now his fierce eyes with sparkling fury glow,
Now sighs steal out, and tears begin to flow:
Persians and Greeks like turns of nature found,   380
And the world's victor stood subdued by sound!
The power of music all our hearts allow,
And what Timotheus was, is Dryden now.
 Avoid extremes, and shun the fault of such,
Who still are pleased too little or too much.
At every trifle scorn to take offense,
That always shows great pride, or little sense;
Those heads, as stomachs, are not sure the best,
Which nauseate all, and nothing can digest.
Yet let not each gay turn thy rapture move;   390
For fools admire, but men of sense approve;
As things seem large which we through mists descry,
Dullness is ever apt to magnify.
 Some foreign writers, some our own despise;
The Ancients only, or the Moderns prize.
Thus wit, like faith, by each man is applied
To one small sect, and all are damned beside.
Meanly they seek the blessing to confine,
And force that sun but on a part to shine,
Which not alone the southern wit sublimes,   400
But ripens spirits in cold northern climes;
Which from the first has shone on ages past,
Enlights the present, and shall warm the last;
Though each may feel increases and decays,
And see now clearer and now darker days.
Regard not then if wit be old or new,
But blame the false, and value still the true.
 Some ne'er advance a judgment of their own,
But catch the spreading notion of the town;
They reason and conclude by precedent,   410
And own stale nonsense which they ne'er invent.
Some judge of authors' names, not works, and then

Nor praise nor blame the writings, but the men.
Of all this servile herd the worst is he
That in proud dullness joins with quality.
A constant critic at the great man's board,
To fetch and carry nonsense for my lord.
What woeful stuff this madrigal would be,
In some starved hackney sonneteer, or me?
But let a lord once own the happy lines,   420
How the wit brightens! how the style refines!
Before his sacred name flies every fault,
And each exalted stanza teems with thought!
    The vulgar thus through imitation err,
As oft the learned by being singular;
So much they scorn the crowd, that if the throng
By chance go right, they purposely go wrong;
So schismatics the plain believers quit,
And are but damned for having too much wit.
Some praise at morning what they blame at night,   430
But always think the last opinion right.
A Muse by these is like a mistress used,
This hour she's idolized, the next abused;
While their weak heads like towns unfortified,
'Twixt sense and nonsense daily change their side.
Ask them the cause; they're wiser still, they say;
And still to-morrow's wiser than to-day.
We think our fathers fools, so wise we grow;
Our wiser sons, no doubt, will think us so.
Once school-divines this zealous isle o'er-spread;   440
Who knew most sentences,[6] was deepest read;
Faith, gospel, all, seemed made to be disputed,
And none had sense enough to be confuted.
Scotists and Thomists, now, in peace remain,
Amidst their kindred cobwebs in Duck Lane.[7]
If faith itself has different dresses worn,

[6] Possibly a reference to Peter Lombard's *Sentences*, a collection of the *sententiae* or opinions of the church fathers and theologians.
[7] A section in which old and second-hand books were sold.

What wonder modes in wit should take their turn?
Oft, leaving what is natural and fit,
The current folly proves the ready wit;
And authors think their reputation safe,   450
Which lives as long as fools are pleased to laugh.
    Some valuing those of their own side or mind,
Still make themselves the measure of mankind;
Fondly we think we honor merit then,
When we but praise ourselves in other men.
Parties in wit attend on those of state,
And public faction doubles private hate.
Pride, malice, folly, against Dryden rose,
In various shapes of parsons, critics, beaus;
But sense survived, when merry jests were past;   460
For rising merit will buoy up at last.
Might he return, and bless once more our eyes,
New Blackmores and new Milbournes[8] must arise:
Nay, should great Homer lift his awful head,
Zoilus[9] again would start up from the dead.
Envy will merit, as its shade, pursue;
But like a shadow, proves the substance true;
For envied wit, like Sol eclipsed, makes known
The opposing body's grossness, not its own.
When first that sun too powerful beams displays,   470
It draws up vapors which obscure its rays;
But even those clouds at last adorn its way,
Reflect new glories, and augment the day.
    Be thou the first true merit to befriend;
His praise is lost who stays till all commend.
Short is the date, alas, of modern rhymes,
And 'tis but just to let them live betimes.
No longer now that golden age appears,
When patriarch-wits survived a thousand years;
Now length of fame (our second life) is lost,   480
And bare threescore is all even that can boast;

[8] Sir Richard Blackmore and Luke Milbourne, critics of Dryden.
[9] Zoilus, a Greek grammarian and critic of Homer.

Our sons their fathers' failing language see,
And such as Chaucer is, shall Dryden be.
So when the faithful pencil has designed
Some bright idea of the master's mind,
Where a new world leaps out at his command,
And ready nature waits upon his hand,
When the ripe colors soften and unite,
And sweetly melt into just shade and light,
When mellowing years their full perfection give,   490
And each bold figure just begins to live,
The treacherous colors the fair art betray,
And all the bright creation fades away!
    Unhappy wit, like most mistaken things,
Atones not for that envy which it brings.
In youth alone its empty praise we boast,
But soon the short-lived vanity is lost!
Like some fair flower the early spring supplies,
That gaily blooms, but even in blooming dies.
What is this wit, which must our cares employ?   500
The owner's wife, that other men enjoy;
Then most our trouble still when most admired,
And still the more we give, the more required;
Whose fame with pains we guard, but lose with ease,
Sure some to vex, but never all to please;
'Tis what the vicious fear, the virtuous shun,
By fools 'tis hated, and by knaves undone!
    If wit so much from ignorance undergo,
Ah let not learning too commence its foe!
Of old, those met rewards who could excel,   510
And such were praised who but endeavored well:
Though triumphs were to generals only due,
Crowns were reserved to grace the soldiers too.
Now, they who reach Parnassus' lofty crown,
Employ their pains to spurn some others down;
And while self-love each jealous writer rules,
Contending wits become the sport of fools;
But still the worst with most regret commend,

For each ill author is as bad a friend.
To what base ends, and by what abject ways,
Are mortals urged through sacred lust of praise!
Ah ne'er so dire a thirst of glory boast,
Nor in the critic let the man be lost.
Good nature and good sense must ever join;
To err is human, to forgive, divine.

But if in noble minds some dregs remain
Not yet purged off, of spleen and sour disdain;
Discharge that rage on more provoking crimes,
Nor fear a dearth in these flagitious times.
No pardon vile obscenity should find,   530
Though wit and art conspire to move your mind;
But dullness with obscenity must prove
As shameful sure as impotence in love.
In the fat age of pleasure, wealth, and ease,
Sprung the rank weed, and thrived with large increase;
When love was all an easy monarch's care;
Seldom at council, never in a war,
Jilts ruled the state, and statesmen farces writ;
Nay, wits had pensions, and young lords had wit;
The fair sat panting at a courtier's play,   540
And not a mask went unimproved away;
The modest fan was lifted up no more,
And virgins smiled at what they blushed before.
The following license of a foreign reign
Did all the dregs of bold Socinus drain;
Then unbelieving priests reformed the nation,
And taught more pleasant methods of salvation;
Where Heaven's free subjects might their rights dispute,
Lest God himself should seem too absolute.[10]
Pulpits their sacred satire learned to spare,   550
And vice admired to find a flatterer there!
Encouraged thus, wit's Titans braved the skies,
And the press groaned with licensed blasphemies.

[10] A reference to the spread of deism and of Socinianism, which developed into Unitarianism.

our darts engage,
exhaust your rage!
dalously nice,
nto vice;
ected spy,
iced eye.

[237]

520

Part III

Learn then what morals critics ought to show,   560
For 'tis but half a judge's task, to know.
'Tis not enough, taste, judgment, learning join;
In all you speak, let truth and candor shine,
That not alone what to your sense is due
All may allow, but seek your friendship too.
    Be silent always when you doubt your sense,
And speak, though sure, with seeming diffidence;
Some positive, persisting fops we know,
Who, if once wrong, will needs be always so;
But you, with pleasure own your errors past,   570
And make each day a critic on the last.
    'Tis not enough, your counsel still be true;
Blunt truths more mischief than nice falsehoods do:
Men must be taught as if you taught them not,
And things unknown proposed as things forgot.
Without good breeding, truth is disapproved;
That only makes superior sense beloved.
    Be niggards of advice on no pretense,
For the worst avarice is that of sense.
With mean complacence ne'er betray your trust,   580
Nor be so civil as to prove unjust.
Fear not the anger of the wise to raise;
Those best can bear reproof, who merit praise.
    'Twere well might critics still this freedom take,

But Appius[11] reddens at each word you speak,
And stares, tremendous, with a threatening eye,
Like some fierce tyrant in old tapestry.
Fear most to tax an honorable fool,
Whose right it is, uncensured, to be dull;
Such, without wit, are poets when they please,   590
As without learning they can take degrees.
Leave dangerous truths to unsuccessful satires,
And flattery to fulsome dedicators,
Whom, when they praise, the world believes no more,
Than when they promise to give scribbling o'er.
'Tis best sometimes your censure to restrain,
And charitably let the dull be vain;
Your silence there is better than your spite,
For who can rail so long as they can write?
Still humming on, their drowsy course they keep,   600
And lashed so long, like tops, are lashed asleep.
False steps but help them to renew the race,
As, after stumbling, jades will mend their pace.
What crowds of these, impenitently bold,
In sounds and jingling syllables grown old,
Still run on poets, in a raging vein,
Even to the dregs and squeezings of the brain,
Strain out the last dull droppings of their sense,
And rhyme with all the rage of impotence.
   Such shameless bards we have; and yet 'tis true,   610
There are as mad abandoned critics too.
The bookful blockhead, ignorantly read,
With loads of learnèd lumber in his head,
With his own tongue still edifies his ears,
And always listening to himself appears.
All books he reads, and all he reads assails,
From Dryden's *Fables* down to Durfey's *Tales*.
With him, most authors steal their works, or buy;
Garth did not write his own *Dispensary*.

[11] John Dennis; see note 3 above.

Name a new play, and he's the poet's friend,   620
Nay, showed his faults—but when would poets mend?
No place so sacred from such fops is barred,
Nor is Paul's church more safe than Paul's churchyard;
Nay, fly to altars; there they'll talk you dead,
For fools rush in where angels fear to tread.
Distrustful sense with modest caution speaks,
It still looks home, and short excursions makes;
But rattling nonsense in full volleys breaks,
And never shocked, and never turned aside,
Bursts out, resistless, with a thundering tide.   630
    But where's the man, who counsel can bestow,
Still pleased to teach, and yet not proud to know?
Unbiased, or by favor, or by spite,
Not dully prepossessed, nor blindly right;
Though learned, well-bred; and though well-bred, sincere;
Modestly bold, and humanly severe;
Who to a friend his faults can freely show,
And gladly praise the merit of a foe?
Blest with a taste exact, yet unconfined;
A knowledge both of books and human kind;   640
Generous converse; a soul exempt from pride;
And love to praise, with reason on his side?
    Such once were critics; such the happy few
Athens and Rome in better ages knew.
The mighty Stagirite first left the shore,
Spread all his sails, and durst the deeps explore;
He steered securely, and discovered far,
Led by the light of the Mæonian star.[12]
Poets, a race long unconfined, and free,
Still fond and proud of savage liberty,   650
Received his laws, and stood convinced 'twas fit,
Who conquered nature, should preside o'er wit.
    Horace still charms with graceful negligence,
And without method talks us into sense,

[12] Maeonia, or Lydia, was the reputed birthplace of Homer.

Will, like a friend, familiarly convey
The truest notions in the easiest way.
He, who supreme in judgment, as in wit,
Might boldly censure, as he boldly writ,
Yet judged with coolness, though he sung with fire;
His precepts teach but what his works inspire.   660
Our critics take a contrary extreme:
They judge with fury, but they write with phlegm;
Nor suffers Horace more in wrong translations
By wits, than critics in as wrong quotations.
See Dionysius[13] Homer's thoughts refine,
And call new beauties forth from every line!
Fancy and art in gay Petronius[14] please,
The scholar's learning, with the courtier's ease.
In grave Quintilian's[15] copious work, we find
The justest rules, and clearest method joined.   670
Thus useful arms in magazines we place,
All ranged in order, and disposed with grace,
But less to please the eye, than arm the hand,
Still fit for use, and ready at command.
Thee, bold Longinus! all the Nine inspire,
And bless their critic with a poet's fire:
An ardent judge, who, zealous in his trust,
With warmth gives sentence, yet is always just;
Whose own example strengthens all his laws
And is himself that great Sublime he draws.[16]   680
Thus long succeeding critics justly reigned,
License repressed, and useful laws ordained.
Learning and Rome alike in empire grew,
And arts still followed where her eagles flew;
From the same foes, at last, both felt their doom,
And the same age saw learning fall, and Rome.

[13] Dionysius of Halicarnassus, the Greek rhetorician and critic.
[14] Petronius Arbiter, the Roman satirist and critic.
[15] Quintilian, the Roman rhetorician.
[16] Pope's praise is in keeping with the reputation and influence of Longinus in eighteenth century England.

With tyranny, then superstition joined,
As that the body, this enslaved the mind;
Much was believed, but little understood,
And to be dull was construed to be good;   690
A second deluge learning thus o'er-run,
And the monks finished what the Goths begun.

At length Erasmus, that great injured name,
(The glory of the priesthood, and the shame!)
Stemmed the wild torrent of a barbarous age,
And drove those holy Vandals off the stage.

But see! each Muse, in Leo's golden days,
Starts from her trance, and trims her withered bays;
Rome's ancient Genius, o'er its ruins spread,
Shakes off the dust, and rears his reverend head.   700
Then sculpture and her sister-arts revive;
Stones leaped to form, and rocks began to live;
With sweeter notes each rising temple rung;
A Raphael painted, and a Vida sung.
Immortal Vida: on whose honored brow
The poet's bays and critic's ivy grow:
Cremona now shall ever boast thy name,
As next in place to Mantua, next in fame![17]

But soon by impious arms from Latium chased,
Their ancient bounds the banished Muses passed;   710
Thence arts o'er all the northern world advance,
But critic-learning flourished most in France:
The rules a nation, born to serve, obeys;
And Boileau still in right of Horace sways.
But we, brave Britons, foreign laws despised,
And kept unconquered, and uncivilized;
Fierce for the liberties of wit, and bold,
We still defied the Romans, as of old.
Yet some there were, among the sounder few
Of those who less presumed, and better knew,   720
Who durst assert the juster ancient cause,

[17] M. Hieronymous Vida of Cremona (1490?-1566), a critic and author of Latin poems.

And here restored wit's fundamental laws.
Such was the Muse, whose rules and practice tell,
"Nature's chief masterpiece is writing well."
Such was Roscommon,[18] not more learned than good,
With manners generous as his noble blood;
To him the wit of Greece and Rome was known,
And every author's merit, but his own.
Such late was Walsh[19]—the Muse's judge and friend,
Who justly knew to blame or to commend; 730
To failings mild, but zealous for desert;
The clearest head, and the sincerest heart.
This humble praise, lamented shade, receive,
This praise at least a grateful Muse may give:
The Muse, whose early voice you taught to sing,
Prescribed her heights, and pruned her tender wing,
(Her guide now lost) no more attempts to rise,
But in low numbers short excursions tries;
Content, if hence the unlearned their wants may view,
The learned reflect on what before they knew: 740
Careless of censure, nor too fond of fame;
Still pleased to praise, yet not afraid to blame;
Averse alike to flatter, or offend;
Not free from faults, nor yet too vain to mend.

[18] Wentworth Dillon, Earl of Roscommon, translator of Horace's *Art of Poetry* and author of *An Essay on Translated Verse.*
[19] William Walsh, a poet who had befriended Pope.